The Search for Organic Growth

To remain successful, companies must respond to the challenge of achieving continual internal or core growth. But how is this done, and why do some strategies work better than others? In *The Search for Organic Growth*, leading writers on business strategy and organization offer authoritative analysis and practical guidance on implementing a strategy for organic growth. All businesses go through cycles, and momentum can be created in many ways, from new products and market extensions to add-ons and enhancements. The book also answers crucial questions such as how to keep customers happy during periods of change, how to foster an entrepreneurial environment and satisfy individual potential, and how to turn the immense short-term revenue pressures of a push towards growth to your advantage. A lively resource for business school faculty, MBAs and executives, this book is ideal for any reader interested in connections between latest business thought and practice.

EDWARD D. HESS is Adjunct Professor of Organization and Management, Executive Director of the Center for Entrepreneurship and Corporate Growth, and Executive Director of the Values-Based Leadership Institute at the Goizueta Business School, Emory University.

ROBERT K. KAZANJIAN is Professor of Organization and Management at the Goizueta Business School, Emory University.

The Search for
Organic Growth

EDITED BY

EDWARD D. HESS AND
ROBERT K. KAZANJIAN

CAMBRIDGE
UNIVERSITY PRESS

CAMBRIDGE UNIVERSITY PRESS
Cambridge, New York, Melbourne, Madrid, Cape Town, Singapore, São Paulo

Cambridge University Press
The Edinburgh Building, Cambridge CB2 2RU, UK

Published in the United States of America by Cambridge University Press, New York

www.cambridge.org
Information on this title: www.cambridge.org/9780521852609

First published 2006

Printed in the United Kingdom at the University Press, Cambridge

A catalogue record for this publication is available from the British Library

ISBN-13   978-0-521-85260-9 hardback
ISBN-10   0-521-85260-9 hardback

Contents

Figures

Tables

Contributors

Philip Anderson is Alumni Fund Professor of Entrepreneurship, Director of the 3i VentureLab, and Director of the International Centre for Entrepreneurship at INSEAD.

Douglas Bowman is Associate Professor of Marketing at the Goizueta Business School, Emory University.

Robert Drazin is Professor of Organization and Management at the Goizueta Business School, Emory University.

Raghu Garud is Associate Professor of Management and Organizations at the Leonard Stern School of Business, New York University.

MaryAnn Glynn is Professor of Organization and Management at the Goizueta Business School, Emory University.

Andrew Hargadon is Associate Professor of Management and Director of the Technology Management Programs Graduate School of Management at the University of California at Davis.

Edward D. Hess is Adjunct Professor of Organization and Management, Executive Director of the Center for Entrepreneurship and Corporate Growth, and Executive Director of the Values-Based Leadership Institute at the Goizueta Business School, Emory University.

Michael A. Hitt is Professor of Management, the Joe B. Foster Chair in Business Leadership, and the C. W. and Dorothy Conn Chair in New Ventures at Mays Business School, Texas A & M University.

R. Duane Ireland is Professor of Management and the Foreman R. and Ruby S. Bennett Chair in Business Administration at Mays Business School, Texas A & M University.

William F. Joyce is Professor of Strategy and Organization Theory at the Tuck School of Business at Dartmouth.

Robert K. Kazanjian is Professor of Organization and Management at the Goizueta Business School, Emory University.

Arun Kumaraswamy is Visiting Associate Professor of Management at the Lee Kong Chian School of Business, Singapore Management University.

Rita McGrath is Associate Professor of Management at Columbia Business School, Columbia University.

Das Narayandas is Professor of Business Administration at Harvard Business School, Harvard University.

Chad Navis is a doctoral student in the Organization and Management Department at the Goizueta Business School, Emory University.

Erich R. Reinhardt is President and Chief Executive Officer of Siemens Medical Solutions.

Vallabh Sambamurthy is Eli Broad Professor of Information Technology at the Graduate School of Management, Michigan State University.

Tom Taylor is Executive Vice-President, Merchandising, Marketing of Home Depot Stores, The Home Depot, Inc.

Christopher S. Tuggle is Assistant Professor of Management at the College of Business, University of Missouri, Columbia.

Acknowledgments

Organizational growth has always been a topic of interest to executives and researchers. Recently, however, we have noted that although organic, or non-acquisitive, growth has been pursued more aggressively by companies, there exists a paucity of research on the topic. This recognition led us, along with our colleague and friend Bob Drazin, Professor of Organization and Management at the Goizueta Business School of Emory University, to organize a conference entitled *Hitting the Growth Wall: Growth in Large Organizations*. The conference was unique in that the participants included both leading scholars who study growth-related issues and executives from a number of companies with extraordinary growth records.

The conference was hosted by the Center for Entrepreneurship and Corporate Growth at the Goizueta Business School. We wish to acknowledge the generous contributions made by Siemens Medical Solutions, the sponsor of the conference. We are particularly indebted to Thomas N. McCausland, President of Siemens Medical Solutions, USA who worked closely with us in the design and delivery of the conference. We are also indebted to Dr. Erich R. Reinhardt, CEO and President of Siemens Medical Solutions and member of Siemens AG for his endorsement of the conference and his participation. We also wish to extend our appreciation to Bob Drazin, Faculty Director of the Center of Entrepreneurship and Corporate Growth, and Tom Robertson, former Dean at Goizueta, for their support of our efforts.

Following the conference, we worked with the executives and scholars who participated to organize the papers into this book. We greatly appreciate the cooperation of our co-authors who contributed to this book, all of whom responded positively and quickly to our requests. We wish to express our appreciation to Katy Plowright, Business and Management Editor at Cambridge University Press, for her thoughtful guidance and patience in working with us. We also appreciate the assistance of Lynn Dunlop, Assistant Editor, as we worked through the final stages of the publication process. Finally, both Carol Gee and Gail Moody here at Goizueta were invaluable in the manuscript preparation and final editing process.

1 | The challenge of organic growth

ROBERT K. KAZANJIAN, EDWARD
D. HESS, AND ROBERT DRAZIN

THROUGH much of the 1990s, corporations realized extraordinary growth in revenues and earnings. As this trend unfolded, senior executives began to experience significant pressure from financial analysts, shareholders, and others for continued growth as measured by quarterly reports of performance against forecasts. In the aftermath of the technology bubble, and as the accounting and financial scandals of 2001 and 2002 surfaced, it was apparent that a portion of the earlier reported growth was the product of a mix of widespread earnings management and financial engineering, serial acquisitions, and the utilization of accounting and tax manipulations to create specific financial results. The vitality and substance of those results are now being questioned in various regulatory, legal, and legislative forums. In other cases, firms may have developed innovative strategies or products that led to high growth, but as the firm matured or approached market saturation, growth slowed. For a range of reasons, then, many firms have "hit the wall," experiencing flat revenues after an extended period of high growth.

As a result, executives in many companies now struggle with an increased emphasis on internally generated, or organic, growth, which is qualitatively different in the substance and character of the key tasks central to success, from growth via acquisition. As Rita McGrath notes in Chapter 9, with a sample of over 900 large companies she examined, approximately 6% of all companies who were growing at even a modest rate overall could be accurately described as growing organically. This suggests that although more firms must pursue organic growth strategies, few are endowed with the skills, processes, and experiences necessary for success. Additionally, the economic environment for growth presents daunting obstacles in the form of saturated markets, the inability to raise or even maintain prices in the face of intense competition, and economic uncertainty due to geo-political conditions.

1

Therefore, the purpose of this book is to identify the central problems, both strategic and organizational, of organic growth and to propose both conceptual and practical approaches to these problems. The chapters that follow are contributed by both leading scholars working on growth-related issues and senior executives from successful growth companies. This work was originally presented at the "Hitting the Growth Wall: Growth in Large Organizations" conference at the Goizueta Business School of Emory University, hosted by the Goizueta Center for Entrepreneurship and Corporate Growth and sponsored by Siemens Medical Solutions.

Although there is a burgeoning literature on growth via acquisition (Hitt, Harrison, & Ireland, 2001; Sirower, 1997), there is little on organic growth. Most is captured within sub-questions related to product/service innovation (Kazanjian, Drazin, & Glynn, 2002) or geographic market expansion (Zook & Allen, 2003). Given the paucity of research on organic growth *per se*, we chose to take a fresh look at this issue. First, we profile four companies selected because of their challenging but novel approaches to organic growth. Each of these companies offers a grounded example of the organic growth challenges and solutions from a general manager's perspective. Additionally, we invited recognized research experts to share their current perspectives on organic growth. Based on these inputs, three central themes of organic growth emerged. We have organized the book into three sections that correspond to these themes.

Case examples of successful growth companies: the general management perspective

Given that most of the academic research on organic growth is highly specialized and narrow in scope, we felt it important to capture several integrated perspectives on the issue. Therefore, this first section of the book presents the specific growth-related challenges and successes of four highly successful companies. These case examples point to several central strategic and organizational themes that we address later in this chapter. In Chapter 2, "Profitable growth at Siemens Medical Solutions," Erich R. Reinhardt describes the path to growth originating with a focus on internal operating problems. In 1995, Siemens Medical Solutions (MED) faced a dramatic challenge when the FDA temporarily shut down four manufacturing plants for non-compliance with

Good Manufacturing Practice (GMP). Additionally, with higher over-head costs than competitors and excess manufacturing capacity, MED was projecting a financial loss for 1996. Following a detailed diag-nosis, senior management identified three main objectives: restructure the business, continuously improve operational efficiency, and capi-talize on new business opportunities. Reinhardt's detailed description of the activities and decisions provides a road map to the creation of renewed offerings, capabilities, and assets that fed organic growth. Sub-sequently, MED realized seven years of profitable growth and increases in market share.

In Chapter 3, "UPS: Brown's organic growth story," Edward D. Hess describes the dramatic growth of the company from its origins in Seat-tle, Washington in 1907 as a local delivery service, to a \$36 billion global logistics and distribution company. Hess describes several ele-ments central to growth at UPS. Geographic expansion was the orig-inal focus, as UPS extended its reach nationally and then, in 1975, expanded to other markets outside the United States. With a global distribution system in place, UPS pursued growth in related markets for synchronous commerce and supply chain management with indus-trial and commercial customers. This required approximately thirty small acquisitions and a significant investment in information tech-nologies to complete the full range of assets and capabilities needed to compete effectively. Hess pointedly notes that these acquisitions were executed to gain specific capabilities, not market share. Subsequently, the strategy was to concentrate on organic growth across both the con-sumer and synchronous commerce markets. Finally, Hess describes the organizational characteristics and UPS practices of focusing employee efforts on successful execution, highlighting the role of measure-ment systems, promote-from-within policies, local hiring in interna-tional operations, and the employee-centric ownership culture of the company.

Chapter 4, "Execution: making growth happen at The Home Depot" by Tom Taylor, tells the story of extraordinary organic growth since the founding of the firm in 1978. The path of growth mirrors that described in earlier chapters in some regards. Established in Atlanta, Georgia, The Home Depot initially grew with the increase in the number of stores, eventually covering the Southeast and ultimately the entire country. Through this process, The Home Depot became the fastest growing retailer in US history, while at the same time twenty-five of their top competitors in the "do-it-yourself" retail market failed. However, in 1999 The Home Depot "hit the wall." Between 1999 and 2002, sales growth declined 13 percentage points and same-store sales dropped for eight consecutive quarters. With the forthcoming retirement of the founders of the company, and recognizing the coming decline, the Board chose a successor from outside the company. Bob Nardelli joined The Home Depot in 2000 and launched a process to integrate strategy and operations. The strategic emphasis centered on enhancing or strengthening the core business, extending into services and related areas, and finally expanding into new markets such as government customers and high-end consumers. In executing this strategy, Taylor describes a range of changes including expanded measurement and accountability, heavy investment in technology accelerators, and balancing decentralization of field operations with increased centralization of procurement and merchandising. With these changes came increased emphasis on analysis by senior management and a focus on details. This altered strategy and organizational approach led to fundamental questioning of earlier assumptions about the customer base and their shopping preferences, which then led to over $1 billion invested in store design, merchandising, and location. Resulting recent performance indicates increases in growth and same-store sales.

In Chapter 5, Edward D. Hess also profiles the remarkable growth achieved by SYSCO, the largest food marketing and distribution company in North America. With sales of over $30 billion and 157 profit centers, SYSCO has delivered double-digit growth in sales and net earnings for more than thirty years. Hess describes the evolutionary character of growth as the company expanded geographically throughout the United States. In similar fashion, new food products, non-food products, and services were added to satisfy the needs of existing customers more effectively. Further, SYSCO segmented its customer market into four price points for greater market focus. Finally, it emphasized internal cost efficiencies through supply chain management innovations and the aggressive adoption of enabling technologies. It is noteworthy that the company was created through the merger of nine separate family-owned foodservice operations, creating the infrastructure and network of assets that generated subsequent growth. None the less, Hess indicates that SYSCO has grown more via internally generated growth than as a result of acquisitions. He then presents SYSCO's internal

organizational practices emphasizing broad-based employee ownership of company stock, a highly decentralized operating structure, and
human resource strategies emphasizing promote-from-within, a rigorous measurement regime, an aggressive performance management
system, and a highly open and entrepreneurial culture.

Strategic alignment for organic growth

The chapters in this second section of the book concentrate on central strategy questions related to organic growth, underscoring issues
reflected in the experiences of Siemens, UPS, The Home Depot, and
SYSCO. These questions include: (1) if organic growth is to be the
strategic priority of the firm, how is it defined? (2) what is the relationship of acquisitions to organic growth? and (3) what resource align-
ments and practices are associated with successful growth companies?

In Chapter 6, "Strategic position, organic growth, and financial performance," William F. Joyce extends his recent well-regarded study
of the determinants of performance with a sample of 200 firms in
fifty industries to investigate organizational elements that influence
organic growth (Joyce, Nohria, & Roberson, 2003). The original study
was designed to identify four firms per industry, tracking their performance over a ten-year period. Within each industry, the four firms
selected for study were: a "loser" whose performance lagged throughout the decade; a "climber" whose performance improved throughout
the decade; a "tumbler" whose performance rose for the first five years,
then dropped off for the remaining five years; and, finally, a "winner"
whose performance led the industry by a significant margin throughout the decade. Winner firms demonstrate several characteristics significantly related to growth. Thus, growth is heavily emphasized in
the strategy of the firm throughout the study period. Interestingly, he
finds that "winners" begin by emphasizing acquisitive growth in the
first five-year period, but emphasize organic growth in the final five-
year period. Additionally, he finds that successful organic growth firms
excel at disciplined execution, operate within formal structures that are
flat, enhancing responsive decision-making, and build performance-
oriented cultures.

A strategic focus on organic growth assumes a clear, specific definition, but the measurement of organic growth is a complex task.

In Chapter 7, "Defining and measuring organic growth," Edward D. Hess offers such a specific measure with supporting rationale, and then applies that measure to identify the leading organic growth firms for 2001 and 2002. He argues that total corporate growth can result from four sources: (1) internal operations or organic growth; (2) acquisitive growth; (3) growth from investments; and (4) growth that results from aggressive interpretations of Generally Accepted Accounting Principles (GAAP) and associated financial reporting practices. These four sources of growth are not only distinct, but are produced by separate organizational skills and processes. For example, financial engineering is a very different competence than repetitive, organic growth. In this chapter, Hess sets forth a financial model that attempts to quantify and discriminate among various types of growth, with the result being a better definition of organic growth.

As discussed earlier, because of the tremendous pressure for growth, many firms engage in acquisitions. In Chapter 8, "The make or buy growth decision: strategic entrepreneurship versus acquisitions," authors Michael A. Hitt, R. Duane Ireland, and Christopher S. Tuggle argue that while acquisitions can be successful, many of them produce negative returns while providing growth (Hitt, Harrison, & Ireland, 2001). Thus, while producing immediate growth, they may not maintain a level of market value that meets or exceeds investors' expectations unless they are integrated with other growth-creating strategies. They argue that many firms therefore must generate value-creating growth through other ventures. These ventures include expansion into new international markets or engaging in entrepreneurial activities (Hitt, Ireland, Camp, & Sexton, 2001, 2002). To do so, firms can invest internally in R&D (in high-tech industries, as does Siemens Medical Solutions) or otherwise develop creative opportunities for growth (as does The Home Depot). They then argue that firms should engage in "strategic entrepreneurship" (Ireland, Hitt, & Sirmon, 2003) to make these types of efforts successful. They also note that these organic growth initiatives may be aided by the infusion of ideas, knowledge, and competencies gained through previous acquisitions. This chapter explores the means by which firms can become strategically entrepreneurial, including developing an entrepreneurial mindset; allocating resources to growth projects proportionate to their strategic priority; and fostering creativity and innovation through an entrepreneurial culture and leadership style.

Organizing for organic growth: understanding key roles and processes

The following chapters, in the final section, address the role and leverage of organizational resources that emerged as a critical challenge to growth at Siemens Medical Solutions, UPS, The Home Depot, and SYSCO. The direction and marshaling of those resources to creative, innovative ends is central to performance. More specifically, these chapters explicate: (1) the role of sponsoring managers in nurturing and spawning new ideas; (2) the challenges to the subsequent internal corporate venturing process; and (3) the processes of linking and leveraging internal and external knowledge and resources as vehicles for organic growth.

There is consensus in the academic literature that innovation and creativity are central to organic growth. Much of this work highlights the role of senior management in allocating resources to entrepreneurial projects and fostering a climate conducive to risk-taking. Much less has been written on the critical role of middle managers in identifying and championing new ideas that comprise the core of new products, services, and businesses. In Chapter 9, "The misunderstood role of the middle manager in driving successful growth programs," Rita McGrath describes the role of middle managers in the internal innovation process that is so central to organic growth. She offers a detailed description of the activities and tasks critical to success. These include developing an inventory of opportunities as well as the articulation of relevant screening criteria. Once an initiative has been selected, tasks shift to funding, monitoring, making choices of structural reporting relationships, and establishing connections with other relevant corporate resources. Finally, as the project succeeds and grows, middle managers are central to the acquisition of new skills and capabilities as well as buffering the effort from dysfunctional political pressures.

Philip Anderson opens Chapter 10, "Organic growth through internal corporate ventures," with a presentation of growth options available to firms that have "hit the wall" and have experienced flat revenues. Although noting that firms can grow by acquisition of other companies, he concentrates on the variations of organic growth. Following a brief discussion of two approaches to organic growth – extending an organization's geographic reach, and expanding into new roles along its existing value chain – the remainder of the chapter develops the option of new business creation through the use of new internal corporate ventures (Kazanjian, Drazin, & Glynn, 2002; O'Reilly & Tushman, 2004), an option that has been in and out of fashion several times over recent decades. Anderson frames the challenges of managing intra-corporate new ventures by contrasting their growth and development with that of independent start-up new ventures, describing domain restrictions and conflict over charters within the firms as restrictions not faced by independents. He then offers the example of Singapore Technologies' launch of their new-venture incubator, Incubators@Work!, as one approach to addressing these challenges.

Within the alternatives for growing organically, increasing revenue from existing customers in core businesses has clearly emerged from the case examples of UPS, Siemens, The Home Depot, and SYSCO. Douglas Bowman and Das Narayandas also note in Chapter 11, "Linking customer management efforts to growth and profitability," that a natural tack for many firms is to seek more business with their current customers. This approach may be more effective and profitable than to search for and develop new customers. A challenge, however, is how to invest firm resources to achieve this goal. Bowman and Narayandas propose profit-chain-link (or cascading) frameworks (Heskett, Jones, Loveman, Sasser, & Schlesinger, 1994) as useful for linking operational resources (under the influence of vendor managers) to sales and profits at the customer level. Vendor managers also support investments in customer satisfaction programs and customer loyalty programs. According to such a framework, resource inputs are invested to deliver product/service value; product/service value, in turn, is a determinant of customer satisfaction; customer satisfaction influences customer loyalty; and customer loyalty is a contributing factor for customer profitability. When properly specified, profit-chain-link frameworks allow for a rich description of the complex linkages between firm effort and customer sales and profitability, namely, nonlinear linkages and differential responsiveness occasioned by customer-specific (or situation-specific) factors. According to Bowman and Narayandas, controlling for situation-specific factors illuminates, to some degree, why similar levels of customer management effort and/or performance can yield quite different customer-level sales and profitability outcomes. It also leads to guidelines for adapting customer management efforts at the customer level with an eye towards doing more business with a given customer and improving profitability.

Raghu Garud, Arun Kumaraswamy, and Vallabh Sambamurthy carefully develop the role of organization-specific knowledge as a foundation for organic growth in Chapter 12. In "Harnessing knowledge resources for increasing returns: scalable structuration at infosys technologies," they argue that knowledge-infused resources (such as knowledge workers, proprietary technologies, and internal work processes) can increase with use, and at an increasing rate. Further, they argue that existing knowledge produces new knowledge via the application process. They identify mechanisms that firms might apply to induce the scalability of organizational knowledge – what they call "scalable structuration." The authors then describe a case example of Infosys, a company that relied extensively on a knowledge-based approach to organic growth. Through the case, they find that in exploiting existing knowledge, firms must explicate the knowledge for future use, and then develop that knowledge to make it a collective asset available to all. They finally caution organizations to avoid the potential for competence traps that result from rigidities associated with over-reliance on existing perspectives and knowledge stocks (Leonard-Barton, 1992; Levitt & March, 1988).

Knowledge management also emerges as a central theme in Chapter 13, "Stay tuned: knowledge brokering via inter-firm collaboration in satellite radio," as Chad Navis, MaryAnn Glynn, and Andrew Hargadon explore how firms assemble knowledge through inter-firm collaborations to enable innovation and organic growth. They argue that collaborative partnerships serve as integrating mechanisms that can amass new resources and overcome the institutional constraints to the creation of new growth platforms. They illustrate their ideas with case illustrations of two satellite radio firms, XM and Sirius. They propose that collaboration of this type occurs in two stages. In the first stage, collaborations are aimed at securing legitimacy for the new venture. This entails positioning the service to be familiar to mass market outlets, in this instance multi-channel radio service to automotive vehicles, which requires collaboration with partners with strong reputations in automotive and technology sectors. The second stage leverages the positional advantages of the first stage by targeting more specialized niche markets. Such specialized niches pursued in this case were the marine/boat market, weather reporting for the aviation

Table 1.1. *Organic growth issues by chapter/author*

Issue	Case examples										
	Siemens	Home Depot	SYSCO	UPS	Joyce	Hitt et al.	McGrath	Anderson	Bowman & Narayandas	Garud et al.	Navis et al.
Organizational transformation	✓	✓									
Developing a platform for growth	✓	✓	✓	✓	✓	✓	✓			✓	✓
Growth via geographic expansion	✓	✓	✓	✓	✓	✓		✓			
Developing innovative products and services	✓	✓	✓	✓	✓	✓	✓	✓	✓	✓	✓
Efficiency and the use of technology	✓	✓	✓	✓	✓						
Role of people and leadership	✓	✓	✓	✓		✓	✓			✓	✓
Role of measurements, rewards, and employee ownership	✓	✓	✓	✓	✓						
Organizational structures and processes				✓	✓	✓	✓	✓	✓	✓	✓
Customer centeredness	✓	✓	✓	✓							

and marine markets, and home receivers. These collaborations create growth opportunities available to all collaborating firms. Navis, Glynn, and Hargadon conclude with implications for theory and practice.

Central themes in organic growth

A close reading of this book will indicate a number of central themes developed by the authors that emerge as essential to successful organic growth. Table 1.1 presents an issue-by-author matrix. The rows indicate nine specific issues that we have identified as significant elements central to the arguments and positions of the authors of at least two chapters. In the columns are specific authors. The case chapters are indicated by company name. (In this analysis, we have omitted Chapter 7, "Defining and measuring organic growth," by Edward D. Hess because he restricts his discussion exclusively to questions of definition and measurement and does not examine elements associated with attaining growth.) Although authors may have briefly referenced some or all of these issues, to be indicated on the matrix, the issue had to be central to their line of argument. The issues identified are as follows.

Organizational transformation

Several of the case chapters present the need to address organizational problems that detracted from the firm's competitiveness. These include excess operating capacity, above-average cost structures, lack of focus on customer needs, and inadequate investment in enabling technologies. For example, at Siemens Medical Solutions the successful realization of organic growth was precipitated by a drop in financial performance which led to renewed commitment to competitiveness and an aggressive campaign to restructure operations and product/service offerings. Similarly, at The Home Depot, the experience of "hitting the wall" coupled with the arrival of new management led to fundamental changes in supply chain integration and store design that were part of the return to growth. In some circumstances, transforming the competitive capability of a firm may be a first step in the pursuit of organic growth.

Developing a platform for growth

All of the case chapters, as well as several other authors, identify the need for what we term a platform for growth as the basis for organic expansion. We define a platform as the collection of products, services, and related support functions offered to customers, as well as the assets and competencies of the firm to deliver them. For UPS, this might entail a full range of delivery and logistics services available to segmented markets of consumers, small to medium companies, and global enterprises, as well as the skilled employees, fleet of trucks and aircraft, sorting hubs, and enabling technologies to support them. For SYSCO, the platform would be the collection of food and non-food products and services offered to their highly segmented customer groups, as well as their complex of trucks, warehouses, logistical processes, and skilled employees that deliver them. It is interesting to note that several chapters indicate that elements of the platform are commonly realized through acquisition of other companies, typically small or medium-sized firms, specifically for their assets or capabilities, which complement the platform and therefore support further organic growth. This concept of a platform for growth has not been widely discussed in the growth literature.

Growth via geographic expansion

One commonly pursued option for organic growth mentioned by several authors is expansion to new geographic markets. As presented, this usually assumes extending the same collection of products and services into the new markets. Specific examples of this type of growth include UPS's global expansion and SYSCO's shift from being a local or regional competitor to become a national distributor. Of course, each different geographic target presents different product preferences, infra-structural support requirements, as well as systems of regulatory oversight, all of which may require some modification to the platform for growth.

Developing innovative products and services

Almost all authors see innovations in products and services as a central mechanism for growth. The case chapters all discussed the need for innovative products as central to market share and revenue growth, and several identified the opportunity to extend their customer offerings from core products to new product categories as well as to services. At Siemens Medical Solutions, this included the development of cutting-edge medical imaging equipment as well as the development of information technology support services to facilitate the processing, storage, and retrieval of patient data. Several of the other chapters discussed management challenges associated with the organizational processes that are central to new product development. Garud, Kumaraswamy, and Sambamurthy discuss the importance of the leverage and extension of existing knowledge and capabilities as a basis for such innovation, while McGrath carefully describes the specific role of middle managers in developing new products and businesses.

Efficiency and the use of technology

Much of the existing perspective on organic growth has emphasized geographic market expansion and innovation in products and services, discussed above. Few references are found that relate efficiency to organic growth. However, all of the case chapters emphasize the need for operational efficiency and adequate investment in enabling technologies as central to the competitiveness required for growth. Interestingly, much of the academic literature equates efficiency with a strategy of competing on cost, which is usually associated with slower growing, mature industries. We find here that all of the case examples of successful organic growth companies see this as central to their success.

Role of people and leadership

Several authors within the general management and academic perspectives emphasized the role of human capital in organic growth, whether as central to the general implementation process, the innovation process, or in the knowledge development process. For example, both SYSCO and UPS adopted a promote-from-within practice as a mechanism to foster and retain an extensive knowledge and experience base necessary for growth and innovation. Hitt, Ireland, and Tuggle make a compelling argument that initiating the pursuit of strategic entrepreneurship requires consistent focus and appropriate allocation of resources by senior leadership. Within this view, shared by several other authors, the articulation of a clear strategy with a specific focus on organic growth as well as the design of the associated social architecture required for implementation is the product of effective leadership.

Role of measurements, rewards, and employee ownership

The SYSCO and UPS case examples emphasize the importance of identifying and measuring those critical organizational processes that are closely tied to organic growth. This enables the organization to highlight expectations, to monitor results, and ultimately to reward employees commensurate with performance, thereby creating a clear sense of accountability and a performance culture within the firm. At The Home Depot, the adoption of these measurements was part of their transformation process. This approach enables the firms to align individual objectives and motivations with those of the shareholders, creating a sense of ownership among employees. UPS and SYSCO take this a step further by rewarding performance with stock, thereby making employees owners directly. In his description of the strategic and organizational alignment associated with organic growth, Joyce also highlights these factors.

Organizational structures and processes

Several of the scholars of growth highlight the importance of formal structures and coordination processes central to organic growth. Joyce finds a direct relationship of organizational structures that are flat, facilitating responsive decision-making, to performance. Both McGrath and Anderson in their chapters each discuss structural options and the associated critical process milestones for the incubation of new businesses. In their chapter, Garud, Kumaraswamy, and Sambamurthy present ideas for the sharing and development of organizational knowledge that is a foundation of innovation and new product or new business development. Finally, Navis, Glynn, and Hargadon describe the alliances and inter-organizational collaboration necessary to launch a new service offering.

Customer centeredness

Finally, all of the case chapters recognize customer centeredness as an imperative for successful organic growth. Each, to one degree or another, describes careful and detailed analysis of customer requirements as the primary consideration in the design of products, services, operations, supply chain dynamics, and customer support systems.

In developing this further, Bowman and Narayandas in their chapter present a specific framework and logic for allocating resources to those factors found integral to the growth of revenue from existing customers. They argue that such an approach is more profitable and effective than the perennial search for new customers.

Beyond these central issues, an examination of the body of the matrix suggests some interesting patterns in the perspectives of the general management orientation presented in the case chapters and those of the academic researchers presented in the rest of the book, raising several possible new areas for productive research related to organic growth. We will discuss Table 1.1 again in Chapter 14 as a basis for proposing several areas worthy of future research suggested by these patterns.

References

Heskett, J. L., Jones, T. O., Loveman, G. W., Sasser, W. Earl, Jr., & Schlesinger, L. A. 1994. Putting the service profit-chain to work. *Harvard Business Review*, 72(2): 164–174.

Hitt, M. A., Harrison, J. S., & Ireland, R. D. 2001. *Mergers and Acquisitions: A Guide to Creating Value for Stakeholders*. New York: Oxford University Press.

Hitt, M. A., Ireland, R. D., Camp, S. M., & Sexton, D. L. 2001. Guest editors' introduction to the Special Issue "Strategic entrepreneurship: entrepreneurial strategies for wealth creation." *Strategic Management Journal*, 22 (Special Issue): 479–491.

2002. Strategic entrepreneurship: integrating entrepreneurial and strategic management perspectives. In M. A. Hitt, R. D. Ireland, S. M. Camp, & D. L. Sexton (eds.), *Strategic Entrepreneurship: Creating a New Mindset*. Oxford: Blackwell.

Ireland, R. D., Hitt, M. A., & Sirmon, D. G. 2003. A model of strategic entrepreneurship: the construct and its dimensions. *Journal of Management*, 29: 963–989.

Joyce, W., Nohria, N., & Roberson, B. 2003. *What Really Works: The 4+2 Formula for Sustained Business Performance*. New York: Harper Business.

Kazanjian, R. K., Drazin, R., & Glynn, M. A. 2002. Implementing strategies for corporate entrepreneurship: a knowledge-based view. In M. A. Hitt, R. D. Ireland, S. M. Camp, & D. L. Sexton (eds.), *Strategic Entrepreneurship: Creating a New Mindset*. Oxford: Blackwell.

Leonard-Barton, D. 1992. Core capabilities and core rigidities: a paradox in managing new product development. *Strategic Management Journal*, 13: 111–125.

Levitt, B. and March, J. G. 1988. Organizational learning. *Annual Review of Sociology*, 14: 319–340.

O'Reilly, C. A. & Tushman, M. L. 2004. The ambidextrous organization. *Harvard Business Review*, 82(4): 74–83.

Sirower, M. L. 1997. *The Synergy Trap: How Companies Lose the Acquisition Game*. New York: The Free Press.

Zook, C. & Allen, J. 2003. Growth outside the core. *Harvard Business Review*, 81(12): 66–75.

2 | *Profitable growth at Siemens Medical Solutions*

ERICH R. REINHARDT

B ENJAMIN FRANKLIN once said: "Drive thy business or it will drive thee." This statement is true for any business in any industry and it is vital to understanding the concept of business growth. No business wants to go stale or get into a rut. Executives want to continually drive business growth, optimize profits, and ultimately be the best.

Webster's Dictionary defines growth as "an increase in size, number, value or strength." The next entry, for a growth company, is: "a company whose rate of growth markedly exceeds that of the average in its field or the overall rate of economic growth." Many believe that growth at large companies is difficult and more often than not these organizations "hit the growth wall" or become victims of their own size. While some companies do meet such a demise, Siemens Medical Solutions (MED) has been able to transform its business strategy, processes, and culture to overcome financial and industry downturns and drive sustained profitable growth (Knowledge@Emory, 2003).

Company background

MED is part of the global electronics leader, Siemens AG, which ranks first among the world's electronics and electrical equipment companies, with €74 billion in sales and more than 425,000 employees.

MED has a long history in the healthcare industry that dates back to 1877 when Erwin Mortiz Reiniger started manufacturing medical devices at the company's headquarters in Erlangen, Germany. After the discovery of the X-ray, the company successfully developed the first tube and equipment, and trend-setting innovations continued to drive the growth of the company (Table 2.1) (Mills & Kurz, 2003).

Today, with more than €7 billion in sales and 31,000 employees around the globe, MED is one of the largest suppliers to the healthcare industry (Figure 2.1). The company is known for bringing together

Table 2.1. *Siemens Medical Solutions: significant innovations*

1896	Industrially manufactured X-ray tubes for medical diagnostics
1911	First electrocardiogram with electronic signal intensification
1913	First electric hearing aid worldwide
1956	Universal measurement system for nuclear medicine
1958	Implantable cardiac pacemaker developed in Sweden
1966	First ultrasound echography device with real-time display
1975	First instant image in computed tomography produced on a Siemens device
1982	Erlangen technicians install first Siemens magnetic resonance imaging system in the United States
1992	First digital network in a radiology department, installed in Vienna Hospital
1995	First UFC detector
1999	Introduction of Syngo software platform for all modalities and workstations
2002	First European installation of Biograph, a combined position emission tomography (PET) and computed tomography (CT) system

innovative medical technologies, healthcare information systems, management consulting, and support services, to help its customers achieve tangible clinical and financial outcomes. MED is composed of nine divisions with offerings that range from imaging systems for diagnosis, e.g. CT (computed tomography), MR (magnetic resonance), and ultrasound, to therapeutic equipment, to healthcare information systems, to hearing instruments and beyond (Table 2.2).

The United States is particularly important to the company. Almost 50% of MED's sales are made in that country and four of the nine divisions have their headquarters there. Overall, MED employs more than 12,000 people in the United States.

Most recently, MED has achieved six consecutive years of profitable growth (Figure 2.2). In fiscal year 2003, it generated a profit of €1.1 billion on €7.4 billion in sales. This is impressive because the company reported a loss of €84 million on €3.4 billion in sales in fiscal year 1997 and, at that time, was facing a great number of external and internal challenges.

The company's profitable growth since then – as well as its corresponding market share gains – have been achieved through a broad range of actions that can generally be classified into three main

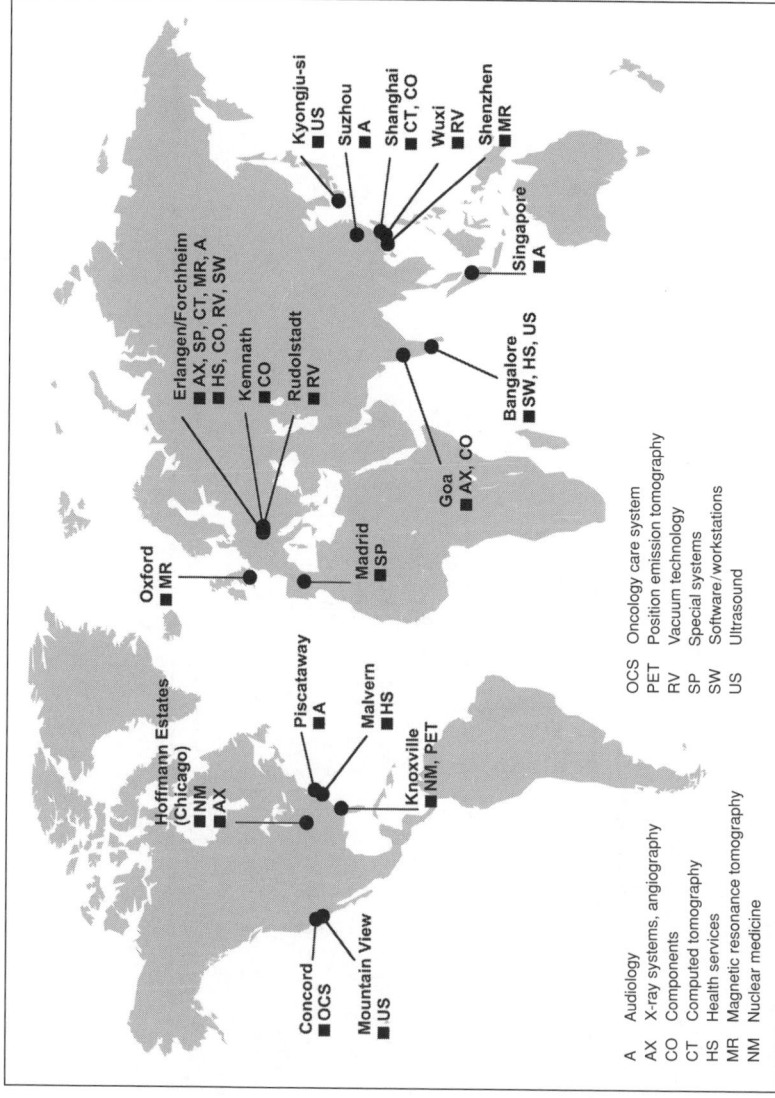

Figure 2.1. A global company.

Table 2.2. A customer-oriented organization

External

| According to customer requirements | Customers Sales and service | | | | | | | |

Internal

| According to operational requirements | X-ray systems Angiography (AX) | Special systems (SP) | Computed tomography (CT) AXIOM Artis of TA | Magnetic resonance tomography (MR) | Nuclear medicine (NM) | Ultrasound (US) | Oncology care systems (OCS) | Health services (HS) | Audiology (A) |

Joint management
(Strategy, Finance, Business Administration, Human Resources)

Joint functions
(Basic R&D, Service Support, Group Communications, Environmental Protection . . .)

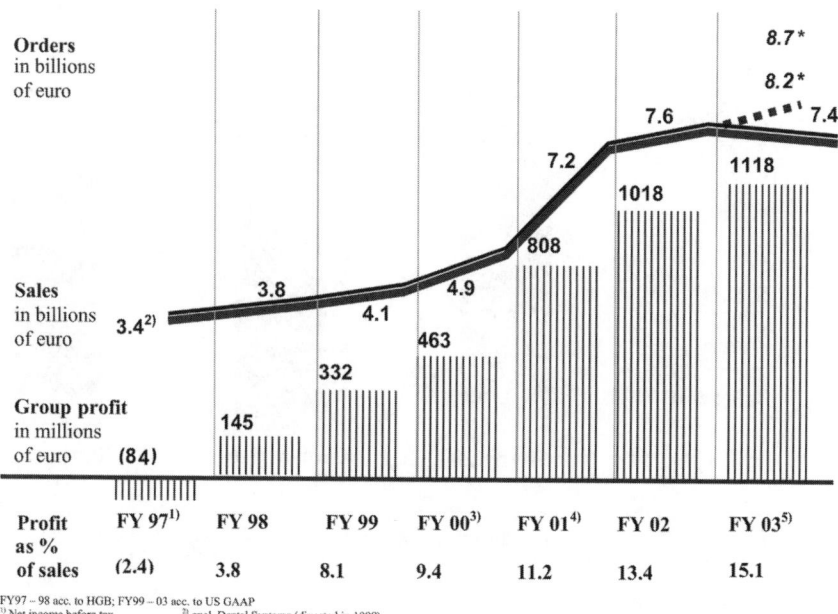

FY97 – 98 acc. to HGB; FY99 – 03 acc. to US GAAP
[1] Net income before tax   [2] excl. Dental Systems (divested in 1998)
[3] incl. Shared Medical Systems in Q4   [4] incl. 11 months Acuson   * *Comparable basis*
[5] Group profit included 63 mill. euro gain from portfolio transactions

Figure 2.2. Continual profitable growth.

objectives: initially restructure the business; continuously improve operational efficiency; and capitalize on new business opportunities. The following story describes in more detail the situation in the mid-nineties and explores each of these objectives, highlighting some of the challenges and identifying key success factors.

The changing (and challenging) healthcare industry

In the mid-nineties MED was facing several industry challenges. Healthcare providers were continually challenged with trying to reduce costs (Mills & Kurz, 2003). In addition, these same groups were changing the way they purchased medical equipment. In the past, equipment was purchased for superior technical performance and quality, but as a result of cost pressures, healthcare providers began looking much more closely at the bottom line before purchasing equipment. With healthcare providers facing severe cost pressure, the medical equipment industry was left with overcapacity and continued price erosion.

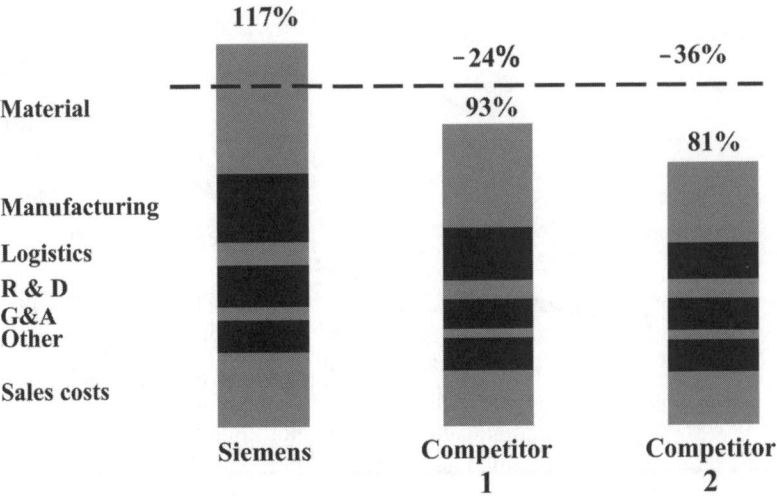

Figure 2.3. Business cost disadvantages.

Competition in the healthcare market was also changing. Before the nineties there were several medical equipment providers, but cost pressure and declining sales forced several competitors to close or to be acquired by the larger companies. Competition was intense during this period and three major players ultimately emerged: Siemens, General Electric, and Philips.

However, MED was at a significant cost disadvantage compared to its competitors. For example, a 1995 benchmarking study demonstrated that the cost disadvantage for computed tomography (CT) equipment was 25% to 35% compared to other major competitors (Siemens Medical Solutions, 1995) (Figure 2.3). A large portion of the gap was in two areas: materials and manufacturing. When the company conducted an investigation, it learned that manufacturing overcapacity was worse than previously thought and that overhead costs were also higher than those of competitors. Furthermore, the increased rates of technical innovation were causing continual erosion of manufacturing content.

While these external and internal factors already provided a difficult foundation, a routine investigation into the company by the US Food & Drug Administration (FDA) identified areas of non-compliance with Good Manufacturing Practice (GMP) regulations. The resulting

Table 2.3. *MED's main objectives for profitable growth*

	Part 1 Reduce manufacturing	Part 2 Consolidate
Moment of truth	capacity	manufacturing facilities
Restructuring		
Operational efficiency	Top+ P³	
New business opportunities		
1996	1998	Today

citation from the FDA forced MED temporarily to shut down four facilities in 1995. Subsequent compliance efforts took almost two years (1,400 man-years) and cost approximately €250 million. Just as important, the time dedicated to ensuring that GMP requirements were met delayed the company in making necessary productivity improvements.

MED faced its moment of truth in 1996 when it was clear that the situation was not improving. In fact, exactly the opposite was true: instead of the €90 million profit forecast for the upcoming year (1997), a loss was likely. It was clear that the time had come to make dramatic changes and consequently to set the company on a course for profitable growth. So how does a large, multi-national company handle a task of this magnitude? MED started with a top-down approach involving more than twenty executives in daily intensive one-on-one and plenary sessions over a three-week period. The aggressive program initially created shock among the company's management, but it very quickly stimulated survival energy and a sense of urgency; generated support for strategic initiatives; and resulted in agreement on the major actions to be initiated. From these meetings, MED defined three broad objectives (Table 2.3):

– restructure to align the company's resources better;
– introduction of the Top+ program to increase operational efficiency; and
– identify new business opportunities to generate growth for the future.

In terms of financial goals, the company's target at the time, an 8% return on sales by 2000, did not change (Mills & Kurz, 2003). Management's mantra was clear: "We stick to our targets!"

Mastering objective number 1: Restructuring

To achieve this goal, MED restructured its operations, concentrating on manufacturing, work force, and internal group structures. The first step was to achieve a significant reduction of manufacturing capacity. To do this, the company reduced the scope of the activities that were handled internally. Many low-value-added steps – such as basic parts or cable manufacturing – were outsourced.

The second step was to consolidate manufacturing facilities. Resources that were freed up were shut down or sold off. For example, consolidation and process improvements allowed the manufacturing facilities at the company's headquarters in Erlangen, Germany to be reduced by 30% in space, reducing total facility costs by 40%. Buildings with almost 700,000 sq. ft. of space were demolished. The company has invested in new facilities with a process-oriented layout near where the old buildings stood. According to internal reporting, cost productivity increased by 26% and employee productivity by 43% in three years as a result of these actions (Siemens Medical Solutions Internal Report).

In addition to the consolidations and efficiency programs it was also necessary to adjust the company's work force. During this period, approximately 1,200 employees in Germany (about 20% of the work force at the time) lost their jobs and 800 jobs in other countries were also eliminated.

Structural changes in the group organization and adjustments of administrative functions were also made. For example, each division's software activities were bundled into a software center of competence that acts as an internal supplier to the divisions. This not only allows the company to be faster and more efficient in developing software, but it also provides tremendous benefits to customers as all MED products include software with a common look and feel. Shared service organizations that consolidated functions such as general accounting and payroll were formed as well.

Results: The actions implemented during MED's restructuring period helped the company to regain its competitiveness, and effectively set the stage for the implementation of a comprehensive, ongoing initiative to drive the company's growth.

Targeting objective number 2: Operational efficiency

While changes were being made to the manufacturing processes and other functions, significant changes were also initiated to improve the company's overall operational efficiency. These changes were organized under the Top+ Program called P^3, or "P to the Power of 3," a business excellence initiative focused on p̲eople, p̲rocesses, and p̲roducts. The program proved to be, and remains today, the enabler of the company's sustained profitable growth.

Understanding the value of employees

The *people* component of the P^3 program focuses on motivation and leadership. In 1996, an assessment of the management at MED revealed that there were deficiencies in the leadership team (Mills & Kurz, 2003). The company dedicated much time to human resources initiatives including training and shifting managers to roles that better suited their talents. It was, and still is, absolutely essential that the company attract and motivate the best talent worldwide and continuously improve leadership quality. To achieve the latter, a program was launched through which up to 1,000 managers around the globe are evaluated every year. This mechanism to review managers formally on a regular basis allows actions, such as training, job rotation, and if necessary, dismissal, for performance improvement to be defined and implemented with vigorous control. In addition, the company instituted competency programs that include the Siemens Graduate Program and KnowledgeSharing.

The Siemens Graduate Program is focused on identifying and developing employees who could assume leadership positions at MED in the future. These employees are rotated to different business divisions, taking on new responsibilities at each assignment.

The KnowledgeSharing program exemplifies a key focus of the organization – continual innovation and access to new ideas. Innovation and process management are driving forces behind MED's continued growth in sales and earnings (Birk & Muller, 2002). The initiative was developed for real-time information-sharing, allowing knowledge created by employees anywhere within the Siemens network to be available to all other employees. KnowledgeSharing is a holistic approach to an organizational need and is supported from the top. Six factors are crucial for the implementation and continued success of the program: top management support, a common topic structure, identification and support of communities of practice, user-friendly IT, support structures and processes, and incentive structures. The basic structure of this program was fashioned on a model developed by the European Foundation for Quality Management (EFQM), an organization focused on assisting corporations with improving customer and employee satisfaction as well as business results (Birk & Muller, 2002).

Process-focused initiatives to drive efficiency

While people are an important component of the foundation for growth, the company also focuses strongly on improving all operational *processes* for greater efficiency and increased speed to market.

In particular, this aspect of P[3] often meets with a number of barriers or challenges including reluctance to change, adjustments to culture, mistrust, functional vs. departmental thinking, and fears of losing power. In order to address the potential employee conflict with change, barrier removal teams were implemented and charged with identifying and prioritizing areas of conflict, defining removal action plans, implementing and controlling the transition, and then identifying new barriers. By becoming a process-oriented organization, the company has been able to create the capability to cooperate with several groups, including customers and partners, on a local, regional, and global basis; develop customer orientation throughout the organization; create a culture sensitive to changes in the marketplace; and develop a lean organization that can respond quickly to change. It is important to note that cultural change is the result of living the process, not a prerequisite!

The migration to a process-driven organization culminated in the introduction of the "Process House," which is focused on optimizing and standardizing the company's management, customer relationship management, supply chain management, product life cycle management, and support processes. In the "Process House" processes are defined "from the customer, to the customer." Customers are an integral part of the company's processes and all activities are focused on providing solutions that help meet their needs.

**Delivering innovative solutions that meet the healthcare
industry's needs**

The third P in the program is *product* and describes MED's commitment to developing trend-setting, innovative technologies that drive growth. This approach requires that the company intimately understands customers' workflow, e.g. their clinical and operational processes, their process interfaces as well as the interfaces between MED's equipment, IT, and services, and the interaction of all these components.

Partnerships with customers and academia have also been essential in developing the trend-setting technologies that help improve healthcare efficiency. As partnerships create a stimulating atmosphere to drive innovation, the company refocused its efforts on defining and maintaining close relationships with the scientific community and customers. For example, in the MR (magnetic resonance) division, there are now more than 800 agreements for on-site development with customers. MED also regularly conducts workshops with customers all around the world to help identify their needs and to ensure that the company's products, IT solutions, and services help to solve real problems. These partnerships not only provide MED with direct access to customers and their needs, but also with access to other great thinkers to help propel the company to the front lines of product innovation and healthcare issues. Finally, R&D spending has remained continuously at approximately 8–9% of sales.

Also in 2003, MED continued to focus on innovation and partnership with the foremost authorities in healthcare by undertaking several new activities to further the field of molecular imaging. Molecular imaging allows non-invasive measurement of molecular and biological processes within the living body. Compared to conventional diagnostic imaging, molecular imaging probes the molecular abnormalities that are the origin of disease, rather than imaging the resulting conditions caused by the disease. The company extended its partnership with the Center for Molecular Imaging Research at Massachusetts General Hospital and Harvard Medical School, one of the world's leading molecular imaging centers, to further develop and test cutting-edge imaging applications in laboratory models and clinical studies. In August 2003, the company also introduced *bon*SAI, a fluorescence optical imaging technology that could have a profound impact on the way drugs are developed and diseases are understood and treated. This prototype

Table 2.4. *Profitable growth through innovation*

	Increase in revenue, 1998–2003 (%)	Increase in market share, 1998–2003 (% points)
CT	122	10
MR	69	6
X-ray	23	8

product is now in use in the pre-clinical environment, and could have vast future potential in human imaging.

Results: The actions associated with MED's Top+ Program, P^3, as well as the actions implemented during the company's restructuring, have directly contributed to the company's profitable growth by helping to decrease its cost base and increase its power to innovate.

The P^3 Program resulted in total cost productivity of €3.0 billion between September 1997 and September 2003, which was, in effect, money directly to the company's bottom line. However, cost productivity is not only important to improve the company's financial results. Continual cost productivity also puts the company in a good position to continue to grow, i.e. to gain market share, even when market conditions become difficult, such as with overcapacity and price erosion.

The commitment to increasing the company's innovation power has proven valuable. For example, in 2003 the company disclosed an average of three patents per workday. More importantly, many of the divisions have realized substantial sales growth and achieved significant market share gains with their trend-setting technologies that help to increase healthcare efficiency, as shown in Table 2.4. These experiences speak for themselves: innovation drives growth.

Meeting objective number 3: New business opportunities

As MED began to reshape itself, management quickly realized that changes in the healthcare industry also demanded a new vision and strategy to drive future business growth. The company, therefore, defined a new vision to meet the market's changing needs: high-quality, patient-centered healthcare with best processes and proven outcomes (Figure 2.4). The corresponding strategy to achieve this was defined as improving healthcare efficiency, which means improving the quality

Vision:
High quality, patient-centered healthcare with best processes and proven outcomes

Strategy:

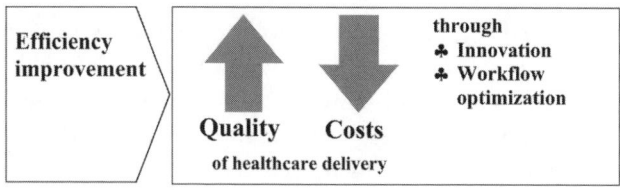

Figure 2.4. The goal: improve healthcare workflow.

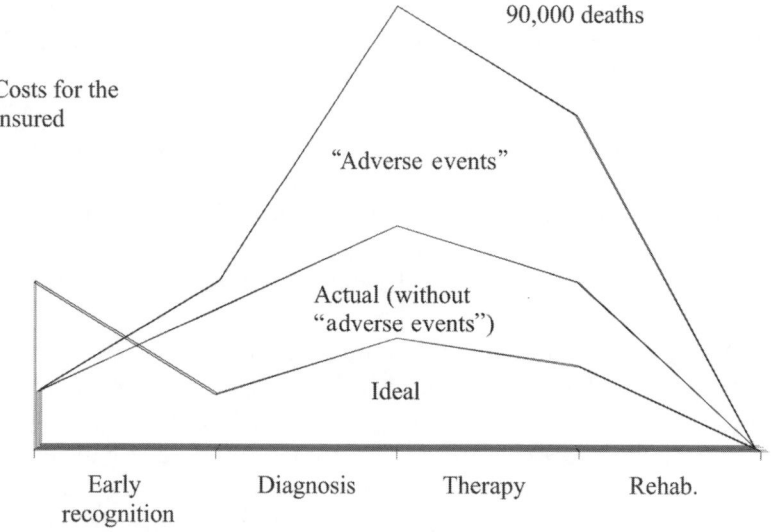

Figure 2.5. Improvements in the quality of care reduce healthcare expenses. (*Source:* Institute of Medicine, 1999, p. 26; American Hospital Association, *Hospital Statistics*, Chicago, 1999.)

of care while simultaneously reducing its cost, through innovation and optimization of healthcare processes. Simply stated: the company had to position itself to help improve healthcare workflow. There is tremendous potential to achieve this goal. For example, according to an Institute of Medicine (IOM) study, *To Err is Human*, approximately 90,000 patients in the United States die each year simply because of medical errors (Institute of Medicine, 1999) (Figure 2.5).

For the company, this meant that its business focus had to change from medical equipment to integrated solutions. In other words, it had to offer a broader range of services and move towards being a solutions provider not just a medical device company.

The company defined the necessary portfolio components to help improve healthcare efficiency and adjusted its portfolio accordingly, e.g. businesses with annual sales of more than €1.1 billion have been divested. More importantly, however, the company also set out to grow the business by obtaining the elements it needed in order to become a supplier of integrated solutions. MED realized that one of the key components to improve healthcare efficiency was healthcare information technology (IT), which can also be seen in the following quote from the IOM: "Healthcare delivery has been relatively untouched by the revolution in information technology that has been transforming nearly every other aspect of society. The development and application of more sophisticated information systems is essential to enhance quality and improve efficiency" (Institute of Medicine, 2001). IT's overall business value is to allow people to work faster and for outcomes to be better than without the technology. IT plus medical devices would establish the company as a leading solution provider focused on improving healthcare efficiency and would be the cornerstone to drive profitable growth.

Acting on this insight, MED purchased Shared Medical Services (SMS), the leading supplier of IT systems and services for administrative and clinical processes in the healthcare industry, in July 2000 for $2.1 billion. After the acquisition of SMS, MED had diagnostic and therapeutic equipment, which could be connected via a hospital-wide network, and software applications that could help manage billing and patient data. Therefore, MED became the first company to develop compelling offerings of both medical equipment and IT systems and services, in essence offering value that is greater than the sum of the parts. This proposition has been very well received by customers.

Another key portfolio component that was added was the purchase of Acuson, an innovation leader in ultrasound solutions with a strong brand name, in November 2000 for just less than $700 million. This acquisition propelled Siemens from sixth or seventh in the world ultrasound market to the leading position.

Results: These portfolio changes not only prepared the groundwork for MED's on-going transformation and a new market positioning, but they also substantially expanded the size of the company's addressable

Table 2.5. *Continued market growth*

	Global market (€billion)			
Product segment	FY 1996	FY 2003	FY 2008 (est).	Projected annual growth (%)
Imaging systems (X-ray, CT, MR, NM, US)	8.8	14.2	16.2	2.5
Oncology care systems	0.4	1.4	1.8	5
Electromedical systems	0.9	2.9	3.4	3
Audiology	1.9	1.8	2.1	3
Product-related services	5.1	8.0	10.0	5
Health services	n.a.	12.7	20.5	10

market – and did so in market segments that are growing significantly faster than the company's traditional market (Table 2.5). For example, healthcare IT is anticipated to grow on average approximately 10% annually to 2008, whereas the company's traditional imaging market is expected to grow considerably more slowly at 2.5% (Siemens Medical Solutions Internal Report).

Furthermore, with each acquisition, the company was granted greater access to innovative thinkers and inventions. These deals gave the company skills and competencies it did not possess – and, in turn, an advantage in the marketplace. In short, they helped pave the way for future growth.

Success factors

Many factors led to the successful MED turnaround and, more importantly, sustained profitable growth. Key factors include:
(1) *Each division head is the worldwide entrepreneur* (i.e. each division is responsible for program implementation). Management works with each division to define clear goals and objectives, but it is the division's responsibility to meet these goals.
(2) *Support of cross-divisional activities.* One particularly important skill that entrepreneurs in a large organization must have is the ability to recognize and efficiently use internal cross-division synergies. The company's division heads must see where there are synergies with other divisions (i.e. where products, software, and services

can be effectively combined to optimize healthcare workflow) and then must work together accordingly. Here it is also important that top management be able quickly to identify and resolve conflicts that may arise between divisions.

(3) *Transparency with top-down goals/targets and bottom-up measures and personalized responsibilities.* This component allows employees to take ownership and drive the initiative. Actions are identified by each division according to the specific impact to the bottom line, deadline, and responsibility.

(4) *Stringent implementation controlling, which incorporates ongoing reviews with fast consequences.* This helps employees quickly understand the repercussions of their actions.

The future of growth in healthcare

The transformation and changes at MED allowed the company to position itself for growth and become a world leader in healthcare. Some of the many examples of the company's concrete contribution to increased healthcare efficiency are outlined in the following paragraphs.

Addressing efficiency and effectiveness

Cincinnati Children's Hospital Medical Center, the 2003 recipient of the prestigious Healthcare Information Management and Systems Society's (HIMSS) Nicholas E. Davies Award of Excellence for Electronic Health Record (eHR), was able to reduce medication errors by 35% and decrease medication turnaround time by 52% through the use of an integrated clinical information system.

In addition, South Carolina Heart Center has reduced the time it takes to get a cardiac cath lab report from two days to just fifteen minutes, and the resulting time savings have enabled greater efficiencies, generating an increase in revenue of more than $700 million.

An all-digital hospital: Scott & White Center for Advanced Medicine

Scott & White's Center for Advanced Medicine in Temple, Texas, is the first comprehensive, all-digital healthcare facility in the United States and opened in 2005 with the assistance of MED, as well as many other Siemens divisions. A truly integrated hospital, Scott & White will utilize Siemens healthcare information technology solutions for patient monitoring and for connecting all hospital departments to allow more effective and efficient patient care. Siemens was chosen as a partner for this alliance because of the company's ability to provide high-end technology products and integrate complex systems across various locations and hospital departments (Siemens Medical Solutions Internal Report).

Conclusion

The transformation and profitable growth achieved at MED is an example of the results of many excellent practices coming together. The company's initial reorganization allowed it to align its resources better to a changing and challenging market environment; it enabled the company to improve its cost position substantially and to concentrate better on its core competencies. By continually striving to improve operational efficiency, especially by focusing on people, processes, and products, the company became leaner and more tuned to customer needs. And, finally, by defining and establishing a portfolio based on current and future market needs – this especially involved adding information technology and therewith the ability to create integrated solutions that increase efficiency in healthcare – the company has established the foundation to drive growth well into the future.

While the company is well positioned for growth in the future – all of its divisions are in a number one or two position in their respective markets – it understands that this will require many of the same, as well as many new, practices that have helped to drive growth to date. One thing is for certain: competition is intensifying and MED can only be in the world class by having the strongest cost position and the most innovative products, as well as continually improving. As Oliver Cromwell, the seventeenth-century British leader, once said, "He who stops being better, stops being good."

References

Birk, D. & Muller, M. 2002. KnowledgeSharing@Med – turning knowledge into business. In T. H. Davenport, J. B. Gilber, & J. Probst (eds.), *Knowledge Management Case Book*, 2nd edn. Hoboken, NJ: Wiley.

2001. *Crossing the Quality Chasm: A New Health System for the 21st Century*. Washington, DC.

Institute of Medicine 1999. *To Err is Human: Building a Safer Health System*. Washington, DC.

Knowledge@Emory 2003. Can large companies be entrepreneurial? Emory
    University   (October).   http://knowledge.emory.edu/index.cfm?fa=
    viewArticle&id=720.
Mills, D. Q. & Kurz, J. 2003. Siemens Medical Solutions: strategic
    turnaround. Harvard Business School Case.
Siemens Medical Solutions 1995. Analysis result of a Boston Consulting
    Group Study. Unpublished report.

3 | UPS: Brown's organic growth story

EDWARD D. HESS

THIS is UPS's growth story from its birth in 1907 in Seattle, Washington when nineteen-year-old Jim Casey started a messenger and home delivery service for city department stores. Today UPS is a global public company with more than $36 billion of revenue, and operations in over 200 countries and territories.

This chapter will discuss how UPS grew organically and explain how UPS's culture and internal processes have relentlessly focused the company on growing organically. We will attempt to answer the following questions: How does UPS keep evolving? Why has it not become arrogant, complacent, or insular? How has UPS institutionalized organic growth into its culture, processes, and business model?

What is UPS?

UPS is headquartered in Atlanta, Georgia and employs 384,000 employees worldwide. Of these, approximately 40,000 work in countries other than the United States and fewer than 40 of those 40,000 employees are US expatriates. UPS is the fourth largest employer in the United States.

UPS's worldwide revenues of $36 billion are derived primarily from the delivery of packages and documents. In the last five years, UPS has expanded the scope of its services to provide freight forwarding, customs clearance, inventory management, pick and pack, export financing, and customer returns and repairs so as to be a service provider along the entire supply and distribution chain.

UPS is a vertically integrated company. For example, it operates the world's eleventh largest airline, maintaining its own air fleet of 569 jets and employing over 2,500 pilots. The UPS airline moves more than 2 million packages and documents daily, flying over 1,800 flight segments to more than 850 airports in the world.

UPS is also a large technology company and a telecommunications company. It operates the largest DB2 database in the world with 412 terabytes of dynamic memory. Its mainframe capacity allows for the transmission of more than 22 million instructions per second. UPS employs over 4,700 employees in its technology unit, and it also operates the world's largest phone system. UPS's mobile radio network transmits more than 3 million packets of tracking data each day. Its communication scale is further illustrated by the fact that it has over 145 million hits per business day on its website with peak days of 252 million hits. It processes 10 million tracking requests a day.

UPS delivers over 14 million packages a day and is the Internet's largest fulfillment source. It serves nearly 8 million customers daily, and it has the capacity to deliver a package or document to every address in the United States. And it delivers those 14 million packages 99% plus on time and defect-free. The company operates one of the largest truck fleets in the United States – more than 88,000 vehicles, including 1,800 modern alternative-fuel vehicles.

UPS's growth can best be illustrated by its revenue growth from $29.4 billion in the year 2000 to over $36 billion in the year 2004. UPS's business model has produced operating margins which are the best in its industry and UPS has averaged 12% annual growth over the past decade and generated an average return on equity in excess of 20%.

The scale of UPS can further be illustrated by its Worldport technology and package hub at Louisville, Kentucky. This automated "airport" and package sorting center has an area of 4 million square feet, the equivalent of eighty football fields, and processes some million packages a night over a four-hour period.

UPS's employment turnover is low, less than 6% a year. The tenure of its average driver is sixteen years. Its driver turnover is less than 2% a year. The average tenure of its district managers is fourteen years. Nearly 60% of its work force is unionized. UPS's 85,000 drivers hold an esteemed position in the company. Drivers who are unionized can earn up to $70,000 a year and senior drivers get nine weeks paid annual leave and 100% of their health insurance premiums paid. The UPS work force is also diverse. Over one-third are members of minority groups and over 25% of the company's US managers are members of minority groups. Women represent 27% of its US management team and 21% of its overall work force.

UPS's promotion from within and employee-centric culture can be illustrated by the fact that over 50% of its full-time drivers began as part-timers. Over 70% of its full-time managers were promoted from within. Likewise, 75% of its vice-presidents started at UPS in non-management positions. Over 50% of its full-time work force owns UPS stock.

Tenure and low turnover permeates UPS from its front-line employees to its twelve-person executive team. This Senior Management Team averages thirty years of UPS service and eleven of those twelve executives, who include one woman and one African-American, have spent their entire working lives at UPS. Nine of the twelve members of the Senior Management Team have only an undergraduate college degree. Interestingly, no one has an MBA from Harvard, Wharton, Northwestern, Stanford, or any other top-ranked MBA school. Most went to public colleges like Purdue, Delta State, Portland State, Rutgers, and the University of Illinois.

One member of the twelve-member Senior Management Team, Kurt Kuehn – Senior Vice-President of Sales and Marketing – stated that, "Most senior managers like me began at UPS when part-timers in college as package sorters or assistants. We loved it and we stayed."

UPS became a public company in 1999, going public in the largest IPO in the history of the New York Stock Exchange. Today, about half of UPS stock is owned by its current and former employees and their families. UPS has a market capitalization of $46 billion and is one of only seven public companies with an AAA credit rating from both S&P and Moodys.

The UPS growth story

So, UPS is big and UPS is global. It has over 14 million customer deliveries every day to nearly 8 million customers. Its customer contact points include 3,700 UPS stores in the United States, 1,500 global Mail Box, etc. stores, 1,000 UPS customer centers, 18,000 UPS authorized outlets, and 45,000 UPS drop boxes. UPS is focused on efficiency and productivity and recently spent over $10 billion integrating its processes and technology to make the company a real-time 24/7/365-day operation.

Behind every driver is a sophisticated technology and operations support team that can track the exact location of any package or document anywhere, anytime, and UPS can, on a daily basis, organize every part of the logistics chain for maximum efficiency down to the order in which packages are loaded. Technology has made UPS more adaptable, agile, and quick to respond to daily glitches.

In September 2003, UPS unveiled a new technology system that will further improve customer service and provide greater internal efficiency. When fully deployed, the new system is expected to reduce mileage by more than 100 million miles and save the company almost 14 million gallons of fuel. It features advanced tools that allow UPS to analyze and edit dispatch plans to optimize delivery routes and times.

The UPS factual story would not be complete without looking into its corporate "heart." Two examples of UPS's corporate citizenship stand out. In 1968, at the height of the Civil Rights Movement in the United States, UPS began a diversity awareness program that is to this day unique in corporate America. Called the Community Internship Program, it has placed more than 1,200 senior managers into inner-city poverty or Appalachian poverty environments. These UPSers spend several weeks working in soup kitchens, homeless shelters, and other community service roles.

UPS also issues an annual Corporate Sustainability Report. It is more than eighty pages long and details how UPS balances its economic success with social and environmental objectives, and how it measures such performance. To this end, UPS and its employees were for the past four years the largest contributor to the United States United Way Campaign, contributing more than $57 million in 2005.

In summary, UPS is a large, global, socially and environmentally responsible company, owned primarily by its employees and operates consistently at the top of its industry by emphasizing a promote-from-within policy.

One can look at UPS's growth over a period of ninety-eight years simplistically as an iterative geographic expansion. First, UPS began in Seattle in 1907. The company expanded its intra-city business first to Oakland, California in 1919 and then, over the following fifty-eight years, across the United States, opening its first location in New York City in 1930. UPS expanded its service by opening new locations in new states just like an expanding retailer.

Geographical expansion went international in 1975 when UPS opened in Ontario, Canada, and in 1976 it began operations in Europe, in Düsseldorf, Germany. Since 1975, UPS has expanded throughout the world – Asia Pacific region in 1988 and Latin America in 1989 – and it now operates in over 200 countries and territories, having entered its last untapped market – China – in 1995. So, UPS has grown geographically, operating the world's largest small package delivery network, serving every address in the United States and delivering to every major global center.

Another way to look at UPS's growth story is to look at how its business has changed over its ninety-eight years from a customer viewpoint. UPS began in 1907 and operated for forty-six years as an intra-city delivery business. UPS began delivering packages for large department stores to customers' homes. It then expanded to other types of businesses needing residential and then business deliveries. Changes in the American lifestyle and shopping patterns, beginning with the creation of suburbs, the building of regional malls, and development of the interstate highway system, generated a new UPS focus.

The company responded to these changing demographic, transportation, and customer needs by transforming itself first into a national delivery company and ultimately, in the 1990s, to a global delivery company. UPS's broadening of its customer focus continues today with UPS delivering over 50% of the packages bought over the Internet. UPS's customer base today includes most business types, large and small, from Dell Computer to an entrepreneur selling his or her products over the Internet.

When UPS ran out of geographical areas in which to grow, at least three things could have happened. First, it could have "hit the growth wall" and plateaued; or second, it could have sought to sell new complementary services to its existing customer base; or third, it could have made a major diversification move through acquisition. Not surprisingly, UPS did the second in 1998 when it announced its move to provide synchronized commerce services and solutions to its customer base. Synchronized commerce expanded UPS's market space. Mike Eskew, UPS's chairman and CEO, stated, "Our new mission is ambitious. It propels us from an $80 billion market into a $3.2 trillion market."

In effect, synchronized commerce allows UPS to sell more products and services to its existing customers. To effectuate this model, UPS acquired nearly thirty service providers with expertise in different areas of synchronized commerce: freight forwarders, customer clearers, a bank for export financing, fulfillment services, customer returns and repairs. Eskew defined synchronized commerce as the coordinated and efficient movement of goods, information, and financing along the supply and distribution chain. This initiative, which began in 1998, is still in its infancy – producing $2.4 billion in revenue in 2004.

Arguably, before 1998, UPS grew by moving into new geographic areas and by doing there what it had done well in other places. In 1998, I suggest, UPS in one move redefined its market space. It redefined itself as a solutions company, offering a broad menu of services that could be tailored to an individual customer's supply chain and business-process need chain.

This change was big. It challenged UPS's sales force and it changed the focus of UPS's operations research division. Rather than working exclusively to improve UPS's efficiencies and productivity, the focus shifted to that of a consulting group selling those skills to UPS customers. Up until 1998, UPS primarily increased the geographic scope of its operations; from 1998 it magnified the scope of its offerings.

UPS did not stop with its synchronized commerce initiative, which, in my judgment, was more revolutionary then evolutionary. Chairman Eskew also codified and explained to UPS employees and to Wall Street, UPS's new organic growth strategy. And Eskew named this strategy the "Four Quadrant" model based on the University of North Carolina basketball team's use of the four-quadrant offense. As he stated, "We will call our offense for innovation 'The Four Quadrants' which focuses on innovating existing business operations internally and externally and, likewise, focuses innovation on new entrepreneurial ventures both internally and externally."

The Four Quadrant growth model reemphasized UPS's long-standing principle of maintaining the core while seeking to grow new revenue sources. UPS is adamant that it cannot fail in servicing its core business, and that it must keep adding services onto its existing service model. Kurt Kuehn, Senior Vice-President of Marketing, stated, "The more value we can add for our customers on top of, or within, our existing business model, the more value we will create for our customers and for UPS."

As Kuehn further stated, "Our organic growth strategy is simple: it is the business model."

UPS's entrepreneurial activities are driven by its venture capital fund and alliances with universities and partners. Here UPS understands that it will have a high failure rate but strives to manage its risks so that much can be learned quickly at low cost.

One could stop here and have a good overview of UPS's organic growth story. But that story would miss the rich, underlying drivers of UPS's organic growth. To understand how UPS has institutionalized its organic growth processes into its DNA, one must understand what makes UPS "tick."

To understand how UPS has maintained its vigilance and continued to grow its business over a ninety-eight-year period while avoiding the death spiral of corporate arrogance, hubris, and insularity, one has to understand the UPS culture and the UPS operations research mentality. The two are so integrated and intertwined that they are seamless and both are perpetuated today at UPS through stories, processes, measurement systems, human resource policies, and leadership acts.

Culture

Jim Casey built UPS over a fifty-year period with a distinct and well-defined culture which continues today. That culture embraced the values of integrity, quality, dignity, respect, stewardship, partnership, equality, and humility. To understand UPS you must understand Jim Casey, a man who went to work at age nine because his father was ill and a man who founded UPS as an entrepreneur at age nineteen. He became a self-made success, rising from a humble background and never forgetting his roots. He never forgot to treat every individual and employee with the dignity and respect each is due.

Jim Casey wrote and spoke often about the values which UPS should hold and the type of company it should be. He left a large imprint upon UPS, which today is taught to every employee. And when you ask UPS executives, they talk about their duty to make sure those values, those ways of doing business, and those ways of taking care of employees, continue. They do not want UPS's culture to change or fail "on their watch."

The richness of the culture is evidenced by the Employee Policy Manual which every employee receives and the compendium of Jim Casey speeches in the "Legacy of Leadership" document. Jim Casey wanted to build a business where every employee could actualize their potential. He wanted them to achieve all they could. He also wanted them to take pride in working for a business that conducted itself as an outstanding corporate citizen.

The UPS culture can be summarized as:

(1) a performance culture with partneurial mutuality of accountability, no matter what your position;

(2) a constant challenge-and-be-critical and be-better culture described as constructive dissatisfaction; and

(3) an employee-centric ownership culture with executives being stewards of the business.

When I asked Kurt Kuehn to describe the UPS culture in a few words, he thought a while and stated, "A culture of mutual accountability. Everyone is accountable to everyone else for performance – doing what's right and doing it well." He continued by saying, "With our measurement system, we try to take personalities and politics out of judging performance."

At UPS the CEO is as accountable to employee Jim or Jane as they are to him. And Jim or Jane can and should hold Mike Eskew accountable. This mutual accountability is partneurial because employees are viewed as partners. And most are actual owners of the business. This mutual accountability breeds a more equalitarian culture which discourages or devalues arrogance, hubris, or self-aggrandizement. As examples, all of UPS's top twelve executives have offices on the fourth floor, not the top floor, of the headquarters building. All have the same size office, and almost all share senior administrative assistants. UPS executives are not provided limos or cars with drivers and UPS has no corporate jets. Executives fly with commercial airlines and follow the same travel policies as other employees. There is no executive dining room. It is rare to see French cuffs, Italian suits, or Hong Kong or London tailored, made-to-order shirts on the fourth floor. Eleven of the twelve executives have spent their entire careers at UPS and most have had several different jobs working their way up the organization. The UPS culture frowns on "tooting one's own horn," and UPS works very hard at living daily Jim Casey's values and ideals.

When talking about this mutual performance culture in my talk with Mr. Kuehn, I asked him to describe the performance culture in one word. His choice is informative and gives you a good feel for the passion at UPS. He stated, "RELENTLESS."

UPS is relentless about improving. UPS works at a problem until they get it right. UPS emphasizes the details – the blocking and tackling of business. They are into process – efficiency – productivity. This iterative learning culture is illustrated by a Jim Casey story. When he started his business, he wrote to over a hundred delivery companies across the United States and asked them how they made a profit. He said, "We found no singular idea that was really revolutionary. It seemed to be a matter of learning as we went along, and that is about all that we have done" (UPS Archives, 1947).

The UPS culture is one of the relentless pursuit of constant, incremental improvement. How can we be faster, smarter, more efficient? This leads to the rewarding and honoring of constructive dissatisfaction. Dissent, inquiry, questioning, challenging, and critiquing are all valued and encouraged because it helps UPS be better; it helps UPS compete; and it negates insularity, arrogance, and complacency. UPS people work at it until they get it right. UPS takes a long-term approach. As an example, it took international operations twenty-eight years before it was profitable. UPS just works at a problem or a process incrementally and iteratively until it improves. UPS is like the "little engine that could." UPS believes it can always be better and devalues being satisfied, smug, or complacent.

The third strong aspect of the UPS culture is the partneurial, employee-centric ownership and leaders' duty of stewardship to help everyone achieve their potential.

Jim Casey said it best:

One measure of your success . . . will be the degree to which you build up others who work with you. While building up others, you will build up yourself. (UPS Archives, 1945)

Good management is not just organization. It is an attitude inspired by the will to do right. Good management is taking a sincere interest in the welfare of the people you work with. It is the ability to make people feel that you and they are the company – not merely employees. (UPS Archives, 1944)

On the subject of future leaders, Jim Casey said:

Who will those leaders be? They will be people who now, today, are forging ahead – not speculating or with fanfare, but modestly and quietly. They are the plain, simple people who are doing their best in their present jobs with us, whatever those jobs may happen to be. Such people will not fail us when called on for bigger things. It is for them, our successors, to remember that all the glamour, romance, and success you have in our business at any stage

of its existence, must be the product of years resulting from the work of
many devoted people, and there can be no glamour, no romance, no truly
great success unless shared in by all. (UPS Archives, 1957)

UPS's employee-centric culture is further evidenced by:
(1) its promotion-from-within policies and actions;
(2) its employee stock ownership plans;
(3) its diversity programs;
(4) its employee education programs;
(5) hiring local employees in its international operation; and
(6) its employee internal free agent program which allows any UPS
    employee to move anywhere in the company and to advance.

Jim Casey believed and acted on the policy that it is your employees
who make you successful, not the executives, and UPS has an obligation
to fairly share its success with those who make it happen.

These three aspects of the UPS culture: a mutually accountable performance culture, an emphasis on constructive dissatisfaction, and
employee-centric policies and ownership, are the foundation of UPS's
way of doing business.

Recipes for success

Integrated with these cultural values and policies is the UPS operations
research mentality. "We have a saying at UPS," explained Kuehn. "In
God we trust; everything else we measure."

The second ingredient of the UPS recipe for success is its engineering
process and measurement mentality. To be a high-performance company, you need real-time measurements. And UPS measures everything:
from CO_2 emissions – to the time it takes to wash a windshield – to the
correct speed a driver should walk to a customer's house – to the most
efficient way to start a package van's ignition – to the optimal way to
load a package van – to defining the optimal daily delivery routes.

Jim Casey hired his first industrial engineer in 1921 to do time-
and-motion studies for efficiencies. This started UPS down the path of
process engineering which over the years institutionalized itself into
a powerful operations research division. That division spent its first
eighty-seven years internally focused on measuring everything that
could be measured – studying, modeling, and simulating the move-
ments of people, conveyor belts, and packages.

For example, UPS developed 340 methods for drivers to follow to increase their efficiency and to insure safety. This measurement mentality teaches everyone to pay attention to the details and the little things that can impede safety and destroy on-time delivery. Another example of this passion for measurement is the way UPS measures its managers. The company uses a balanced scorecard and publishes sixteen UPS key performance indicators, including economic, social, and environmental measures. UPS measures water consumption, ground network fuel efficiency, and global aircraft emissions. The purpose of this measure-everything mentality was expressed by Jim Holsen, VP of Engineering, when he said, "We're never satisfied with the way things are, if they can be improved."

This measurement compulsiveness would lead you to think that UPS is a micro-managed, rigid, robotic work place with every action dictated by best practices. UPS overcomes that tendency through its performance culture, paying its people very well, holding everyone from the sorter to the CEO to these high standards, and by being a predominant employee-owned company. Strong controls are offset by local autonomy, from the district manager level to the driver having the power and authority to do what is right to serve the customer. In 1942 Mr. Casey stated, "Each local manager is in charge of his district. We want him to look upon it exactly as if it were his own business. We want him to solve his problems in his own way." Centralized measurement, accountability, standards, and controls were balanced by local autonomy.

What is interesting about UPS is how they have integrated, fused, and blended their performance culture, constructive dissatisfaction mindset, and engineering process measurement mentality into a seamless accepted way of doing things. It all fits together. And when you add the mutuality of accountability and employee ownership, you have executives working for employee owners and you devalue hubris, complacency, and insularity.

This culture is perpetuated by a promote-from-within policy and insularity at the top is mitigated by its active diversity policy and the fact that almost 50% of its board of directors are minority group members. UPS works at diversity just like it works at everything else. It works hard at the daily things needing to be done – measures everything – and keeps at it day in and day out.

UPS's current growth challenges

UPS's growth has historically been evolutionary and organic. The company had trouble in its initial international expansion efforts because it tried to export UPS people to foreign countries and to override local culture and customs. But it learned. UPS has now reinvented itself by moving from the package or document delivery business to serving the entire supply and distribution chain.

UPS has changed what it is selling and it has changed the level in corporations to which it must sell – up to the CEO, CIO, and COO levels. The challenge to UPS's culture and way of doing business is at least fivefold:

(1) Will UPS need to recruit large numbers of outsiders to sell and execute this new business? Does it need to scale faster than it can develop the talent from within?

(2) Will the types of people needed to do this new business have the mentality, personality, and willingness to "play" in the UPS culture? Will consultants fit in the UPS culture?

(3) Will this new focus on the customer's process and the exporting to customers of the UPS operation research expertise dilute its internal focus and will efficiencies decline internally?

(4) As part of this new strategy, UPS went public in order to have public-stock currency to do acquisitions to acquire capabilities and competencies in the freight forwarding, customs clearance, financing, etc. areas. Will the public markets allow UPS to be as patient as it historically has been in working at a problem until UPS gets it right? And

(5) How well will UPS integrate employees assimilated from its recent acquisitions into its culture and mission?

Will UPS be able to manage short-term public market earnings goals and its long-term movement into this new market space? UPS has never been a short-term manager. They have a saying: "We manage not for a quarter but for the next quarter-century."

UPS hires people that will fit into its culture and who will fit into this iterative improvement and measurement work place. Remember, the people that UPS avoids are those wanting a fast track to the top. UPS is looking for those who want to be part of a team that is the best at what it does and who love the blocking and tackling of business. The payoff for a job well done is the opportunity to work for a company or employer that values career and professional development.

In recent years, UPS has changed its focus to be more customer-centric. It has redefined its market space to the entire logistics chain. It has gone public, and elected a new chairman/CEO. Taken together, these are significant changes. In one fell swoop, UPS expanded the scope of what it is selling and expanded the scale of its potential customer base. From an internally focused engineering efficiency expert, it wants to be a supply chain efficiency expert for all its customers.

One of the executives leading this new charge is Kurt Kuehn. He stated that the public market is one more scorecard for UPS management, which they welcome. He thinks the public market will increase UPS's focus and intensity. He views the recent redefining and expansion of the business as an enhancement of the UPS business model, one which the company can execute.

Role of acquisitions

No discussion of organic growth is complete unless one addresses the role of acquisitions in UPS's strategy. To expand into the full scope of the logistics chain, UPS had to acquire new capabilities. Rather than build these capabilities, the company made thirty acquisitions to buy this expertise. UPS is adamant that such acquisitions bought capabilities, not market share, and this does not violate its organic growth strategy, nor does it make UPS a serial acquirer of revenue to meet Wall Street expectations. Mr. Kuehn stated: "We acquired thirty companies in the last five years to buy capabilities to add to our business model. In total the value of all the acquisitions was less than 3% of our market capitalization."

As UPS moves towards its hundredth anniversary in 2007, it faces the challenges of growth as discussed above. When one talks to people at UPS about these issues, what you hear is not denial and not that it will be easy. You hear enthusiasm for the challenge, and you hear acceptance of the burden of the challenge in a dutiful, stewardship way. You can feel the perseverance and commitment to the UPS way; they will work at it every day until they get it right, and then they will work every day to make it better. If you visit UPS, you can feel the passion, intensity, and focus on the challenges at hand.

As Jim Casey said in 1948 (UPS Archives):

We must keep our eyes on the distant horizon and at the same time master the day-to-day problems that lie immediately before us. We must be a step ahead in our thinking – never once believing that we reached perfection in anything. We must be ready to move quickly in any direction to meet new conditions of a progressive world.

Jim Casey is watching and everyone at UPS understands and welcomes that.

4 | Execution: making growth happen at The Home Depot

TOM TAYLOR

THE HOME DEPOT is a remarkable growth story. In the late 1970s, co-founders Bernie Marcus and Arthur Blank invented the large-scale home improvement category and helped set off the wave of big-box shopping that has changed the face of retailing in the United States and around the world. Growing from a handful of stores in 1979 to over 1,890 in 2004, The Home Depot is now the world's third largest retailer (after Wal-Mart and France's Carrefour Group) and the number one home improvement retail chain in the United States, more than double the size of its largest direct competitor. The company ranked thirteenth on the 2003 Fortune 500 list of US companies, up from its twenty-third ranking in 2001.

With more than 325,000 "orange-blooded" associates, The Home Depot is the eighth largest employer in the United States. In the last two years, the company has created over 20,000 net new jobs, more than any other US business. Since its founding, the company has employed over 1.2 million people.

The company's financial growth has been equally staggering. Annual sales in 1979 were $7 million; today, The Home Depot rings up that sum in just one hour. Sales have grown tenfold in twenty-five years and are expected to top $70 billion in 2004, marking another record year. Along the way, the company became the youngest retailer ever to reach $30 billion, $40 billion, $50 billion, $60 billion, and soon $70 billion in revenue. Along with revenue have come strong earnings – a record $4.3 billion in 2003 – and impressive returns for investors. An investment of $1,000 during the company's initial public offering in 1981 would be worth over $1 million today. Between the second quarter of 1987 and the third quarter of 2004, investors received seventy consecutive quarterly dividend payments. And in 2002, Merrill Lynch named The Home Depot first in a quality-of-earnings study of large, publicly traded US companies.

But shareholders have not been the only beneficiaries of The Home Depot's success. While the business itself was growing, its impact on consumers and the home improvement industry in general has been dramatic. The Home Depot has made home improvement more affordable for millions of consumers. Professor David Bell of the Harvard Business School compared The Home Depot's prices today on a basket of everyday home improvement items to a comparable basket from 1978, adjusted for inflation, and found that the company has reduced prices by an average of 54%. For example, the cost of redoing a kitchen floor with 45 square feet of vinyl tile was $35 in 1978. Today, customers can buy it at $26. Back then a refrigerator's average price per cubic foot was approximately $77. Today it is only $48. Overall, the study found that The Home Depot shoppers have saved more than $500 billion over the past twenty-five years.

The remarkable growth of this company and the ensuing impact it has had across the entire retail sector would surely make for a fascinating study of entrepreneurship and rapid business growth. No doubt the evolution of The Home Depot and the keys to its success will be examined by students of business far into the future. My perspective, however, is not that of a detached business scholar. Instead, I have watched and participated in the growth of the company from the inside. Since age sixteen, when I began as a part-time employee in a store in Florida, The Home Depot's growth has been not just an expanding set of business metrics, but a series of significant changes to a business I know intimately. It has been an exhilarating professional experience, and all of us now in the company remain optimistic about more growth ahead. But having lived through the tumultuous times that such growth invariably brings to any organization, I can attest that very rapid growth is not merely a result of good fortune and prosperous economic times. Sustained growth is a product of sound strategy and, perhaps more importantly, consistently superb execution.

In any company undergoing repeated growth spurts, execution becomes a necessary management and survival exercise. But it rarely comes consistently over a twenty-five-year period. That is why I tend to look at The Home Depot's history as one of growth accompanied by change. Those changes were both a product of the growth and a reaction to it. The changes in the company, in turn, fostered new approaches to management and execution. In this chapter, I will try to trace those changes and distill the lessons the company has absorbed from them in its quest to remain a growing company.

Four phases of growth

Although many of the measurements of growth, like the ones I have already cited, might present a portrait of a company that has enjoyed a seamless path of expansion, the actual experience from innovative start-up to global brand has been less direct. I recognize four phases in our quarter-century history: early start-up, explosive growth, slow growth, and transition transformation.

The early start-up years of 1978–83 were marked by all the excitement and uncertainty that goes with testing a brand-new concept and building a company from the ground up. We turned our first profit ($856,000) in 1980 and made our public debut on the NASDAQ in 1981, listing at $12 a share and raising over $4 million. Success, however, was not immediate. After The Home Depot's initial stock offering of $12 in September of 1981, the stock dropped under $11 a share in August 1985 and it took six months for the price to get back above $12 again. Yet despite the financial uncertainty that accompanies a young company, a clear culture was emerging. It was during this early period that our founders instilled The Home Depot with the eight core values we still live by today: taking care of our people; giving back to our communities; doing the right thing (in addition to doing more things right); providing excellent customer service; creating shareholder value; building strong relationships based on trust, honesty, and integrity; upholding the entrepreneurial spirit; and showing respect for all people.

With its distinctive corporate culture, the company expanded quickly during those first five years, moving from its home base in Atlanta, Georgia, into Florida, Louisiana, Texas, and Alabama. But the truly explosive growth came during the next phase of evolution from 1983 through 1998. This was the period during which we racked up tremendous market share gains while leading a dramatic consolidation of the industry. When The Home Depot opened its first store, it was a distinctive arrival in what was otherwise a crowded field of competitors in the home improvement market. But while our company expanded, the rest of the industry was rapidly shrinking. Only five of the thirty top home improvement players in 1980 survived the nineties: The Home Depot, Lowe's, Menard's, Sears, and Scotty's. In 1990, The Home Depot surpassed Lowe's as the market leader. During this period we also began to look outside the United States for growth. We opened stores in Canada in 1994 and in Chile and Puerto Rico in 1998, and by 2002 we had stores in forty-nine of the fifty states.

In 1999, however, we hit the wall. Our reliable strategy of "build it and they will come" was no longer enough to ensure growth. Our competitors were essentially doing the same thing, and in some respects they were beating us at our own game. Between 1996 and 2003, there was a rapid build-out by the top three players: The Home Depot, Lowe's, and Menard's. Collectively, we increased the number of big-box home improvement stores in the United States by 173% during this period, which meant that the number of households served per store plunged from 104,000 to fewer than 42,000. In effect, we were cannibalizing our own stores, and sales dropped. Between 1999 and 2002, sales growth at The Home Depot declined 13 percentage points. Same-store sales dropped for eight consecutive quarters during 1999 and 2000.

Realizing this decline, the board decided to seek new leadership, for the first time ever, from outside the company. In December 2000, it turned to Robert Nardelli to become its CEO, and within a year, chairman of the board. To many of The Home Depot employees, the choice initially seemed puzzling. Bob, as he would quickly come to be known throughout the company, had spent nearly thirty years at General Electric. He was a proven leader, having run GE Power Systems and helped to shape several enormous business units. Yet he had never worked in retail, and to some, the notion that someone trained in the rigorous GE system of management and measurement could fit into the loose, decentralized entrepreneurial culture of The Home Depot seemed a dubious proposition. Yet Bob and others, myself included, realized that The Home Depot was unlikely to earn its next $50 billion operating in the same way that it had earned its first $50 billion. Simply adding more stores was no longer a viable growth option. So under Bob's leadership, The Home Depot underwent a huge change process over the next three years, creating the fourth phase of the company's growth. New systems of company-wide processes were gradually put into place along with a large infusion of technology. The result transformed the company into a much more thoroughly managed organization, while retaining the best of its entrepreneurial spirit.

The changes came in many forms: a centralized merchandising system; replacing the hundreds of different employee hiring and evaluation processes with a clearer, more uniform system; an aggressive plan of employee communication and training to improve customer service. But these many changes were a result of a broader vision of how to systematically improve every aspect of a large enterprise with hundreds of thousands of employees spread across the map. It required a new type of thinking about our purpose and strategy.

To spark creative yet disciplined thinking, Bob introduced SOAR – Strategic Operating And Resource planning – an integrated strategic planning process for identifying growth opportunities, setting priorities, and allocating capital, people, and other resources. For a company like The Home Depot, it was an entirely new way of thinking about our business as a whole. Modeled on GE's approach, SOAR combines a three-year *strategic* planning process that meshes growth plans from the regional sales divisions and the functions (e.g. logistics, operations, merchandising and marketing, human resources); a one-year *operating* planning process that lays out key metrics such as productivity, operating leverage, cash conversion, accountability, and compliance; and a one-year *resource* planning process that addresses staffing, leadership capabilities, performance management, communications, and other organizational issues.

The SOAR process led us to set our sights on achieving sustained growth on a massive scale through a three-pronged strategy: enhancing the core, extending the business, and expanding the market.

Enhancing the core is about getting more sales out of each store, by revamping all aspects of the stores and by adding entirely new merchandising categories. Throughout its history, The Home Depot never carried major appliances – it did not seem to be our market. But executing a strategic plan required rethinking those assumptions, listening to customers, and understanding how our own customer base was changing. Many store leaders – including me – had quizzical looks on their faces when they saw the first washers and dryers unloaded at our stores. Just four years after launching this category, we already rank third in appliance market share in the United States. This is a $21 billion market, and one we see as a strong, long-term growth opportunity. To take advantage of it, we really needed to create a systematic way of evaluating how we could create growth.

Extending the business means offering new services to our existing customer base. For example, we are pursuing huge opportunities in the market for at-home improvement and repair services such as plumbing, decorating, and carpentry, where currently we have just a small piece of the $180 billion rapidly growing pie. We are also working to capture bigger shares of the professional contractor market and the tool rental business, which already yields our highest profit per square foot.

Expanding the market involves creating different store formats for different customers and pursuing attractive opportunities in fast-growing international markets. Different formats include Expo Design Center, which caters to high-end, more fashion-conscious customers. The Home Depot Supply stores offer opportunities through channels such as Builder Solutions, which sells to new home builders, Government Solutions, which sells to government organizations, and the recently acquired White Cap, which caters to large and medium-sized construction contractors. These businesses allow us to capture a higher portion of the professional market.

We have recently added unique urban formats on both coasts of North America. We opened two stores in Manhattan and a successful urban store in Park Royal, Vancouver. Virtually everything about these stores from their design and layouts to their merchandising selection and use of technology was specifically designed to meet the needs of their local communities and provide us access to an almost entirely new and untapped customer base. These stores demonstrate another opportunity for new store growth by bringing The Home Depot to previously underserved markets.

Another part of our expansion strategy is to grow beyond the United States. One of these expanded markets is Mexico, where in less than two years, we went from zero to number one and are now the country's largest home improvement retailer. Mexico gave us the opportunity to take the culture and the merchandising, and provide a shopping experience for customers who were already cross-border shopping. In 2004 we announced that we would be expanding into China, a nearly $50 billion market that is growing at a double-digit rate.

The success of this three-pronged strategy hinges largely on executing well. That's not new. Excellence in execution has always been part of the lifeblood of The Home Depot. Our founders knew that great execution was the key to providing customers with knowledgeable, friendly, personalized service and the best selection of products at the best prices. It also has enabled us to replicate our model very quickly, which is essential when a company is opening, on average, a new store every forty-eight hours.

Lessons in execution

Our experience has led me to conclude that execution is not just a matter of running a tight ship. Execution helps drive growth. How? Based on The Home Depot experience, particularly during the recent years of transformation, I see five important lessons of execution that apply to us and to many other companies.

(1) Superior execution demands a sharp focus on the details that shape the customer experience, right down to the cleanliness of the floors.
(2) It's impossible to execute well unless you sell the strategy to employees at all levels; if you want people to embrace new ways, they must understand the rationale for change as well as the benefits.
(3) As a company matures, efficient execution requires finding an appropriate balance of power between headquarters and the field – or, in our case, between entrepreneurship and anarchy.
(4) There's no way of knowing how well you are executing unless you are measuring the things that matter and holding managers accountable for results.
(5) Technology enables faster, better execution, and is a powerful tool that we at The Home Depot are still learning to master.

The remainder of this chapter explores and elaborates on these five lessons and how we came to learn them at The Home Depot.

Lesson 1: Focus on details that shape the customer experience

Our core purpose at The Home Depot is "to improve everything we touch." Retailing is a tough game, and to survive – and thrive – we must deliver on our brand promise at every touch point. In other words, what we tell our customers must be exactly what we execute, with no disconnects between what people see in our advertisements and what they experience in our stores. If we run a TV commercial about a father and son building a treehouse and picking out the lumber at The

Home Depot, the lumber departments in our stores had better look as appealing as they do in the ad.

To ensure that we get the details right, we try to examine every aspect of store operations through our customers' eyes. When we launched the SOAR process a few years ago, we analyzed a host of economic, competitive, and demographic trends in different businesses and product classes and realized that our merchandising mix and operational priorities were out of sync with the market. In addition, we found that we were under-investing in our stores relative to the competition.

Here's what had changed. In the old days, The Home Depot was largely a transaction business: customers came into the stores, bought a garden hose or a couple of 2×4s, and they left. The business was not terribly complicated, provided we had the products in stock that people sought. In the late 1990s, we began to see signs of an evolution from simple transactions towards the project business, with increasing sales from categories like special-order carpets and kitchen installations. For example, growth in special-order carpets shot up from modest rates to 30–40% gains each year while sales of garden hoses and other staples stayed pretty constant. And, as our customers took on bigger, more complicated projects, the nature of their purchases and their service expectations became much more complex.

This change in customer needs got us thinking about our overall store environment. People who are shopping for a garden hose are usually in and out of the store pretty quickly, and as long as the price is right most of them do not mind what the store looks like. People who are remodeling their kitchens, on the other hand, typically spend a few hours with an expert at The Home Depot, talking about the design, scheduling installation, and picking out cabinets, fixtures, flooring, and the like – and who wants to hang around in a dirty, disorganized place? Market research told us that 50% of customer visits to The Home Depot were made by couples, but that women, who influence 85% of major purchasing decisions for the home, were not comfortable shopping in our décor departments. We recognized, therefore, that winning this lucrative project business would require a dramatic overhaul of our stores and operating approaches.

Addressing the store environment led to changes across the board, from creating a brighter, cleaner, and more comfortable shopping environment, to updating the merchandising mix and reconfiguring store operations in order to enable better customer service. In 2004, for example, we invested roughly $1 billion in store modernization and technology. In some locations, we did a complete gut and renovation, making the stores like new. In others, we were doing extensive refreshes and updates, such as sprucing up our design centers, installing brighter lighting, updating displays to be more shopper-friendly, and improving direction signage in the stores.

From my perspective, reconfiguring store operations has involved the most significant changes, illustrating the extent to which we hone in on the details that make or break the customer experience. For anyone who has been with the company for more than five years, what we are doing now marks a reversal of everything we were taught in the old days. For example, when I was a store manager back in the eighties and early nineties, I would get in trouble if more than 5% of my payroll went to operations during "dark hours," when the store was not open for business. Back then, we were striving to give the stores the look and feel of warehouses – not too clean and not too organized, with cluttered aisles that were difficult to navigate; in fact, we put a lot of products on the floor in the hope that customers would browse and buy more. We deliberately pushed some products deeper into the shelf space to avoid the look of a polished showroom. If you came into one of my stores on a Saturday, you would find it difficult to get a shopping cart down the aisle because we had so much merchandise on the floor.

Around 1999 we took a 180-degree turn and revamped operations based on what customers told us they valued: "shop-ability," cleanliness, and convenience. This initiative was called SPI (Service Performance Improvement), which moved tasks like unloading inventory and restocking shelves to the overnight shift so it is less distracting and safer for the customer to shop. When I walk a store these days, I talk to the managers about whether the aisle is wide enough to accommodate three or four customers at the same time. In short, it is a completely different way of operating and managing.

We know our investments and new strategies are paying off because customer satisfaction – which we measure through our "voice of the customer" initiative – has risen significantly over the last eighteen months. We've shown steady improvement in categories like ease of shopping and cleanliness. But most importantly, we have enhanced the shopping experience; customers have spent more: our average ticket size has increased almost $7, from $48 to over $55 in the past couple of years.

Lesson 2: Make sure employees understand the benefits of change

One of the hardest lessons we have learned at The Home Depot is about the value of good internal communications, both telling and listening. We know now that you cannot expect employees to execute well if they do not understand why and how they are being asked to change and if they do not feel they have a stake in the process. Indeed, research shows that high employee engagement is critical to driving customer satisfaction and business results, yet only 20% of workers are highly engaged (Tower Perrin, 2003).

In my view, the best way to engage your work force and get them to change is to help them see the benefits of the change. Because we under-estimated this communications challenge, we turned over roughly 50% of our management team through the transition, and remodeling and revamping store operations proved much harder than anticipated. In retrospect, we simply did not do a good enough job of explaining to managers and associates beforehand why the changes were critical to our competitiveness and our ability to execute the new growth strategy. Our people needed to know the facts, like the relative age of our stores, and they needed to hear insights from our market research, including what customers were saying about The Home Depot shopping experience and how we were falling short.

We also failed to appreciate the magnitude of the cultural shift we were undertaking and how the front line would react to being told to do things just the opposite of how they had done them for years. Having grown up in a culture that taught, "If it's not broken, don't fix it," our people needed to understand exactly what *was* broken and why it needed fixing. They needed to understand that the changes we were making – including the about-face on dark-hours staffing and cluttered aisles described earlier – were not merely arbitrary but essential, not only to strengthen competitiveness, but also to ensure the safety of our customers and our associates. For example, we never really explained to associates why we were moving tasking and receiving to the night shift. We should have told the full story behind that change – details like how many people had been hurt because of forklifts in the aisles and what was happening to our workers' compensation claims. Associates needed to hear that, no. 1, it's just not safe to transport thousands of pounds of equipment while there is customer traffic in our stores. And, no. 2, we can be more efficient by deploying busier daytime associate hours to the sales floor. The change alone ensured a satisfying customer experience; there is no misunderstanding about that now.

Once we realized that success hinged on changing people's mindsets, our leadership team started communicating much more intensively and extensively. At times it seemed like we were saying the same things again and again, but we found that it paid to over-communicate. Making sure the right messages flowed through middle management to the front line in a consistent and timely manner took great patience and persistence. For example, I would have a Monday morning call with my district managers to review a new plan, and the next day I would round up twenty store managers on the phone and ask what they had heard about the changes. If they knew what was happening, I was delighted, but most times I would have to explain things again and ask them to brief their associates. More often than not, I would tell the district managers one thing and by the time it got down to the hourly associates, it was a completely different story. So I learned to keep drilling the messages through, holding managers accountable for informing their teams, and checking that people down the line knew what they were supposed to know.

This sort of rigor is essential to changing people's behavior, especially in a highly entrepreneurial culture like ours. Communicating as I have described here takes a very large investment of time and energy not only on the part of senior management – including board members – but all the way down the line. The truth is, change cannot be driven solely by the people at the top. In our case, even the division presidents were not totally sold on the new strategy at first, let alone the folks in the field. Three or four years ago, you would hear a lot of people saying we had to do something because "Bob [Nardelli] wants the change." Luckily, those people have either come around, or they have left the company. What we like to hear now is, "We need to do this because it's what customers demand."

As Bob puts it, "Many companies make the mistake of thinking that their senior executives are the drivers of success and the people in the field are the pit crews. In fact, it's the other way around." Each level of management – and especially the front-line leadership – needs to sell the change like they own it personally. Our experience has been that when a store manager gets behind a new merchandising category, or a new technology, or a new incentive program, it wins every time.

To ensure an effective cascade, we now hold managers at every level accountable for communicating with their direct reports, and we follow up to ensure that important messages are getting through. We also hold many more meetings than we did in the past for all types of leaders. In these meetings, we provide extensive background information about the root causes of change, explaining not just *what* needs to be done differently but *why* we need to do those things in order to keep the company growing. In our experience, it is this combination of honesty and facts that makes difficult change more acceptable.

Recognizing that communication is a two-way street, we do a lot of listening as well as talking. One of the ways we stay in sync with our people is by conducting a regular "employer of choice" survey – a full census every two years and a shorter pulse check on an annual basis. The survey measures employee satisfaction along seven dimensions: inclusive culture, challenging work, developing potential, growth and advancement, recognition and reward, communication, and work environment. Questions include: How long do you plan on staying with The Home Depot? Are you thinking about leaving? What needs to change? We track our performance on key issues year to year and compare our scores to norms for the home improvement industry and all consumer services.

Based on the survey feedback, HR partners with managers at every level of the organization – divisions, regions, and stores – to develop game plans for fixing specific problems. These problems, along with the results, are shared with all associates. Among the company-wide initiatives that have evolved from the survey are a front-line bonus program ("Success Sharing"), merit programs, accelerated tuition reimbursement and other benefits, and increased learning opportunities for our associates.

Within the Eastern Division, which I lead, the survey has been extremely helpful in identifying concerns we can address through proactive communications at a very granular level. For example, through the survey we learned that associates felt there was little opportunity for advancement. That's worrisome: if people in a retail organization start feeling that they cannot get ahead, you fairly soon have a place that is no fun to work. But in this case, the perceptions were out of line with the facts. In truth, the Eastern Division was promoting roughly 1,000 people a month; we just were not doing anything to publicly celebrate those promotions. The solution in this case was simple. Each month we put up a poster, called the "career board," in the store break-rooms. The poster has a photo of me shaking an associate's hand, and it lists the name and store of every person who's been promoted that month. Now people can see for themselves how good are the opportunities for advancement.

The survey also revealed that people did not understand the benefits of working at The Home Depot, and they felt they did not have any outlet for asking questions or raising concerns about HR issues. So once a month, in every store, we now have "HR Information Day," where HR representatives are available to talk with associates and answer any questions they might have.

At a broader level, the survey suggested that communication was a huge issue in our division and that store associates wanted more information and more direction. In response, I started hosting an hour-long conference call every Monday for all of my district managers. During these calls, we cover last week's results, set priorities for things that need to get done in the stores in the coming week, and then deal with any questions managers want to raise. Those calls did not exist before we did the employer-of-choice survey and heard directly from associates in the stores.

These and other efforts to strengthen communication over the past few years have made us a more flexible organization, and one that is much more open to new ideas. Our associates wanted to tell us how they felt about working for The Home Depot, and as we have acted on the results, we have improved in the areas that we targeted to improve. Participation levels in the survey are off the charts, and employee turnover is down. And, as noted earlier, our average ticket is up, which we attribute partly to happier and better-motivated associates who simply sell more effectively.

Lesson 3: Strike the right balance between entrepreneurship and anarchy

Sooner or later, nearly every fast-growing company grapples with finding the right balance of power between headquarters and the field. For The Home Depot, this was a particularly difficult challenge because the company was built on entrepreneurial spirit, which in practical terms meant that store managers had tremendous decision-making power *vis-à-vis* the corporate center. Today, we are trying to cultivate that entrepreneurial spirit and be much more thoughtful about how entrepreneurship delivers real value to our customers and our business.

Our highly decentralized model generally served us well through our first decade or so, giving store managers ample flexibility to make merchandising choices based on local needs and to adjust prices in response to local competition. However, as our growth pace quickened in the 1990s and we became a much larger organization, the bias towards decentralized functions and local decision-making led to unnecessary complexity and costs as well as confusion for customers. With eleven regional buying offices – one for each geographic division in North America – and each division president running his or her own merchandising and marketing show, we had huge variations in sales catalogs and stock counts across the country; some stores carried as many as 50,000 SKUs, while others had less than 20,000.

Worse, entrepreneurial spirit became the ticket to noncompliance. In effect, we had over 1,800 different businesses under one roof – each of our stores was run like a separate company. People said, "Hey, I'm an entrepreneur; that means I'm not going to do what you tell me." As a company, that meant we could not go to a vendor like Ortho, buy an end cap of home pest control, and put it in every store. When we sent it to the stores, the store manager might well invoke the entrepreneurial spirit and say, "It's my store; I choose not to participate." As a store manager, I was just as guilty of this as everyone else, second-guessing every decision that came out of the Store Support Center at corporate headquarters.

The notion of entrepreneurship above all also made it very difficult to measure and reward performance fairly. Until 2001, for example, the regional operations VPs could decide who got promoted to district manager without consulting anyone else or putting candidates through a standard assessment process. We had more than 150 different performance evaluation processes and no pay bands in our stores. And Atlanta did not give store managers any direction on pay levels for hourly associates. Imagine the complexity: in the Eastern Division alone, I have more than 600 stores and almost 130,000 associates. When individual managers have the power to decide what a person who sells floor tile should be earning, you end up with enormous pay variations from store to store.

In the last few years, we have made dramatic changes to address these issues and strike a new balance. We still want managers to be entrepreneurial in taking care of customers and sales, but when it comes to operations – things like configuring the store and managing associate performance – we have put company-wide policies and procedures in place and we expect people to follow them. Instead of over 1,800 different businesses, we now have one.

On the merchandising front, in 2001 we pulled the very best buyers out of all the regional divisions and put this "A team" in charge of making merchandising decisions and managing vendor relationships for the entire company. Today all of our buying is done centrally, and it is the sole job of stores to execute. We still tailor the product mix for certain geographies, but there is much more consistency across the board and everyone is closer to the average. We have been able to leverage our buying power by developing strategic, exclusive alliances with vendor partners, whose relationship with us ensures their own longevity. As a result, they can drive down their manufacturing costs, pass on the savings to us, which we, of course, pass on to our customers. Our customers want top-tier merchandise at the best prices. By centralizing merchandising, we are able to offer just that, leaving no area in the store without distinction and innovation, and value. That is why we have experienced increases in average ticket. The impact on the bottom line has been huge.

At the store level, managers remain empowered to make decisions about the things they know best: sales and customer service. If a PVC plumbing item is selling really well, we expect them to buy as much inventory as they need to meet demand. If they have to jump through hoops to take care of a customer, they should go ahead and do that. Indeed, it is that kind of entrepreneurship that has enabled some of our company's proudest moments – like in 1995, when The Home Depot district manager for Oklahoma City got truckloads of donated rescue supplies to the bomb scene before the firefighters even got there. He knew exactly what to do without calling Atlanta first. More recently, I saw the same sort of response when a series of hurricanes hit Florida. I arrived at our Venice, Florida store and found 200 customers lined up out the front door. The damage to the community was devastating and our store, like most of the surrounding area, had no power. But it was still open for business, even though only six associates were able to get to work that day. They were serving customers one at a time, helping people find what they needed by taking them into the store with flashlights because there was no power. They had to use an old-fashioned cash box to handle the money and manually process credit card numbers if people did not have the cash. I did not tell the store manager to do that; she was an entrepreneur who knew how to take care of her community.

This was exactly the sort of entrepreneurial spirit that The Home Depot's founders had in mind when they created the company twenty-five years ago, and we have every intention of preserving it.

Lesson 4: Measure the things that matter

A key lesson for The Home Depot over the past ten years has been the need to pay close attention to tracking performance along multiple dimensions. We now have many more metrics – and much more granular ones – in place than we did in the early years, allowing us to respond to competitive trends and address customer service issues more quickly.

When The Home Depot was still a relatively new concept and the competition was less intense, growth came easily: pretty much all we had to do was open new stores and customers would come. And, as long as we were growing fast and launching new stores without cannibalizing existing ones, we did not need to pay attention to most items below the sales line. So there was not much discussion of – or need for – performance metrics beyond sales.

Focusing solely on sales was fine during the go-go years, but managing in a slower-growth environment meant we needed more information. Today we have a broad range of internally and externally focused metrics in place that signal when things start to deteriorate before sales do. As a result, we can manage the business to a symptomatic level, get out in front of trends, and fix little problems before they become big ones.

To highlight key drivers and the linkages between them, we use a performance management tool called "four-block metrics." Every manager at every level has a set of four-block metrics, tracking results along four dimensions: financial, operations, process (e.g. acceptance of Six Sigma), and people. To measure store management performance, for instance, we track hundreds of metrics, everything from the number of pallets handled per minute to how many transactions a store processes before we get a customer complaint. In some cases, we have found some interesting linkages; for example, increases in associate turnover are often a leading indicator of increases in shrink because new associates tend to make more mistakes in receiving product and ringing up sales. Now, because we are talking about both shrink and turnover in quarterly performance reviews, we can anticipate potential shrink problems and manage them through better associate training and better in-store processes.

Not surprisingly, we faced some resistance to the new system at first because it made it much easier to see what was really going on in the stores. And, frankly, the early four blocks contained too many metrics – pretty much everything you could measure in a store was on there – which made it hard to prioritize which ones were most important to manage. Once we pared them back to a more reasonable number, people began to recognize the benefits of having greater transparency and holding everyone to the same standards. In my division, for example, I hold a quarterly staff meeting where we get every district manager in one room and everyone sees who the top performers and bottom performers are. There is no hiding, and people are inspired to do better.

In addition to taking a much closer look at how our stores are performing, we are also doing a better job of watching our competitors and listening to our customers. We used to analyze market share by doing telephone surveys in our major markets through an outside company; now we do that ourselves, and I can tell you what any store in my division is doing from a market share standpoint. In terms of service metrics, we have several vehicles to collect customer feedback on the shopping experience and how we stack up against competitors. For example, customers can log onto our website after making a purchase and rate us on twenty different attributes, including associate knowledge, speed of service, and choice of product styles and price points. All of these tools give better insights into how well we are executing and what we need to improve.

Lesson 5: Harness the power of technology as a competitive advantage

Our goal on the technology front is not to be equivalent with the competition. We want to leapfrog the rest and be the leader. To that end, we are spending twelve times more on information technology than we did prior to 2001.

Technology enables competitive advantage in terms of both the quality and speed of the customer experience and management decision-making. We want to get customers into and out of the stores faster. We want to move products in and out faster. And we want to get information to managers and executives faster.

Recognizing that out-of-stock problems and slow checkout lines can mean lost sales and, potentially, lost customers, we have spent over $300 million on systems that will differentiate The Home Depot in the customer's eyes. First, we have installed self-checkout machines in more than 800 stores so far, and over 30% of our customers are using them. Second, we have given our cashiers handheld scan guns, which enable them to move customers through the checkout lines much faster than in the past. Thanks to these two changes, average checkout waiting time has dropped 40%. Third, we have put in mobile ordering carts with automated UPC look-up so if a customer wants a product that is not on the shelves, an associate can scan a bar code and advise on availability in just a few seconds; in the old days, that would have required flipping through a paper catalog. All of these investments are paying off in terms of increased customer satisfaction and sales.

We also are using technology to collect the information and data we need to make faster, fact-based decisions. This is part of a broader shift from what was largely an emotional decision-making culture to one that is much more analytical. I can remember a time when people predicted that we would never have e-mail in The Home Depot, and as recently as three years ago, our store managers still did not have e-mail. Now they have e-mail as well as a workload management portal right in the stores, which enables store managers to prioritize work more efficiently. Getting there required starting at the ground level and replacing our legacy computer systems with a powerful data warehouse, which now gives executives and store managers a nonstop flow of real-time data on business performance, including critical sales and inventory numbers.

Though we are getting better at mastering the technology game, in all honesty we are still not even half as good as we need to be. Gone are the old days of treating technology merely as a cost of doing business, and while we are still playing catch-up with companies like Target, which sees technology as a differentiator, and Wal-Mart, which views it as the next frontier, we are committed to continually investing more in technology in order to improve our business performance and the customer experience.

Conclusion: Learning to embrace change

So there is much work still to be done. We have learned a lot in the past few years, both from our own successes and failures as well as those of our competitors.

The biggest lesson of all is that growth is not something that just happens. It needs to be aggressively pursued. That requires an execution strategy. In their early years, companies can probably survive without one. After all, that is when simply keeping up and establishing an operating culture is work enough. But once an organization reaches a certain size, it needs to understand that it cannot extend its growth without a plan – a plan that often requires rethinking many of the assumptions about the business that had been with it since the start. Challenging those assumptions is necessary because what worked well five years ago is not always the best approach today, and what works today probably will not be adequate in another five years. The reality is that our customers are going to keep changing, and so are our competitors. So we have to be prepared to change too. We must keep raising the bar. Look at the Toys R Us experience: perhaps they never took Wal-Mart seriously as a competitor, and now Wal-Mart, Target, and others are beating them at their own game.

Winning requires continually reinventing the company. It means staying flexible and open to new ideas, willing to experiment with multiple approaches and to abandon the things that do not work. In other words, the pace of change internally needs to exceed the pace externally.

Looking back, I think we were very slow to change. Before Bob Nardelli came on board, The Home Depot had a hard time trying new things. We became an upstart company that had grown too traditional – too infatuated with our own culture and too entrenched in our beliefs. I was just as guilty of this as the next guy; for example, I resisted introducing the appliance lines, and I did not see the value of selling cases of bottled water either. The truth was, I was not paying enough attention to what our customers wanted and what our competitors were doing.

Of course, talking about listening to your customers, and building a business strategy around that idea, are two very different things. That is where execution becomes a growth tool. It not only allows you to understand what the company strategy is, but forces you to figure out how to achieve it.

Reference

Tower Perrin 2003. Working today: exploring employees' emotional connections to their jobs. Unpublished report, The Home Depot, Atlanta.

5 | SYSCO: how has it achieved thirty-four years of continued growth?

EDWARD D. HESS

S YSCO, based in Houston, Texas, is the largest food marketing and distribution company in North America. SYSCO sells annually over $30 billion of food, related products, and services to over 400,000 customers through 157 separate profit centers which employ in total 46,000 employees. The magnitude of SYSCO's operations is mind-boggling. It sells over 300,000 products to over 400,000 customers and on a daily basis delivers almost 4 million cases of food and related foodservice products to 360,000 customers, 99% on-time and defect-free. Over one-half of SYSCO's 46,000 employees are hourly warehouse and delivery people, and it employs 12,000 sales and business development employees.

SYSCO's industry – food distribution – is a low-margin industry. None the less, SYSCO's financial statistics are impressive. Historically, SYSCO's annual sales growth has outpaced the foodservice industry growth by two to three times. The company's twenty-year compounded annual growth rate through 2004 was 14.6%. Fiscal year 2004 sales increased 12%, while net earnings were up 17%. The company has consistently paid a dividend since its inception and has increased the quarterly cash dividend thirty-six times in thirty-five years. Return on equity, which was 22.2% in fiscal 1998, reached 38.7% in fiscal 2004, while return on average capital steadily grew from 15.0% to 24.9% over the same time period. During the last six fiscal years, SYSCO returned approximately $3.6 billion to shareholders via dividends and share repurchases.

From fiscal 1984 through 2002, SYSCO's compound annual sales growth rate was over 9% as compared to an industry average of 2.6%. SYSCO's historical sales and earnings increases through fiscal year 2004 are shown in Table 5.1. SYSCO's available market space is approximately $207 billion. With sales of almost $30 billion, it has approximately a 14% market share.

Table 5.1. *SYSCO: compound annual growth rates of sales and net earnings (%)*

	Sales	Net earnings
5-year	11.0	20.2
10-year	10.4	15.4
20-year	14.3	22.3
30-year	16.3	18.0

The SYSCO growth story is interesting because the company has gone through an evolutionary growth pattern since going public in 1970. SYSCO's growth evolution took the following seven-step path:

(1) SYSCO initially expanded its footprint geographically throughout the USA;

(2) it expanded its product offerings to non-food supplies for its existing customers;

(3) it segmented its customer market into four price-point segments for greater market focus;

(4) the company then expanded into specialty and ethnic foods, broadening its product offerings;

(5) it added services to help its existing customers be more successful;

(6) it placed additional internal focus on cost efficiencies; and

(7) SYSCO, now, is redesigning its supply and distribution chain for additional cost efficiencies.

SYSCO is the major player in a $200 billion dollar market – even though it only has a 14% market share. Not only is it big but it outperforms its industry competition year in and year out. How does it do this? In trying to crack SYSCO's DNA, my research and site interviews attempted to understand what made the company different.

First, what was interesting was what I did not find. SYSCO's uniqueness does not appear to be either its strategy, its products, its financial expertise, or its employees. Nor did I did find a rah-rah culture or a visible culture. What is unique about SYSCO is that it has figured out how, on a daily basis, to get and keep everyone – from the CEO to the truck driver – focused with the right attitude on doing the little things that count very very much to their customers.

Simply put, SYSCO is an execution champion. They have figured out how to balance and manage the tensions between decentralized entrepreneurial autonomy and centralized controls. They have figured out how not to become complacent, self-satisfied, or arrogant. They have figured out how to measure what is important to their success and how to reward it all the way down the chain to paying productivity incentives to truck drivers on a weekly basis.

SYSCO is a "quiet" company without a lot of cheerleading at the corporate level and without a lot of corporate frills. They are more like farmers, and I am being complimentary, than Wall Street corporate types – they get up every day, "go to the fields, till the soil, water, fertilize, pull the weeds, harvest some crops," and get up tomorrow and do the job again and again very well. They go about the business of doing business in a determined, engaged, methodical way.

History

Let us start at the beginning. SYSCO was formed in 1969 and went public in March 1970 through the merging of nine separate family-owned entrepreneurial foodservice operations. In 1969, Americans were eating out more than ever and industry studies predicted that half of all meals would be eaten away from home by the year 2000. Women who had entered the work force during World War II were continuing to work. With less time to cook, they wanted more prepared food. John F. Baugh, the entrepreneur who founded Zero Frozen Foods Distribution Company in Houston in 1946, envisioned a national foodservice distribution organization.

Active in industry organizations, Baugh shared his idea with friends across the country who had much in common. Each was self-made, each had tight financial controls in their operations, each treated their employees with respect, and each was family-oriented. Baugh believed each could maintain autonomy but gain strength by combining their talents into a new corporation and going public. Investment analysts and industry peers were skeptical, given the strong personalities and egos involved.

Yet the nine merging companies, which included Baugh's Zero Frozen Foods, trusted Baugh to evaluate their companies and to determine the number of their shares they would receive as their value in the new public corporation. They pledged their personal wealth for three years to guarantee its success. To quote from John Baugh's book:

Baugh's "good faith", plan called for all owners of the founding companies to place in escrow approximately 10% of the shares each would receive in the merger. It was envisioned that one-third of the escrowed shares could be returned over each of the three years. However, for this to occur, it would be necessary that SYSCO's operating results for each year (or the aggregate thereof for three years) would include sales growth of at least 10% compounded annually. In addition, the company's net earnings increase would have to equal or exceed 15% compounded for the three years. Failure to reach those goals would result in the forfeiture of all escrowed shares to SYSCO's treasury. Thus, instead of a conventional "going forward" incentive bonus arrangement for obtaining those challenging objectives, it was required that the company reach or exceed those stringent goals in order that the founders' shares of SYSCO stock that had been placed in escrow be returned to them.

This initial partial performance-based compensation earn-out philosophy institutionalized a reward for performance culture in SYSCO. The dream became reality as the nine companies, with aggregate sales of $115 million in a $35 billion industry, became SYSCO (an acronym for Systems and Services Company) in an initial public offering on March 3, 1970. In 1977, SYSCO became the leading foodservice supplier in North America. Since then, it has maintained this position, increasing sales and earnings every year, and in 1988 an acquisition of its next largest competitor gave the company national coverage.

Customer-centric mission

SYSCO's mission is "Helping Our Customers Succeed." Beginning with a promise to assist foodservice operators in building their businesses, many customer relationships have been nurtured and countless dining trends have evolved along the way. Today, consuming meals prepared away from home is as much a necessity as a choice. Committed to helping customers succeed, SYSCO's 300,000-plus products are as diverse as the 46,000-plus employees who support its daily operations. The company's customers are primarily individual restaurant owners – entrepreneurs. The products include not only the ingredients needed to prepare meals, but also numerous preparation and serving items and business solutions to support chefs, cooks, and owners. Such products might be non-food items, like equipment and supplies, paper and disposables, and even the chemicals used to clean and sanitize kitchens. Business solutions could involve menu development and analysis, food safety training, third-party back-office training and systems, etc.

SYSCO continues to develop customer-centric sales and marketing strength through its approximately 12,000 sales and marketing professionals. It has the largest sales force in its industry and this initiative is designed to focus its sales and marketing resources on customers and customer segments in which it can add the most value, deepen partnerships, and increase profitability. SYSCO sales people visit their key accounts on average three times a week. The stories are many concerning its sales people pitching in and helping customers by washing dishes, waiting tables, etc. when employees unexpectedly do not come to work. SYSCO's sales people take their own families to their customers' eating establishments. They build business relationships and friendships. SYSCO recently introduced a new Business Review function which features in-depth business reviews with its most valued customers. This review is unrelated to a sales call and determines customers' wants and needs, what works or what does not work, with recommendations to help the customer's business be more profitable. The Business Development teams also focus on acquiring new customers by targeting high potential competitors' accounts and demonstrating SYSCO's greater breadth of products and the high quality of products and services that can be tailored to the unique nature of each customer's business.

The company has established a relationship management initiative called Customers Are Really Everything to SYSCO (CARES), a program designed to make certain that its customers receive the best service in the basic functions that customers need to run their business, such as receiving all products ordered, on time, and in undamaged condition; receiving accurate invoices; helpful and knowledgeable sales and delivery associates; and the quality assurance inherent in SYSCO brand products.

The CARES program has evolved into its second phase, *i*CARE. Through this initiative, marketing associates are trained to be more effective business consultants for their customers by understanding a foodservice operation's profitability model, thus enabling them to analyze and develop menus, control inventories, and provide food safety training. Through SYSCO's website, customers are able to access a variety of third-party services that can help them drive and

Table 5.2. *SYSCO service profit chain*
The service profit chain rings true at SYSCO. The companies with highly satisfied associates deliver better results.

	Work climate average	Operating pre-tax %	Operating expense as a % of sales	Workers' comp. as a % of sales	MA retention (%)	Delivery retention (%)	Associates per 100k cases
Top 25% work climate	4.01	7.5	13.3	0.07	85	88	4.13
Bottom 25% work climate	3.61	5.3	14.9	0.20	72	78	4.33
Variance	0.40	2.2	1.6	0.13	13	10	0.20

increase customer traffic. These include access to potential lenders to fund expansions or restaurant upgrades; assistance in creating guest birthday cards, table tents, banners, or posters; even access to insurance carriers, credit card services, and other services they might not be able to use cost-effectively on an individual basis.

SYSCO's employees, from the CEO to the warehouse worker, understand the mission: "Helping Our Customers Succeed." Nearly 50% of its employees are customer-facing.

So SYSCO is the industry leader. It is big, national, and an outstanding performer. As expected, it is customer-centric. But why is the company so much more profitable than its competitors? Is it just efficiencies of scale? Or, is it something else? The SYSCO story is more sophisticated and complex than just efficiencies of scale. SYSCO's competitive advantage is the seamless integration of two interrelated systems:
(1) its entrepreneurial culture; and
(2) its performance measurement and reward system.

What makes SYSCO interesting is how they have aligned and seamlessly integrated these two systems so they make sense to the line employees. Its employees not only know that their job is to "Help Our Customers Succeed" but they also know what that means performance-wise. The employees know that SYSCO measures what is important and that they will be financially rewarded for doing those things.

SYSCO, through years of iteration and just plain hard work, has implemented the principles: people will do what you measure; and they will do it even better if rewarded.

SYSCO's entrepreneurial culture

SYSCO's entrepreneurial culture is historically based. The company was created by John F. Baugh, an entrepreneur, who convinced eight other foodservice entrepreneurs to merge all their companies on a partial earn-out basis to create the beginnings of his novel idea – a national foodservice distribution company created to meet the future needs of the projected high-growth out-of-the-home cooked meal business.

SYSCO's entrepreneurial culture is emphasized on a daily basis in the following ways.

(1) Ownership: 65% of SYSCO's employees own stock (a share of the results of their hard work) in the company.

(2) Its 157 operating units have day-to-day autonomy to operate in their market, subject to strict central financial controls and measurement. As SYSCO's president, Tom Lankford, stated, "Our units have complete autonomy relating to the front-of-the house, customer-facing actions, and very little autonomy on the back of the house – financial controls, accounting, supply chain, ordering, and supplier relationships."

(3) Not only does entrepreneurship mean financial ownership but SYSCO employees are responsible for servicing their customers – they have ownership of and autonomy with respect to the customer.

(4) This entrepreneurial culture is further evidenced by an "open door" policy, transparency, information-sharing within and across business units, and by a best-practices mentality. All of this leads to the industry's best retention rates of 82% for sales people and drivers, which are the key customer-facing positions. At the officer level, retention rates exceed 99% with an average tenure greater than twenty years.

(5) In addition, SYSCO is a promote-from-within company – filling over 95% of its promotions from within the company. And

(6) SYSCO's entrepreneurial culture is further evidenced by the fact that six of its top seven executives are former line operators of its business units. They know the intimate details of the business operations. These executives are 90% internally and operationally focused on a daily basis.

Rick Schnieders, the chairman and CEO of SYSCO, stated that

Table 5.3. *SYSCO human capital (CY04)*

Level	Retention rate (%)	Average tenure (years)	Average age
EVP & above	100	22	55
Sr. VPs	100	26	54
Presidents	97	23	51
OPCO EVPs	98	20	48
Specialty MIP	93	21	49
Corp. VPs	100	20	52
Corp. AVPs	93	12	48

this culture is self-replicating. Our people feel good because many own stock and they see results when everyone works hard and performs. Many, including our truck drivers, are on incentive bonus programs and see compensation results directly and weekly. All this makes people work harder – they feel good about the results which they share in and then they feel good about working hard tomorrow, etc.

SYSCO's focus on its operations – the blocking and tackling of its business – is evidenced also in looking at how its CEO spends his time. Mr. Schnieders spends his time on the following company areas:

10%   External – Wall Street and investor relations
10%   Industry leadership matters
10%   Supplier relationships
30%   Customer relationships, including direct responsibility for three major accounts
20%   Internal corporate processes – e.g. measurement and supply chain
20%   Specific operating company issues
100%

   This entrepreneurial culture produces three important results: (1) an entrepreneurial iterative do-it-better mentality; (2) an openness to change – Tom Lankford, the president, calls this NIHBIDITA – "Not Invented Here, But I Did It Anyway"; and (3) a passionate focus on the details of execution day in and day out.

   This passionate focus on daily execution is necessary when you receive daily orders for over 3.6 million cases of products which have to be sourced, loaded, and delivered the next day on time and defect-free so the food preparer has his or her food and other products to operate their business. As John Stubbefield, the CFO, stated: "We are only as good as our last delivery."

In summary, SYSCO was founded upon values that include integrity, reliability, autonomy, quality, and entrepreneurship, which have been the essence of its culture through the company's history. The autonomous, entrepreneurial, decentralized culture with performance-based reward systems has been one of the keys that has made the company successful and was an integral part of the founding fathers' vision.

John Baugh knew that running local businesses from a central location would not be effective in the foodservice business and Rick Schnieders and Tom Lankford guard that entrepreneurship and autonomy zealously. Each of the company's operating subsidiaries maintains the autonomy to manage and operate their companies in an entrepreneurial fashion, allowing them to respond quickly to customer needs.

Measurement and reward systems

While SYSCO allows its 157 business units to operate "the front of the house" autonomously, the back of the house is centralized and controlled, with a sophisticated measurement system.

Its emphasis on metrics is evidenced by the fact that SYSCO's top ten executive officers meet every Wednesday afternoon and review several hundred metrics for every one of the 157 operating units' prior week's performance. SYSCO measures "everything" related to the receipt, movement, and delivery of products and services to its customers, to new business development, and to every expense and capital expenditure. It measures its return on equity on a weekly basis.

In 1995, SYSCO began working on the design and implementation of a new, all-encompassing technology system that would impact every aspect of the business, the SYSCO Uniform System (SUS). There was no appropriate off-the-shelf package that met all the company's needs, so with the help of a consulting group, the company decided to develop its own system. The first module of SUS was the SYSCO Warehouse Management System (SWMS), which was installed in two phases, SWMS I, a non-directed put away/locator system, and SWMS II, a fully directed warehouse management system. SWMS directs the movement of products through receiving, storing, and shipping to optimize product rotation and freshness.

Modifications of the system continue to be infused as methods and processes improve. In 1998, the SYSCO Order Selector (SOS), another module of SUS, was installed to improve order accuracy and inventory control. A wrist-mounted scanner verifies at the touch of a finger that the product selected is indeed what the customer ordered and virtually eliminates the opportunity for visual errors. Usage of this unit has improved the accuracy of products selected from one error in 800 to one in every three or four thousand items "picked" by the product selector, significantly improving efficiency and customer satisfaction, and reducing restocking costs.

Another enhancement, the SYSCO Loading System (SLS), confirms the accuracy of products selected, then generates a map detailing precise order locations on the delivery trucks so that they are placed in the correct temperature area, are stabilized, and are easily accessible to the driver. Once the trucks are loaded, deliveries are made according to a RoadNet system that assigns optimum delivery routes to minimize driving distances and schedules deliveries within customers' desired time-frames.

The building of the SUS system gave SYSCO the ability to mine data on customers and use that data to provide better service, while using its resources more efficiently. With the new data that were available, it was able to stratify its customer base and determine which customers were the most profitable.

A performance-based system must have strong financial controls and SYSCO maintains a tight rein, requiring that operating company financial results and a myriad of operational and performance metrics be reported to executive management on a weekly basis. While the companies are operated autonomously, they benchmark extensively on performance and operational metrics and share best practices in all areas of the business with peer operating units within the corporation, since it is difficult to find external comparables. The operating units compete with each other for operational recognition and rewards. Likewise, operational units strive not to be on the weekly Wednesday watch list of "under-plan" performers.

The SYSCO measurement system implements the performance-based culture. It is used to determine rewards, and reinforces local autonomy and the entrepreneurial spirit. The culture and the measurement system go hand in hand. Every one of SYSCO's 170 top managers, including its top ten executives, is paid a salary at the industry's 25th percentile. They have to earn their bonus, which can put their total compensation at the industry's 75th percentile. The company's 2,500 top operating company managers work on an incentive reward system, too.

SYSCO is now driving this incentive reward system down to the truck driver and warehouse employee level. The culture, measurement system, and reward system are integrated, internally consistent, understood by line employees, and motivate the desired behaviors.

Chain of growth

SYSCO's DNA is the seamless integration of its culture, measurement, and reward system. These systems drive and focus behavior.

How has SYSCO been able to produce year-in and year-out stellar growth? The company's growth chain has evolved. First, SYSCO grew by expanding its geographical footprint until it covered every major US market. Most of this growth occurred prior to 1988 through the acquisition of many small local family-owned food distribution businesses. Once SYSCO had its geographical footprint, it then segmented the customer market into four segments and created cost-efficient products for each segment from the high-end luxury restaurant to the fast-food carryout restaurant. Then, it entered the ethnic food business – Chinese, Italian, Mexican, Asian – and the specialty foods business – high-end beef and organic fresh vegetables. After rounding out its product offerings within the four customer segments, the company expanded into distributing the hard goods which its customers needed. Customers found it easier, more efficient, and more reliable to place one order with SYSCO than multiple orders with multiple vendors. SYSCO's evolution continued from food to products to the services needed by its customers, including menu design and operational consulting.

SYSCO then focused on its margins – how it could use technology to operate more efficiently. The company measured and iterated until it focused on fifteen to twenty key value-driving metrics which evidenced much of its value creation. And today this journey continues as SYSCO is at the beginning of completely redesigning its supply distribution logistics system into major regional centers, simplifying supplier logistics and maximizing delivery efficiencies at significant cost savings.

SYSCO recently opened its first redistribution center, in Front-Royal, Virginia, which will serve fourteen of SYSCO's broadline distribution centers in the Northeast. SYSCO plans to build seven or eight more regional distribution centers.

When SYSCO talks about its growth, every one of its top officers stresses the importance (and good fortune) of the company having been in an historically good growth industry. The company operates in a market that exceeds $200 billion and has been continuing to grow about 1.5% to 3.0% a year on a real basis (i.e. excluding inflation). SYSCO typically grows by increasing its share of a growing market, as well as by taking market share from competitors. However, in the 2002 and 2003 calendar year periods, the foodservice industry declined 0.7% (in real terms) in 2002 and grew only 0.5% in 2003.

As I stated, SYSCO has been fortunate to be in an industry that has been growing steadily. There are a number of reasons why this is so. There are more dual-income families with both spouses working and having less time to cook; there are more single individuals and single-parent families with less time to prepare meals after a long workday and shuffling children back and forth to activities; also people are living longer, and have more money to spend on meals prepared away from home. The twenty- to forty-year-old segment has grown up with working parents and are familiar with picking up meals at fast-food outlets, enjoying meals at a casual restaurant, or even bringing already prepared meals home to enjoy in the comfort of their own home. Many of these people have neither the skills nor the inclination to cook at home when they can get a tasty meal prepared by someone else at a relatively modest price. As a result, the dollars spent in US grocery stores have continued to decline as the share of dollars spent on food-service has continued to rise, from 37% in 1972 to slightly over 50% in 2003.

Another key aspect of the company's growth strategy has been the development of the SYSCO brand. This brand is the number one brand in foodservice, with more than $12 billion in sales, representing a 43% share of SYSCO's total business and a 56% share of market-ing associate-served or "street" business. According to a NameQuest, Inc. 2002 survey ranking top consumer brands, SYSCO brand sales in fiscal year 2002 would have ranked fourth behind Coca-Cola, Kraft, and Kleenex, a testament to the strength of the brand's recognition and acceptance.

SYSCO introduced its own-brand products in 1975 and, today, more than 40,000 products have the SYSCO name. The original four quality levels comprise Supreme, Imperial, Classic, and Reliance. SYSCO has added expertise in niche product areas like specialty meats, value-added and exotic produce, hotel and lodging industry supplies, Asian cuisine foodservice distribution, and domestic and international custom chain-restaurant distribution.

Since SYSCO does not itself manufacture, a quality assurance team of more than 180 professionals determines specifications for each own-brand item and also sets criteria for raw materials and for the standards that manufacturers and processors must follow for food safety, quality, and consistency, as well as for social responsibility and supplier codes of conduct. This quality assurance team identifies and establishes supply sources and audits those suppliers to enforce SYSCO's strict standards for various factors like facility conditions and sanitary measures. Inspectors are at the plants as bacon comes off the production line, or follow produce from field to cooler to assure proper holding temperatures and product integrity. SYSCO's program is unmatched in the food industry. The number of people and level of resources committed to supporting the integrity of the products are far superior to those of other industry competitors, who may devote merely a handful of personnel to these tasks, if they are undertaken at all.

Role of acquisition

SYSCO's last large acquisition was CFS, a large food distributor, in 1988. This allowed the company to complete its national geographical platform. SYSCO has been acquiring companies since it was formed, and people believe the company's growth has been primarily because of acquisitions. While acquisitions have been important to establish critical geographical footholds, SYSCO has grown faster internally than by acquisitions. The fact that the company has the resources and the internal structure to support the acquired companies in achieving continued growth has been a strength. When making an acquisition, SYSCO usually seeks the premier distributor in a particular market. Often entrepreneurs are willing to sell in order to keep their businesses intact as they get close to retirement, wanting to monetize and realize the equity they have built. Sometimes they have no heirs who are willing or able to step in and run the business. By selling to SYSCO they are able to realize a fair return on their investment, while continuing to grow the business and maintain it as a viable entity. Typically, SYSCO structures its acquisitions with an earn-out provision over a period of years, which motivates the seller to stay involved and maintains profitability during the assimilation. It has been a critical metric for SYSCO's shareholders that acquisition be non-dilutive to earnings and the company typically expects it to be accretive to earnings within the first couple of years. Acquisitions are chosen not only on their position in the market, but also on what they may bring to the table, or the synergies that could be gained by joining with SYSCO, or vice versa. Perhaps it is a location that fills a particular geographical gap or a particular product base. For example, SYSCO, in thirty-five years, has made some 121 acquisitions. In 1999 the company began looking at specialty distributors to fill customer product needs. Since then, not only have broadline distributors been acquired, but also niche distributors, which include nine meat operations, four fresh produce operations, an Asian cuisine specialty company, a distributor to the lodging industry, and a subsidiary that specializes in supplying internationally located chain restaurants. Some may be operations that function as a stand-alone facility, while others may be "folded in" to an existing SYSCO profit center.

Often, a suitable acquisition candidate may not be available in a particular market where the company has been serving customers from SYSCO locations some distance away. In 1995 the company determined that once a specific sales level is established – approximately $125 million to $150 million – then the market can support a stand-alone facility. The business in that marketplace will then be carved away from the existing SYSCO company (or companies) serving those customers from a distant market and a new entity is created – a "foldout." Some advantages to this strategy are that the facility may be built to SYSCO's specifications, with the company's technology systems and a custom-molded, home-grown management team imported from other SYSCO facilities who have the knowledge of the industry and SYSCO's culture to create a new operation. It gives both companies an opportunity to grow in their respective markets, and experience has shown that the seventeen "foldouts" made, including fourteen broadline operations and three specialty company facilities, have grown faster than SYSCO's overall growth rate. It puts SYSCO closer to the customers in that market, makes the company a part of the community, and sets in motion opportunities for continued growth.

Future growth opportunities

SYSCO's long-term financial objectives include growing sales in the low- to mid-teens percentage range, with acquisitions contributing 3% annually on average. The company wants to leverage earnings growth so it outpaces sales growth, while maintaining a 35% return on equity and a 35–40% deb-to-total capital ratio.

How can it do this? First, SYSCO only has a 14–15% market share of a $200 billion market. And, as important, SYSCO on average has captured only 33% of its existing customer total foodservice buys. As CFO John Stubbefield stated, "86% of the customers out there do not think we are the best. And those who do, still buy more products combined from others than they do from us."

So SYSCO's prime growth opportunities, according to president Tom Lankford, are:

(1) acquire new key customers;
(2) sell more products to existing customers and drive the 33% penetration to 60%;
(3) add more specialized disposable products and ethnic foods;
(4) restructure the supply chain to reduce costs substantially so we can compete in the $20–40 billion market of very small customers without lowering our profit margin; and
(5) Expand internationally, where we have less than 1% of our business – especially to the UK and Europe.

To continue its growth, SYSCO has begun over twenty-five Get Better Initiatives in all areas of its business, including sales, marketing, supply chain, safety, diversity, margins, employee retention, incentive compensation, and others.

The following statements by the CEO and president in its 2004 Annual Report summarize SYSCO's focus on operational excellence and the company's top-to-bottom focus on the details of doing business daily.

TO OUR SHAREHOLDERS:

The review of any year should always begin with the recognition that our performance is a credit to our 46,000 associates, who are attuned to every detail, quick to respond to customers' needs and make our success possible. Through their combined efforts we have forged a network of customers, SYSCO operations and suppliers that has proved mutually beneficial and sustainable over the long term. In our industry, it is the attention to every detail – in our own business, as well as our customers' – that makes the difference in our success and theirs.

Daily, we compete in markets throughout North America with thousands of other foodservice distributors, large and small, full-service and specialty distributors. Every day is a new day, another order, another delivery. Our more than 400,000 customers are expecting to receive, literally in many instances, "lunch on the truck." Our warehouses ship approximately four million cases per day and orders for about 85% of those products will have been received yesterday and driven possibly 100 miles before arriving at their destinations – in good condition, on time and with 99-plus % order accuracy.

Since attention to detail is imperative, we continuously strive to improve through benchmarking among our locations on hundreds of metrics, putting to use best practices that continue to raise performance levels. During Fiscal 2004, we continued to see more warehousing and distribution efficiencies in our broadline companies that improved key expense metrics . . .

During my site visit to SYSCO, the founder and chairman, John Baugh, who is 89, was in his office that day. The company's leadership has not become complacent or arrogant even with great success. They, like their warehouse employees, drivers, and sales force go about the daily routine of doing business the SYSCO way – by trying to be better today in helping their customers succeed. It is this improvement mentality culture, which is reinforced through an integrated measurement and compensation system, that makes SYSCO a formidable competitor. Remember what their executives stated:

(1) "We are only as good as our last delivery."
(2) "With only a 14% market share, 86% of the customers are not convinced we are the best."
(3) "With only an average 33% penetration of existing customers, our customers buy more products from others than from us."

This mentality focuses SYSCO daily on the challenges of growth.

6 | Strategic position, organic growth, and financial performance

WILLIAM F. JOYCE

ROWTH remains one of the most intriguing organizational objectives. Research in organization science (OS) has examined growth both as a means to profitability and as an alternative to profitability (Baumol, 1958). With growth as a central concept in OS – either as a means to an end, or as an end in itself – the management literature has variously discussed strategies and structures for growth and varieties of growth (such as organic and inorganic growth), and, indeed, much of the traditional management literature has been concerned with the relationships between functional area strategies and this important outcome criterion.

The large existing literature on growth therefore raises several questions: Is further research on growth needed? What additional contributions can be made to this literature? How can we advance an already voluminous literature and contribute to management practice? Any further research in this area must proceed with at least some amount of hubris, for many, many research efforts have gone before and many issues have been studied.

Research concerning firm growth has tended to follow the path taken by most research in organization science; that is, from general to specific. Research began with an important set of questions, and these have subsequently been fragmented and separated into smaller and smaller parts. This has allowed for the rigorous examination of progressively less and less important problems, and has led us further from the fundamental questions that originally stimulated this field of inquiry. These are: How important is growth, and in particular, organic growth? And second: Depending on our firm's unique strategic situation, what must we do to achieve growth, and through growth, profitability?

It is time, I believe, for us to place growth in context, and to ask these important questions again. It is also time for an integration of growth (as a primary objective of the firm and the means of obtaining profitability) with other critical strategic factors that bear on the ultimate

85

success of the firm. Typically this is done by synthesis of disparate research findings using literature reviews (for qualitative work) or meta-analysis (for quantitative work). Literature reviews place extreme burdens on the cognitive capacity of the researcher, presupposing that he or she is able to remember the findings contained in many studies and reliably integrate them. Meta-analysis averages effect sizes from many empirical studies that often employ quite different measurement methods and definitions of variables that are named similarly. The result is the famous "apples and oranges" problem in which fundamentally and qualitatively different things are averaged, yielding a meaningless result.

An alternative method for answering these questions is to identify and integrate the most important variables affecting profitability (including growth) within a single large-scale study and rely upon rigorous statistical methodology to provide answers to the important and fundamental questions raised above. We are still in need of such answers.

Such a study would have to be large in scale, to ensure that the findings are representative of a broad range of organizations and management practice in general; rigorous, to allow for non-casual interpretation of these large and molar findings; and integrative, allowing the identification and measurement of many potentially important variables and their joint effects in determining firm performance.

This is the approach taken here. The research effort – termed the Evergreen Research Program for its emphasis on determining what factors account for sustained growth in performance – is the largest study of firm performance ever undertaken (Joyce, Nohria, & Roberson, 2003). It provides a new and important perspective on growth both as a means to profitability and as an end in itself.

Growth and the Evergreen research

Literally thousands of books and papers have been published attempting to determine the causes of organizational performance. Unfortunately, this literature remains fragmented, limited in scope, and unconvincing. The Evergreen Research Program was undertaken as an effort to provide a more authoritative answer to the most important question facing management.

How could the Evergreen Project hope to succeed where so many talented researchers and managers had failed? Where had they gone wrong? Essentially, we believed that many of the problems with earlier research could be attributed to four causes. These were: limited resources; an artificial separation between theory and practice; prematurely arriving at the "truth" about the causes of success; and underestimating the difficulty of the fundamental research problem (Joyce, 2005a).

Let us consider each of these. First, almost all management research is very narrow in scope and limited in scale. Most work is done by single researchers with fairly restricted resources. Despite the importance of the problem, we attack it with resources that are modest at best. Often the research is limited to the scale that a single person can accomplish, and because of this it often focuses on a very narrow issue. Real management problems are quite different than this. They are large, both in scope and scale. No one ever encounters a problem that is only a marketing, finance, or accounting problem. These only exist in textbooks. Real problems cannot be solved by treating them in an unreal fashion.

Second, theory and practice are often artificially separated. Researchers talk to other researchers, and practitioners talk to practitioners. It is as if neither one has anything to say to the other, yet they are both trying to determine the same thing: what really works. Practitioners have a rich depth of understanding that is complemented by the rigorous methodologies of researchers. We can scarcely proceed by ignoring one another, and yet we do.

Third, we rely too much on common-sense explanations of management. If this is true, it implies that, because we are human, each one of us is something of an "expert" in managing human behavior. We certainly know more about management from our everyday experiences than we do about physics, or astronomy, or archaeology. For this reason we usually have a starting point for our thinking: what *we* think works, as opposed to what *really* works. We need an approach that is not blinded by these often erroneous assumptions and lets us get to the point – the real point.

Finally, we need to take an approach that recognizes that this is a complex problem. If it were easy it would have been solved a long time ago. Yet over and over, we hear overly simple solutions arrived at through too simple a method. We study ten firms, or interview twenty managers, and draw our conclusions. Who can be surprised that these are often silly and incorrect?

The research that we conducted, the Evergreen Project, was designed to avoid these problems. It was the largest study of its kind ever undertaken. We analyzed over 60,000 pages of information from 200 firms in multiple industries. In all, ten years of data were collected. The firms that were studied varied in size, and we complemented these broad extensive analyses with focused, in-depth exploration of issues of special interest. Both researchers and practitioners were involved. Fourteen prominent academics from Dartmouth, Harvard, Wharton, and other leading business schools were involved. Twenty-one practitioners implemented the study in coordination with the academic researchers. We interviewed journalists, executives, and Wall Street analysts. We let the answers come from the data, and then tested specific hypotheses to explore promising possibilities. And finally, we invented new statistical methodology that is appropriate to this level of complexity.

What really works: basic findings

Each company in our study was assigned to an industry subgroup such as retailing, consumer electronics, or energy (forty in all), and then given a specific performance designation in that subgroup based on their performance relative to peers. These performance differences identified each firm as a Winner, Climber, Tumbler, or Loser over the ten-year period of the study. Winners started out strong and got even better. Tumblers started strong and then faltered. Climbers and Losers both began with weak performance. However, Climbers were able to overcome their problems and rise to a high level of performance by the end of the ten-year period. Losers muddled along, never rising above mediocre performance.

What distinguished Winners from Losers, and Climbers from Tumblers? Surprisingly, only four foundation practices (focused strategy, execution, performance culture, and fast and flat organization) and four secondary practices (securing talent, committed leadership, industry-transforming innovation, and growth through mergers and partnerships) were found to be the most reliable indicators of return to shareholders. Specifically, success required performing well in all four foundation areas plus at least two of the secondary areas. This finding was termed the 4+2 formula for business success. The formula and the specific practices supporting it are discussed in detail in our book *What Really Works* (Joyce, Nohria, & Roberson, 2003) and in subsequent publications extending these findings (Joyce, 2005a, 2005b).

Firms that were unable to meet the requirements of the 4+2 formula dramatically increased their chances of failure and the differences in financial performance among these firms were remarkable. Winners produced total returns to shareholders (TRS) of 945% over the ten-year period of the study, whereas Losers were only able to grow TRS 62%. Sales rose 415% for Winners, but only 83% for Losers. Similar results held for operating income.

Question 1: How important is growth?

Growth seems to be on every manager's mind. But is this concern appropriate? What is it about growth that makes it so pervasive as an object of management's attention? To answer this we have to put growth in perspective.

The two most commonly employed measures of firm performance in organization science are profitability and returns to shareholders, preferred by economists and financial analysts respectively (McGuire, 1964). Other measures have also been used extensively, the most obvious being accounting measures that presumably are predictive of the two measures above. Measures from administrative management theory (Gulick & Urwick, 1937) and systems theory (Kast & Rosenzweig, 1972) have also been proposed. Where does growth fit in this perspective?

It can play one of two roles. First, as an end in itself or as an alternative or adjunct to profitability and shareholder equity, or, second, as an intermediate objective leading to one of these more fundamental outcomes. If we examine the first of these alternatives we see a range of theories that have subordinated profitability to other variables as primary outcomes. For example, research in the economic theory of commercial banking modifies the basic economic goal of profitability to include a superordinate need for liquidity (Cooper, 1949), and Margolis (1958) argues that the context of uncertainty in which business activities are conducted will lead so-called "deliberative" firms to utilize criteria that they believe will lead to profitability in this context. Growth, or revenue maximization, is one such variable (Baumol, 1958).

This literature suggests two conclusions with respect to the role of growth as a primary performance criterion. First, it is only one of many that have been identified, and second, even in this context it is usually addressed as an adjunct to constraints on profitability.

The second role for growth seems therefore more plausible – it is something that firms need to do in order to be economically successful. But here, qualification is needed again. The Evergreen research is authoritative in pointing out that growth is a *complementary* practice. That is, it is not essential to high performance! It is not one of the four essential foundation practices; it is merely one of the further four complementary practices. Only two of these are necessary to ensure success when coupled with the four foundation practices, and the relationships among them are compensatory. That is, high levels of any two can compensate for low levels of the remaining two complementary practices.

In summary, it seems as if growth is merely one of many relevant objectives that might be pursued by organizations, that its relevance lies mainly in enabling profitability, and that for many firms, there are alternative ways of obtaining this profitability without growth. The single-minded pursuit of growth (whether organic, accretive, networked, partnered, or acquired) as an organizational objective therefore seems misplaced, and firms would be well advised to determine its relevance in light of their particular strategic positions and aims. It is to this more important topic that I now turn.

Question 2: Given our strategic situation, how can we grow to ensure outstanding performance?

Should all firms strive for growth? Is it easier for Winners to grow than Losers? Should Losers even attempt growth strategies? How should firms merge growth objectives with other important organizational initiatives? These are all questions that must be answered in the context of a firm's particular pattern of foundational and complementary practices, and must recognize that growth is dynamic, occurring over time.

In order to answer these important questions, I conducted a series of analyses within the fact book coding portions of the broad Evergreen research. So as to understand these results, it is necessary to take a look at the methods involved in greater depth.

Content analyses: fact book coding and sequence comparison

Fact books are collections of publicly available information specific to each of the approximately 200 Evergreen study firms over the period from 1985 to 1995, and comprise written reports and commentaries drawn from a number of sources. These sources include reports by journalists and analysts, as well as other publicly available sources.

I will refer to the analyses based on these sources collectively as the fact book coding and analysis (FCA) portion of the Evergreen studies. It is believed that these analyses represent the largest exploration of text-based secondary source information concerning the causes of firm performance to date. Furthermore, they are based on data sources that have generally not been drawn upon by organizational researchers because of the formidable methodological issues that have to be confronted and addressed for their utilization.

At the completion of this process, 200 detailed Fact Book Coding Reports had been prepared (described in detail below). As a second major step in the analysis, the data from the 200 individual firm reports were aggregated to what was termed the "grand" analysis level, and prepared for further analyses to determine the major clusters of actions or critical success factors that explained performance across firms and over the period (the "Evergreen Decade") of the study. These third and final analyses were accomplished using novel applications of four Quad types, consisting of sequence comparison (SA) methodology to compute metric distances among all linguistic assertions derived from the issues analysis (IA). The inter-item matrix of these metric distances became the input for cluster analyses (CA) and multidimensional scaling (MS) analyses that determined the final set of clusters or critical success factors distinguishing the four Quad types and their associated performance. A number of significant statistical issues had to be overcome in this process since large-scale analyses of this type had never before been accomplished.

The following sections describe the methodology for each of the three major phases of the study described above, beginning with Issues Analysis©, proceeding to aggregation and data preparation, and culminating with a discussion of the sequence comparison analyses.

Issues Analysis©

As described above the primary sources of data for these analyses were "fact books." Each fact book contained a number of reports, articles, and analyses prepared by analysts, journalists, or researchers studying the particular firm of interest. In general, the fact books were voluminous and contained twenty to thirty papers focusing on each of the two study periods. Although a few papers were short, most varied between five and ten pages in length. Over 60,000 pages of textual data were analyzed in the course of the study.

All interviews and articles were reviewed for each firm. Following this, studies were eliminated from further analysis if they did not contain content reflecting the Project Evergreen guidelines (strategy, environment, people), over-sampled particular time-frames (generally selected studies were balanced across both the years and periods of the study, adjusted slightly for publication lag), or lacked source credibility (for example, *Fortune*, the *Wall Street Journal*, and *Business Week* were preferred over obscure journals and publications).

The secondary source of information contained in the fact books was then subjected to a methodology termed Issues Analysis© (Joyce Nohria, & Roberson, 2003). This procedure determines the content and importance of issues that are relevant to firm performance. The process begins by identifying a set of initial issues for the individual firm being studied. The initial issues were selected on the basis of accepted management practice and relevant research in organization theory.

Following this they were weighted by the frequency with which they were mentioned in the secondary source articles constituting the fact book for that particular firm, and ranked in order to clarify which issues were the most important. The ranking of issues determines the relative importance of various causes of firm performance, and was accomplished in both time-periods 1 and 2 of the study.

The issue identification and ranking process was conducted for all of the firms in the study, and an individual firm report was prepared for each Quad for all industry groupings. Each Quad report contained results for the four firm types (Winner, Tumbler, Climber, and Loser) summarized in eight tables, where tables 1 and 2 refer to firm type 1, 3 and 4 to firm type 2, and so on. Each table was followed by a brief summary of the conclusions that could be drawn concerning the dominant causes of performance for a particular firm in each of the two time-periods of the study. Three additional types of analyses could then be conducted based upon these tables.

Type I: Early moves and corrections

These were issues that were mentioned predominantly in time-period 1 but not time-period 2. These characterize actions that were taken in the first period of the study but that were discontinued in the second period. A frequency difference of three or more would represent predominance for a sample of this size at the individual firm level (more sophisticated statistical tests of frequency differences were employed in the grand aggregation stage of this research).

Type II: Later moves and positioning

These were issues that were predominantly mentioned in time-period 2, but not time-period 1. These are actions characterizing the second period of the study but not the first, or critical success factors relevant at the later stages of change. A frequency difference of three or more would represent predominance for a sample of this size.

Type III: Consistent moves and themes

These were issues that were present in both time-periods 1 and 2. These are the ways that the organization has remained the same over time, or has maintained a consistent focus on particular courses of action. These would be issues that did not differ by more than three in frequency counts of importance.

The transition is *larger* the greater the frequency of Type I and Type II issues. The organizational causes for performance *change* will be found in the distinctions between these two types of issues. Higher frequencies of Type III issues indicate that the firm has tended to follow a similar strategy and implementation process over the time-periods of the study.

The analyses described above provide information useful for explaining differences in firm performance among the set of firms comprising each Quad. However, interpretation across Quads, and ultimately across industries, requires that the data be aggregated to a higher level.

Aggregation of issues data to grand level

The next stages of the analysis sought to determine the causes of firm performance across all industries in the study. It was therefore necessary to aggregate the issues that had been identified at the firm level, for each firm type (Winner, Loser, Climber, Tumbler), across all industries. This aggregation was termed the "grand aggregation" (GA) as it contained all of the data of the study without regard to Quad or industry membership. These issues would then be statistically grouped (within firm types, based upon similarity of actions explaining performance) at the next major stage of analysis using sequence comparison methodologies. The resulting clusters of performance-related actions or critical success factors could be contrasted across firm types to explain the relative performance of Winners, Losers, Tumblers, and Climbers.

The final sets of issues contained 250–350 assertions for each issue type (I, II, and III) within firm type (Winners, Losers, Climbers, and Tumblers), or between 550 and 850 assertions for each firm type, posing formidable issues in further managing the complexity of the dataset. These issues were resolved at the next major stage of analysis.

Sequence comparison analyses

The large number of assertions concerning the causes of firm performance precludes conclusions based upon simple inspection of the data. It was therefore necessary to devise a way systematically to aggregate similar assertions to identify and assign priorities to categories of actions responsible for differing levels of performance. Sequence comparison (SA) methodology (Kruskal, 1987; Joyce, McGee, & Slocum 1997) was used for this purpose.

Sequence comparison is a technique for comparing two strings, sequences, or vectors for the purpose of determining the distance between them, and consequently their relationship. The items making up the sequence could be numbers, symbols, tones, letters, or words. We could, for example, compute a metric distance between the names "William" and "Victor." Recognizing this, it is a simple extension to understand that assertions concerning the causes of firm performance are sequences of words, and that sequence comparison methodology can be used to compute similarity measures between these assertions.

Summarizing, sequence comparison allows us to compute the quantitative distance between any two linguistic assertions. In this research, the assertions are those derived from the procedures described above. Once distances (similarity data) are computed that satisfy the metric axioms, the matrix of inter-assertion distances can be analyzed using a variety of multivariate statistical techniques.

The method that was utilized was a naturalistic clustering method that allowed for chaining among assertions. Logical argument, in which a set of assertions is linked to support a conclusion, possesses exactly this type of structure (Govier, 1992). Separate premises in an argument may only be linked through intermediate assertions, and may have no direct connections to one another. They are still essential parts of the overall argument structure. Since our interest is in the issues surrounding the causes of firm performance, as represented in the linguistic assertions and arguments contained in the fact books, naturalistic methods are especially pertinent in this study. All interpretations in the following tables and charts were based upon the single-linkage clustering results using Coggins' D3 measure of similarity.

Clusters were named and weights were assigned to them based upon their size. Compound cluster weights were determined by summing the weights of the parent clusters and all component hierarchical clusters, adjusting for overlapping cluster membership. Clusters were numbered in order based upon the overall importance of the cluster, where 1 indicated the greatest importance. Finally, all clusters were systematically related to the foundation and complementary practices derived in the overall study.

The normalized practice space: visualizing the sequence comparison results

Distinguishing among Winners, Losers, Climbers, and Tumblers

Each of our four firm types has a characteristic profile of foundation practices that is based upon the cluster weights determined above. Figure 6.1 portrays the results of these analyses for the Winner firms in what I call the "normalized practice space" (Joyce, 2005a). Each dimension of the practice space is shown on a scale of 0–100, and has been normalized to allow the use of a common scale for visualizing all

Figure 6.1. Winner foundation practices.

four practices. That is, the total frequency or importance score for each foundation practice has been standardized at 100%, and each Quad type's score is based upon the ratio of its practice weights to those of the Winner firms. These scores are called "practice scores," and the space defined by the scores for the Winner firms is called the "normalized practice space." The Winner firm occupies 100% of the normalized practice space (NPS), since the Winner's frequency or importance scores are divided by themselves.

I have chosen to represent the strategy and execution practices on one axis of the NPS shown in Figure 6.1, with culture and structure on the second axis. Broadly, these correspond to "strategic" and "organizational" dimensions of the NPV. Opposite ends of each dimension focus on longer (strategy and culture) or shorter (execution and structure) term issues in building a 4+2 organization, as shown in the figure.

The foundation practice profiles of each of the remaining three firm types (Losers, Climbers, and Tumblers) may then be identified by computing the ratio of each of their four practice frequencies to those of the Winner profile shown in Figure 6.1. The resulting "practice" scores may be interpreted as the percentage of the Winner profile scores achieved by each of the remaining three firm types on each of

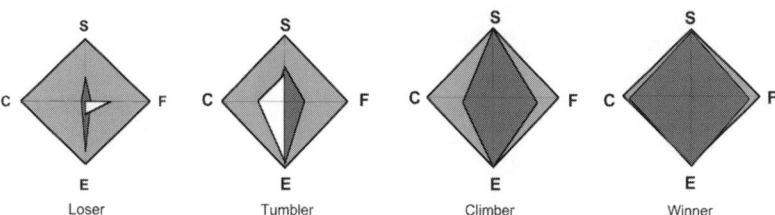

> • All have some ability at execution – this is a <u>survival criterion</u>
>
> • Tumbler retains some strengths from its time as a Winner – <u>Turnaround is easier than transformation</u>
>
> • Winners build culture and organization around effective strategy and execution – and then <u>relentlessly sustain it</u>

Figure 6.2. Lessons from the 4+2 formula.

the four foundation practices. The Winner firm occupies 100% of the normalized practice space, as stated earlier. Each of the remaining three Quad types occupies only a portion of this space.

Comparing foundation practices: *Winners, Losers, Climbers, and Tumblers*

The profiles of Winners, Losers, Climbers, and Tumblers are compared in Figure 6.2. The differences among these, and the implication of these differences for management, are discussed extensively in Joyce (2005a). In this section I will discuss only the major characteristics of each type, in order to provide the necessary context for an analysis of growth and its effects on financial performance. The dark-toned area in these diagrams represents positive actions taken with respect to each of the four foundation practices, and subsequently, for each of the four Quad types. The white area represents negative actions (excess bureaucracy, failed diversification, failing to maintain customer focus, etc.) as identified from the documents analyzed in the FCA portion of the study.

Losers seem to have very few strengths. They perform moderately in execution, but only against a weak strategy. The organizational dimensions are particularly weak: bureaucracy rules and there are few mechanisms for cross-functional coordination. Culture is controlling,

Table 6.1. *Strategic position and growth*

	Loser			Climber			Tumbler			Winner		
	Early	Consis.	Late	Early	Consis.	Late	Early	Consis.	Late	Early	Consis.	Late
Focus on growth (H, M, L)	H ↓	H (Fails) ↑	L ↑	L ↓	M (Learns)	H ↑	L ↓	L (Stumbles)	H ↑	H ↓	H (Sustains)	H ↑
Organic vs. inorganic	Inorg.	Inorg.	Org.	Org.	Org.	Bal.	Bal.	Bal.	Negative inorg.	Inorg.	Org.	Bal.
	↓ Negative path	↑		↓	↑ Positive path	↑	↓	↑ Forgotten path	↑	↓	↑ Any path	↑
Transformation mandates	None	None	Simple	Complex	Complex	Complex	Simple	Simple	Simple	Complex	Complex	Complex
Strategy (S)				S	S	S	S	S		S	S	S
Execution (E)			E	E	E	E	E	E	E	E	E	E
Structure (St)				St	St					St		
Culture (C)				C	C	C	C				C	C

ambivalent, and uninspiring. It is no wonder that these firms consistently underachieve.

Tumblers possess a stronger, yet still troubling profile. First, we notice that Tumblers (who were once Winners) occupy only a portion of the normalized practice space. This indicates that Tumblers have stopped doing a portion of the things that led to their success. This is compounded by many errors; in fact, so many that they virtually offset the positive actions attributed to these firms. Tumblers have ceased many of their winning practices, and then compounded this with many errors in implementing new practices – a dangerous posture indeed.

Climbers seem to have avoided making errors. Climbers attack execution relentlessly, and then build strong strategies on the basis of this improvement. They are on their way to becoming Winners.

Winners do it all. With a strong strategy and execution, Winners build on these strategic practices to strengthen both structure and culture. They make few errors and enjoy the luxury of continually refining and improving already excellent practices.

Strategic position, growth, and financial performance

We are now in a position to discuss growth and financial performance in the context of the strategic position of the firm. We began with the assumption that firms will aspire to the Winner strategic position, and will generally take action to exit the Loser position. Climbers and Tumblers represent "turning points." A Tumbler is a former Winner. We assume that a Tumbler wishes to avoid the practices that have led to its decline and resume its position as a Winner. Climbers have begun the move to Winner status; they aspire to continued success in transformation and to avoid mistakes that would result in returning to the Loser position.

Table 6.1 summarizes the results of the fact book coding and analysis (FCA) for the growth complementary practice of the Evergreen research. Key growth findings are arrayed against the backdrop of the four strategic positions (W, L, C, T) and hypothesized aspirations to move to the Winner category. Critical success factors for growth are indicated based upon the timing of actions identified in the Issues Analysis© described above; that is, (1) early moves and corrections (2) later moves and positioning and (3) consistent moves and themes. Each of the four key strategic positions is discussed in turn.

Growth and strategic position

The Loser firm has a high focus on growth during the early stages of change, and maintains some of this focus over the ten-year period of the study (the Evergreen Decade, ED). In the early stages of attempted improvement in strategic position, Loser firms emphasize inorganic growth and encounter substantial problems in achieving it. Only in the latter half of the ED do they begin to attempt organic growth. This shift in focus is accompanied by an attempt to improve execution, but, in general, Losers do not exert much effort in improving any other foundation practice across the entire ten-year period of the ED.

Tumblers display a quite different pattern. They begin with a balanced growth profile, with roughly equal emphases on organic and inorganic growth. Then, as they encounter performance problems stemming from poor implementation of the foundation practices, they seek a way out of their dilemma by attempting significant inorganic growth. The overall emphasis on growth is low except in the latter portions of the ED where it receives significant emphasis. Perhaps they hope to buy their way out of trouble. Without the foundation practices to support this growth, they stumble. Tumblers maintain some strength in execution from their time as Winners, but make many other mistakes in strategy and culture that offset these positive effects. Attempts to improve the foundation practices and support growth are transitional at best, and focus on only one, or at most two, practices simultaneously.

Climbers avoid the failures of the Tumblers. They have a relatively low emphasis on growth in the early stages of recovery, and often even experience negative growth as they shed poor products, businesses, and geographies. Organic growth is emphasized, and slowly growth becomes a more important complementary practice. The organization learns how to grow by building its competence slowly and carefully in organic growth. Only then, in the latter stages of the ED, do they engage in inorganic growth, yielding a balanced growth profile. Throughout this process the Climber is constantly engaged in activities aimed at improving all of the foundation practices simultaneously. These activities are transformational in this sense; all foundation practices must be in place for radical gains in profitability to take place. This is a significant departure from the merely transitional activities of Losers and Tumblers.

Winners do it all. They seem to begin where the Climbers end. They have a high emphasis on growth across all of the stages of the ED, and emphasize both inorganic and organic growth as opportunities arise. Ultimately this yields a balanced growth profile. Moreover, Winners are constantly engaged in transformation in a manner similar to Climbers. However, unlike the Climber, who must first concentrate on strategy and execution, Winners are already strong in these areas. They continue to emphasize these while seeking additional sources of competitive advantage through organization design and culture.

As we move from Losers, through Tumblers and Climbers, ultimately to Winners, the growth path changes from paths that fail or stumble, to those that learn and sustain high levels of balanced growth. This maturation in skills is accompanied and enabled by a movement to change activities that are fundamentally transformational.

Conclusion

Growth should not be an objective for all firms. It is only one of several potential measures of effectiveness that might be chosen. And, while growth may be a significant contributor to profitability through its role as a complementary practice, other complementary practices such as innovation and talent can compensate for its absence.

The pursuit of growth as a means to financial performance must take account of the strategic position of the firm. Inorganic growth seems to make less sense for Loser and Tumbler firms than for Climber and Winner firms that have developed skills for managing organic growth over time. All growth can only be successful in the context of high levels of all four foundation practices – strategy, execution, fast/flat structure, and culture – and any growth strategy must be accompanied by significant efforts to maintain these at exemplary levels.

References

Baumol, W. J. 1958. On the theory of oligopoly. *Economica*, New Series, 24(99): 187–198.
Cooper, W. W. 1949. Theory of the firm: some suggestions for revision. *American Economic Review*, 39(6): 1204–1222.
Govier, T. 1992. *A Practical Study of Argument*. Belmont, CA: Wadsworth.
Gulick, L. & Urwick, L. 1937. *Papers on the Science of Administration*. New York: Institute of Public Administration.

Joyce, W. 1986. Matrix organization: a social experiment. *Academy of Management Journal*, 29(3): 536–561.

2005a. What really works: building the 4+2 organization. *Organizational Dynamics*, 34: 118–129.

2005b. What really works: HR's role in building the 4+2 organization. *Human Resource Management Journal*, 44(1): 67–72.

Joyce, W., McGee, V., & Slocum, J. 1997. Designing lateral organizations: an analysis of the benefits, costs, and enablers of nonhierarchical organizational forms. *Decision Sciences*, 28: 1–26.

Joyce, W., Nohria, N., & Roberson, B. 2003. *What Really Works: The 4+2 Formula for Sustained Business Performance*. New York: Harper Business.

2005. HR's role in building the 4+2 organization. In S. Meisenger, M. Losey, and D. Ulrich (eds.), *The Future of HR: 50 Thought Leaders Call for Change*. Hoboken, NJ: Wiley.

Kast, D. & Rosenzweig, J. 1972. General systems theory: applications for organization management. *Academy of Management Journal*, 15: 447–465.

Kruskal, J. B. 1987. *Time Warps, String Edits, and Macromolecules: The Theory and Practice of Sequence Comparison*. Boston: Addison-Wesley.

Margolis, J. 1958. The analysis of the firm: rationalism, conventionalism, and behaviorism. *Journal of Business*, 31(3): 187–199.

McGuire, J. 1964. *Theories of Business Behavior*. Englewood Cliffs, NJ: Prentice-Hall.

7 Defining and measuring organic growth

EDWARD D. HESS

W HAT is organic growth? Why is it important? How has the academic world defined organic growth? How has the business world looked at organic growth?

The interest and focus on organic growth in a meaningful way is a recent phenomenon, which grew out of the financial scandals of the late 1990s and early years of the following decade. What the public learned from these scandals was that (1) there are different types of earnings; (2) companies can create earnings in different ways; (3) earnings can be created by accounting recognition, accounting policies, accounting adjustments, accounting elections, and valuations; (4) earnings can be created by financially engineered transactions, pension fund gains, related party transactions, currency gains, cookie jar reserves, classification of investment transactions, channel stuffing, etc.; (5) earnings management is more widespread than many thought; and (6) yes, earnings management can turn into earnings manipulation A good summary of earnings management techniques can be found in Nelson, Elliott, and Tarply (2003).

Fundamentally, we learned that companies frequently produce non-operating or non-core earnings in order to meet Wall Street's expectations of consistent quarterly earnings growth. Certain types of earnings are derived from one-time non-recurring transactions. Should that type of earnings be valued in the same manner as earnings from the operating business? Should companies be required to disclose the types, character, or quality of their earnings? Which is a more valuable predictor of future business operations and their sustainability – cashflow operating results or the non-operating earnings?

The public learned what CPAs, CFOs, and accounting professors have known for a long time: that GAAP accounting rules give companies broad latitude in recording earnings. Maybe all earnings are not as equal or as valuable in evaluating a company's strategy, execution, sustainability, growth, or management team. Not only do the different types or character or quality of earnings impact the quality, reliability, and predictability of business operations, but the fact that all earnings are not the same impacts years of academic research which generally treats all earnings as equal or of equivalent weight.

Historically, the definition of organic growth has not been the focus of academic or financial analysts. Academic researchers looked at increase in revenues or increase in head-count as evidence of growth. Organic growth was defined as the opposite of acquisitive growth. Almost all academic research counted or evaluated every cent of earnings equally. Academic research into corporate growth has generally focused on absolute sales growth or relative employment growth. Some have looked at market share, assets, and profits. A good summary can be found in Delmar, Davidsson, and Gartner (2003). I respectfully submit that all earnings are not equal if you are trying to evaluate the strength, sustainability, and predictability of a business's core operations and processes.

The first major attempt to evaluate the quality of business operating results was the Stern Stewart EVA computation, a proprietary complicated formula that can make up to 160 adjustments to reported earnings of public companies. A component of EVA is to determine a firm's net operating income after tax and while it may accomplish this objective, it has been criticized because it relies on data that, as stated earlier, can be managed (Brewer & Chandra, 1999). It was more than a decade before Wall Street analysts accepted EVA, and today its use is widespread in the corporate world, but not as much as in the investment world.

The financial scandals of WorldCom, Enron, and others challenged investors' confidence in corporate America. In an effort to restore some semblance of confidence in corporate earnings statements, two Wall Street powers attempted to evaluate the quality and character of earnings. On May 14, 2002, Standard & Poors (S&P) released its Core Earnings Test, a method that would separate a company's earnings into core and non-core classifications.

Core Earnings represented a significant step forward but it was widely criticized in the financial community and by some academics. None the less, S&P's Core Earnings computations were an advance.

In August 2002, Merrill Lynch, the only Wall Street investment banking firm to enter the discussion, issued its Quality of Earnings Report, which used four financial discriminating screens created with Professor David Harkin of the Harvard Business School to evaluate the quality of earnings.

What did we do? First, we studied in detail EVA, S&P's Core Earnings Test, and Merrill's Quality of Earnings Report and we talked to financial analysts at each of the respective firms. Secondly, we researched the academic literature on growth, earnings management, and earnings manipulation. Then, thirdly, we talked with senior audit partners at major accounting firms to learn the common issues they faced in determining GAAP earnings. We then spent one year creating, testing, and iterating different tests to create the Organic Growth Index (OGI), which is our interactive, evolutionary extension of the work by Stern Stewart, S&P, and Merrill Lynch. We adjusted or incorporated into our model what we thought were the best parts of their work and added four new tests.

First, we wanted to expand the definition of growth to include not only sales growth but also growth in cash flow from operations (CFFO) because we thought it was harder to manipulate CFFO than sales volume. Secondly, we wanted a way to normalize results across industries, which negated industry bias in growth numbers. Thirdly, we wanted to include an accounting "shenanigans" test to highlight potential income manipulations and, lastly, we wanted to add a merger and acquisition test to discriminate between serial acquirers who repeatedly or significantly purchased revenues from those companies who grew internally or organically.

At first, the financial community reception to OGI was tepid. The *Financial Times* highlighted our first index in an article published on August 8, 2003. Interest increased in 2004 when *Fortune* magazine talked about our index in an article entitled "Organic growth: big firms, big growth," on June 7, 2004. Our research was further highlighted at Fortune.com, now being looked at by others.

Our research is controversial. To academics, if we are correct that different types of earnings can be created and that not all earnings represent true growth, then years of research which assumes every cent of earnings is equal to every other cent of earnings is called into question.

Wall Street – the prime proponent of the fiction that quarterly earnings growth should be linear – questions our research because they make hundreds of millions of dollars a year selling products of various types to generate or create earnings.

What about the interest of the public? The SEC should enter this arena and require disclosure – "sunshine" on the type, character, and quality of corporate earnings. Companies should be required to state how much of their earnings were created through accounting elections, accounting adjustments, changes in accounting methods, investments, financial engineering, related party transactions, acquisitions, etc. Companies should disclose quarterly earnings management and the details on how the results were achieved.

I submit that all cents of earnings are not equal or as valuable as each other in evaluating a company's business, its operations or its future. Companies that generate organic growth earnings are more likely to be sustainable high-performance organizations and should be valued as such.

A focus on organic growth – its processes and its challenges – will change the way senior management is evaluated and compensated. It is an attempt to find and reward real value creation.

We have completed two OGIs and the third will be released in May 2005. In addition, we have a new research project in place that is trying to find out how those high organic growth companies are able to accomplish what so few companies are able to do. And the preliminary results are surprising and counter-intuitive.

The Organic Growth Index is explained in Table 7.1, while on the basis of our model, Table 7.2 lists the best organic growers in the period 1997–2002 using EVA adjusted by size, sales, and cash flow growth as compared to industry averages and as normalized by industry standard deviations. On a relative basis, these companies did not produce material financial results from non-core earnings, accounting manipulations, aggressive revenue recognition, or serial acquisitions. These companies outperformed their industry competition primarily by growing their businesses organically.

The strength of the OGI model is that it combines the rigor of Stern Stewart's EVA methodology, S&P's Core Earnings methodology, Merrill Lynch's Cash Realization Test, and four additional tests into a new model that, we contend, extends the research in the space of organic growth. The cumulative effect of these tests is powerful

Table 7.1. *What is the Organic Growth Index, 1997–2002?*

Research Sample

Our sample began with the top 1,000 economic-value-added (EVA) companies for 2002 based upon Stern Stewart's MVA database and methodology. We then eliminated banks, diversified financials, REITs, and insurance companies because of accounting and industry idiosyncrasies.

Sample size: 862 companies

↓

Test 1 – EVA/capital

We then narrowed the sample to the top 300 EVA producers for the years 1997–2002. To adjust for size bias, we computed yearly EVA/Capital Invested for each company.

Sample size: 300 companies

↓

Test 2 – Sales & CFFO growth

We then calculated an industry-normalized z-statistic for both Sales and Cash Flow from Operations (CFFO) growth and averaged the two z-statistics. Those companies with positive average z-statistics moved to the next screen. This test defines high growth as performance consistently stronger than industry averages.

↓

Results

By using EVA/Capital Invested and Sales and Cash Flow growth, we utilized commonly accepted definitions of growth and economic value creation to identify growing companies. Now, having the top growth companies, we moved to tests to eliminate material non-organic growers.

Sample size: 189 companies

↓

Test 3 – Core earnings

S&P's Core Earnings Test was applied to the top 189 companies. We eliminated companies with material non-core operating results.

Companies eliminated: 83 – Companies remaining: 106

↓

Test 4 – Accounts receivable (A/R) to sales

We then focused on aggressive accrual of income. We looked at who was growing accounts receivable materially faster than sales. This test included a materiality hurdle so that companies would not be eliminated on immaterial numbers.

Companies eliminated: 37 – Companies remaining: 69

↓

Test 5 – Cash realization

To the remaining companies, we applied Merrill Lynch's Cash Realization Test. We eliminated companies that reported financial net income that materially exceeded cash flow from operations.

Companies eliminated: 7 – Companies remaining: 62

↓

Test 6 – Mergers & acquisitions (M&A)

To the remaining companies, we applied an M&A test, which eliminated companies that acquired at least $33\frac{1}{3}$% of their increase in market value between 1997–2002.

Companies eliminated: 39 – Companies remaining: 23

↓

Rank-ordered results

Twenty-three companies produced significant economic value and outperformed their industry competition primarily through organic or internal growth. The companies are presented in a rank order based on performance on the tests.

Table 7.2. *2002 Organic Growth Index rankings*

1.	NVR Inc.
2.	Family Dollar Stores
3.	Harley-Davidson Inc.
4.	Gentex Corp.
5.	Walgreen Co.
6.	American Eagle Outfitters Inc.
7.	Bed Bath & Beyond Inc.
8.	C. H. Robinson Worldwide Inc.
9.	Outback Steakhouse Inc.
10.	Sysco Corp.
11.	Waters Corp.
12.	Wal-Mart Stores
13.	Ross Stores Inc.
14.	Mylan Laboratories
15.	Anheuser-Busch Cos. Inc.
16.	Tiffany & Co.
17.	Lincare Holdings Inc.
18.	Omnicom Group
19.	Paccar Inc.
20.	Brinker Intl. Inc.
21.	Automatic Data Processing
22.	Best Buy Co. Inc.
23.	Ruby Tuesday Inc.

Notes: Due to Standard & Poors' methodological changes in the calculation of core earnings, core earning data were not available for Columbia Sportswear Co., Cognizant Tech Solutions, and Total Systems Services. These three companies qualified under all other tests as organic growers, but were excluded from the final list due to inadequate S&P core earning information.

and robust, with results that have identified companies that grew their businesses organically from 1997 to 2002, while producing substantial economic value and outperforming their industry competition.

Additionally, as shown in Table 7.3, the twenty-three companies that constitute the OGI significantly outperformed the Dow Jones Industrial Average, the S&P 500, the Nasdaq 100, and the Russell 3000 almost all the time.[1]

---

[1] Performance for the OGI was computed using market value data from Compustat. The compounded annual growth rate for each company was computed. A

Table 7.3. *Growth of OGI company results*

	Jan. 1997– Dec. 1999	Jan. 2000– Dec. 2002	Jan. 1997– Dec. 2002	Jan. 2003– Dec. 2004
DJIA	21.3%	−9.8%	4.4%	20.0%
S&P 500	25.9%	−15.4%	3.0%	22.4%
Nasdaq 100	47.0%	−31.4%	0.7%	44.7%
Russell 3000	24.0%	−14.6%	2.7%	24.9%
OGI2	48.6%	12.0%	25.2%	31.3%

Table 7.4. *Market capitalization of OGI companies*

Market capitalization size	1997	2002
Micro ($50–300 million)	2	0
Small ($300 million–2 billion)	13	2
Mid ($2–10 billion)	4	13
Large ($10–200 billion)	4	7
Mega (greater than $200 billion)	0	1

Further, the OGI firms are described by the market capitalization and industry analyses shown in Table 7.4.

Further research at the Center for Entrepreneurship and Corporate Growth at the Goizueta Business School, Emory University will focus on refinements to the model, its predictive uses, and its use as a basis for developing Organic Growth Best Practices.

Databases

For the economic value creation tests we used Stern Stewart's 2003 US EVA/MVA Annual 1000 ranking database. For all other computations, except the M&A tests, we used Compustat. For the M&A tests, we used the Securities Data Corporation (SDC) database provided by Thomson Financial.

weighted average based upon the ending time-period market value was then calculated. The performance for the market indices is simply a compounded annual
growth rate for each index based on its level on December 31 of the last year of
the period.

Test 1 – EVA/capital invested

Purpose

The purpose of Test 1 was to select a relevant and defensible sample of companies which were acknowledged value creators for the time-period 1997–2002.

Many different samples and indices were considered and critiqued. We chose Stern Stewart's Market Value Added (MVA) database and its Economic Value Added (EVA) methodology because it is an independent attempt to adjust a company's reported financial results to determine who was really creating economic value for shareholders.

Application

From Stern Stewart's list of the top 1,000 MVA creators for 2002, we eliminated 138 companies classified as REITs, banks, diversified financials, or insurance companies by Global Industry Classification Standard codes. Thus, we began with 862 companies.

For these companies, we used EVA (from Stern Stewart's database) created by each of these 862 firms for the years 1997–2002. To adjust for size bias, we then divided EVA for each year by the respective capital invested (again from Stern Stewart's database) – defined as the total equity and debt capital of a company.

Then, for each year 1997–2002, we ranked the results, according to the ratio EVA/Capital Invested. For each company, we averaged their respective ranks for the individual years and created one overall rank of EVA/Capital Invested for the period 1997–2002. If a company was not in the EVA Top 1000 for any year, it was given a rank of –100 for that year.

We arbitrarily chose to take the top 300 companies to Test 2. Those companies are listed in Table 7.5.

Test 2 – Growth screens

Purpose

What evidences growth? Common definitions include either consistent top-line or consistent bottom-line growth. We focused on sales and cashflow from operations growth in the period 1997–2002, as compared to relevant industry growth. The following two sections consider sales and cash flow from operations separately.

We wanted to capture outstanding performers in each industry and to nullify the bias that a company would naturally enjoy should it simply be in a high-growth industry. We dealt with industry bias by comparing each company's growth rate to an industry average (based on the six-digit GICS[2] industry codes) by using z-statistics[3] to normalize across industries.

Finally, we identified the growth companies by averaging sales and CFFO growth z-statistics. Those companies experiencing a positive average passed the growth screen and moved to the earnings manipulation screen.

Test 2A – Sales revenue growth

Purpose

This test is designed to determine which companies are growing their sales at rates greater than their respective competitors. Sales, which can be manipulated more easily than cost flow from operations, is a fundamental indicator of company growth.

Application

Reported sales data were obtained using Compustat. For both the individual company and the industry average, we calculated a sales compounded annual growth rate (CAGR) using the formula:

$$\left(\frac{\text{Final Year Sales}}{\text{First Year Sales}} \right)^{\frac{1}{n}} - 1$$

The formula was then applied to companies with complete sales data in 1997 or 1998 and 2002.

The population of companies used to calculate industry averages was drawn initially from the entire universe of stock information in the Compustat database. If data were not available for both

---

[2] Global Industry Classification Standard.
[3] Z = (Company A change in cash flow from operations – Industry average change in cash flow from operations)/ Standard deviation of industry average.

1997 and 1998, the companies were eliminated. After calculating z-statistics using the six-digit GICS industry groupings, we eliminated those companies outside of three standard deviations as outliers. An industry average was then calculated using the remaining 6,269 firms.

Test 2B-Cashflow from operations (CFFO) growth

Purpose

This test is designed to determine which companies are growing their cashflow from operations at rates greater than the rest of their respective industry. This test assumes that reported CFFO is both an accurate measure of a company's growth and less likely to be manipulated than financially reported net income. A company's CFFO is compared to its industry average CFFO to identify those companies that are outperforming their industry.

Application

Reported CFFO values were obtained using Compustat. For both the individual company and the industry average, we calculated a CFFO growth rate using the following formula:

$$\frac{CFFO_1 - CFFO_0}{\text{Book Value of Assets}_0}$$

We looked at each year's change in cashflow divided by the book value of assets (defined as total assets) in the initial year. We then averaged these yearly results for each company. The formula was then applied to the CFFO data in the period 1997–2002 (1998–2002 if data were missing in 1997) and averaged to determine an overall growth rate for the period. This methodology differs from the sales revenue growth because CFFO during the initial period could be negative, negating the efficacy of the CAGR calculation. We used Book Value of Assets as the denominator in order to create a meaningful ratio that could be averaged to show the magnitude of change over time.

The resulting growth rates were normalized to reduce industry bias using z-statistics according to the six-digit GICS industry codes. This gives a company that grows 2% in a 1% growth industry the same standing as one that is growing 20% in a 10% growth industry.

The population of companies used to calculate industry averages was drawn initially from the entire universe of stock information in the Compustat database. If data were not available for the period 1997–2002, the companies were eliminated. After calculating z-statistics using the six-digit GICS industry groupings, we eliminated those companies outside of three standard deviations as outliers. An industry average was then calculated using the remaining 5,830 firms.

We weighted the z-statistics for CFFO and sales equally and averaged the results by company. If a company had a positive net z-statistic average, the company moved on to the next test. Of 300 companies, 189 moved to the next test.

Test 3 – S&P Core Earnings

Purpose

Standard & Poors' Core Earnings Test is an attempt to identify income associated with "a company's ongoing operations" and excludes revenues or costs that arise from investments or non-operating activities. For our purpose, we assume that a company's S&P Core Earnings are a proxy for organic or internal growth, acknowledging that merger and acquisition activity is included by S&P.

Standard & Poors uses a proprietary formula for calculating a company's ongoing earnings from its central business(es). It is an attempt to eliminate earnings manipulations common in corporate financial reporting. Since our previous study, dated September 2003, S&P has changed its Core Earnings methodology. This study uses their updated methodology for all years. According to Standard & Poors' website,[4] the new Core Earnings calculation includes:

- stock option expenses
- restructuring charges
- write-downs of depreciable or amortizable operating assets
- pension costs

---

[4] This methodology is found on a graphic entitled "Standard & Poors' Equity Research Methodology" and is found at http://www2.standardandpoors.com/spf/pdf/equity/Equity_Research_ Methodology_031604.pdf.

- purchased research and development expenses
- merger/acquisition-related expenses
- unrealized gains/losses from hedging activities.

But, S&P excludes:

- goodwill impairment charges
- gains and losses from asset sales
- pension gains
- litigation or insurance settlements and proceeds
- reversal of prior-year changes and provisions.

Application

This test determines the ratio of average S&P Core Earnings to average reported net income for years 1997–2002 for each of the 189 companies entering this screen. A low Core Earnings to net income ratio implies that a company produced material earnings from non-core operating activities.

The test is performed by dividing each company's average total Core Earnings (as defined by Standard & Poors and as found in the Compustat database) by its average reported net income for the period 1997/1998–2002. We then confronted the question of what is a defensible hurdle rate or passing rate. Keeping in mind our goal – to find the best internal, or organic, or core earnings growers – we performed sensitivity analysis using 85% and 90% as possible "passing" grades. We chose 90% because of our overriding objective – to find the best growers. Using a 90% hurdle rate eliminated 83 companies.

Because both core earnings (CE) and net income (NI) can be negative, the following decision rules were employed to adjust for problems that could arise:

1. If $NI \leq 0$ and $CE \geq 0$, then Pass
2. If $NI > 0$ and $CE > 0$ and $CE/NI \geq 0.9$, then Pass
3. If $NI < 0$ and $CE < 0$ and $CE/NI \leq 1.1$, then Pass
4. If not Pass, then Fail.

Test 4 – Sales / accounts receivable

Purpose

A common accounting manipulation is to change the income recognition policies or business model to accelerate sales revenue. Businesses can do this by granting more liberal credit to buyers, booking revenue earlier than previously booked in the transaction process, or by forcing distributors or buyers to take products earlier than normal or usual in the inventory turn cycle. One method to determine whether these financial games are being attempted is to compare the growth rate of the accounts receivable to the growth rate of sales. If accounts receivable are growing at a rate materially faster than sales, it is a good warning of aggressive accounting to boost sales revenues.

Application

For the 106 companies entering Test 4, we compared their year-by-year growth in both accounts receivable and sales for the six-year time-period and if accounts receivable grew on average 10% or more than sales, we then looked at the size or materiality of 2002 accounts receivable relative to 2002 sales.

For the materiality standard, we chose 5% – that is, the total amount of accounts receivable must be greater than 5% of sales for the test to apply. The impact of this materiality test was to retain some large companies (e.g. grocery stores) in our model whose business model had non-material amounts of accounts receivable but that had greater than 10% growth rate of accounts receivable compared to sales growth for 1997–2002.

Thirty-seven companies failed this test, while sixty-nine companies passed it.

Test 5 – Merrill Lynch Cash Realization

Purpose

Sixty-nine companies entered Test 5. The purpose of this test was to compare reported cashflow from operations to net income. This comparison assumes that the closer the numbers, the less likely a company has participated in non-economic and non-operational accounting or earnings manipulations. This test, combined with the S&P Core Earnings Test, should eliminate companies producing material financial results from sources other than real internal growth (again not taking into account acquired revenue through mergers or acquisitions).

Application

We obtained CFFO and net income (NI) for each of the respective companies for the period 1997–2002 from Compustat. We computed CFFO/NI for each of the six years and averaged the ratios for each company over the six-year period, resulting in an overall average ratio of CFFO/NI for each company.

Again, we had the decision of what hurdle rate to use. Keeping in mind our goal – to find a group of companies that were the best real growers – we arbitrarily chose a high hurdle rate of 90%. This hurdle rate eliminated seven companies from the sixty-nine companies entering this screen.

Like the Core Earnings Test, the Cash Realization Test employs two numbers that can be negative, so the following decision rules were employed to adjust for problems that could arise:

1. If $NI \leq 0$ and $CFFO \geq 0$, then Pass
2. If $NI > 0$ and $CFFO > 0$ and $CFFO/NI \geq 0.9$, then Pass
3. If $NI < 0$ and $CFFO < 0$ and $CFFO/NI \leq 1.1$, then Pass
4. If not Pass, then Fail.

Sixty-two companies passed this screen.

Test 6 – Mergers and acquisitions

Purpose

The final screen that we applied to the sixty-two surviving companies was our mergers and acquisitions (M&A) screen. Here our purpose was to eliminate companies that produced a material part of their growth during 1997–2002 by acquisitions and not through internal, core, or organic growth.

This test was difficult to implement because of the lack of reliable M&A data regarding the amount of income acquired. Therefore, we looked at deal values and compared the sum of the values of acquisitions made by a company during 1997–2002 to the increase in its market capitalization for the same period. For this purpose, market capitalization was defined as total equity and debt capitalization.

Application

Using the SDC database, we calculated the cumulative merger values for each company entering the screen and divided that sum by the

Table 7.5. *Top 300 EVA companies (listed alphabetically)*

3M Co.	Bemis Co.
99 Cents Only Stores	Best Buy Co. Inc.
Abbott Laboratories	Biogen Inc.
Abercrombie & Fitch	Biomet Inc.
AdvancePCS	BJs Wholesale Club Inc.
AGL Resources Inc.	Black Hills Corp.
Air Products & Chemicals Inc.	Block H & R Inc.
Albemarle Corp.	Blyth Inc.
Alberto-Culver Co.	Briggs & Stratton
Allergan Inc.	Brinker Intl. Inc.
Allete Inc.	Bristol Myers Squibb
Alliant Techsystems Inc.	Brown-Forman
Altera Corp.	C. H. Robinson Worldwide Inc.
Altria Group Inc.	Cabot Corp.
Ameren Corp.	Campbell Soup Co.
American Axle & Mfg. Holdings	Career Education Corp.
American Eagle Outfitters Inc.	Carlisle Cos. Inc.
American Power Conversion	CDW Corp.
American Standard Cos. Inc.	Centex Corp.
Amerisourcebergen Corp.	ChevronTexaco Corp.
Ametek Inc.	Chicos Fashion Inc.
Amgen Inc.	Choicepoint Inc.
Amphenol Corp.	Church & Dwight Inc.
Anheuser-Busch Cos. Inc.	Cinergy Corp.
Apollo Group Inc.	Cintas Corp.
Applebees Intl. Inc.	Clayton Homes Inc.
Applera Corp.	Clorox Co./De.
Applied Biosys	Coca-Cola Btlng. Cons.
Aptargroup Inc.	Coca-Cola Co.
Argosy Gaming Co.	Cognizant Tech Solutions
Arvinmeritor Inc.	Colgate-Palmolive Co.
Automatic Data Processing	Columbia Sportswear Co.
Autozone Inc.	Compuware Corp.
Avery Dennison Corp.	Conagra Foods Inc.
Avon Products	Concord EFS Inc.
Bard (C.R.) Inc.	Consolidated Edison Inc.
Barr Laboratories Inc.	Constellation Brands
Baxter International Inc.	Constellation Energy Grp. Inc.
Becton Dickinson & Co.	Convergys Corp.
Bed Bath & Beyond Inc.	Corinthian Colleges Inc.

(cont.)

Table 7.5. (*cont.*)

Covance Inc.	Freeprt. Mcmor. Cop.&Gld.
Coventry Health Care	Furniture Brands Intl. Inc.
Crane Co.	Gannett Co.
Cytec Industries Inc.	Gap Inc.
D. R. Horton Inc.	General Dynamics Corp.
Danaher Corp.	General Electric Co.
Darden Restaurants Inc.	General Mills Inc.
Dell Inc.	Gentex Corp.
Deluxe Corp.	Genuine Parts Co.
Dentsply Internatl. Inc.	Grace (W. R.) & Co.
Diebold Inc.	GraCo. Inc.
Dollar General Corp.	Grainger (W. W.) Inc.
Dollar Tree Stores Inc.	Great Plains Energy Inc.
Dominion Resources Inc.	Gtech Holdings Corp.
Donaldson Co. Inc.	Guidant Corp.
Dover Corp.	Harley-Davidson Inc.
Dpl Inc.	Harte Hanks Inc.
DTE Energy Co.	Hawaiian Electric Industry
Du Pont (E. I.) De Nemours	Health Management Assoc.
Dun & Bradstreet Corp.	Health Net Inc.
Ecolab Inc.	Heinz (H. J.) Co.
Education Management Corp.	Hershey Foods Corp.
EMC Corp./Ma.	Home Depot Inc.
Emerson Electric Co.	Hon Industries
Energen Corp.	Hormel Foods Corp.
Engelhard Corp.	Hovnanian Entrprs. Inc.
EOG Resources Inc.	Hubbell Inc.
Equifax Inc.	Illinois Tool Works
Estee Lauder Cos. Inc.	IMS Health Inc.
Ethan Allen Interiors Inc.	Intel Corp.
Exelon Corp.	Interpublic Group of Cos.
Expeditors Intl. Wash Inc.	Intl. Flavors & Fragrances
Express Scripts Inc.	Intl. Game Technology
Fair Isaac Corp.	Intl. Speedway Corp.
Family Dollar Stores	ITT Industries Inc.
Fastenal Co.	J. M. Smucker Co.
First Health Group Corp.	Jabil Circuit Inc.
Fisher Scientific Intl. Inc.	Jacobs Engineering Group Inc.
Forest Laboratories	Johnson & Johnson
Fpl Group Inc.	Johnson Controls Inc.

Table 7.5. (*cont.*)

Jones Apparel Group Inc.
Kb Home
Kellogg Co.
King Pharmaceuticals Inc.
Knight-Ridder Inc.
Kohls Corp.
L-3 Communications Hldgs. Inc.
Lafarge North America Inc.
Lancaster Colony Corp.
La-Z-Boy Inc.
Lee Enterprises
Leggett & Platt Inc.
Lennar Corp.
Lexmark Intl. Inc.
Lilly (Eli) & Co.
Limited Brands Inc.
Lincare Holdings Inc.
Linear Technology Corp.
Liz Claiborne Inc.
Lubrizol Corp.
Manitowoc Co.
Manpower Inc./Wi.
Marathon Oil Corp.
Martin Marietta Materials
Masco Corp.
Maxim Integrated Products
May Department Stores Co.
Maytag Corp.
McCormick & Co.
McDonalds Corp.
McGraw-Hill Companies
MDC Holdings Inc.
MDU Resources Group Inc.
Medicis Pharmaceut. Cp.
Medtronic Inc.
Merck & Co.
Microsoft Corp.
Miller (Herman) Inc.
Mohawk Industries Inc.
Molex Inc.

Mylan Laboratories
National Fuel Gas Co.
National Instruments Corp.
NBTY Inc.
New Jersey Resources
New York Times Co.
Newfield Exploration Co.
Nicor Inc.
Nike Inc.
Nstar
NVR Inc.
Occidental Petroleum Corp.
Oge Energy Corp.
Ominicom Group
Oracle Corp.
Outback Steakhouse Inc.
Paccar Inc.
Parker-Hannifin Corp.
Patterson Dental Co.
Pepco Holdings Inc.
PepsiCo. Inc.
Performance Food Group Co.
Pfizer Inc.
Philadelphia Suburban Corp.
Piedmont Natural Gas Co.
Pier 1 Imports Inc./De.
Pitney Bowes Inc.
Pixar
Playtex Products Inc.
Polo Ralph Lauren Cp.
PPG Industries Inc.
PPL Corp.
Praxair Inc.
Price Communications Corp.
Procter & Gamble Co.
Progress Energy Inc.
Public Service Enterprises
Puget Energy Inc.
Pulte Homes Inc.
Questar Corp.

(*cont.*)

Table 7.5. (*cont.*)

Radio Shack Corp.	Tiffany & Co.
Renal Care Group Inc.	Timberland Co.
Rent-A-Center Inc.	TJX Companies Inc.
Robert Half Intl. Inc.	Toll Brothers Inc.
Roper Industries Inc./De.	Tootsie Roll Industries Inc.
Ross Stores Inc.	Total System Services Inc.
Ruby Tuesday Inc.	UGI Corp.
Sabre Hldgs. Corp.	United Parcel Service Inc.
Safeway Inc.	United Technologies Corp.
Sanmina-Sci Corp.	Unitedhealth Group Inc.
Sara Lee Corp.	Universal Corp./Va.
Schering-Plough	Universal Health Svcs.
Scotts Co.	Usg Corp.
Sealed Air Corp.	UST Inc.
Sempra Energy	Valassis Communications Inc.
Sensient Technologies Corp.	Valhi Inc.
Sigma-Aldrich	Valspar Corp.
Silgan Holdings Inc.	VF Corp.
Smithfield Foods Inc.	Vintage Petroleum Inc.
Sonoco Products Co.	Vulcan Materials Co.
Southern Co.	Walgreen Co.
Standard Pacific Cp.	Wal-Mart Stores
Stryker Corp.	Waters Corp.
Swift Transportation Co. Inc.	Watson Pharmaceuticals Inc.
Sysco Corp.	Wiley (John) & Sons
Talbots Inc.	Winn-Dixie Stores Inc.
Target Corp.	WPS Resources Corp.
Teleflex Inc.	Wrigley (Wm.) Jr. Co.
Tellabs Inc.	Wyeth
Terex Corp.	Yum Brands Inc.
	Zebra Technologies Cp.

Table 7.6. *2002 and 2001 studies*

2002 OGI (rank-ordered)	2001 OGI (alphabetical order)
1. NVR Inc.	1. American Eagle Outfitters Inc.
2. Family Dollar Stores	2. Apollo Group Inc.
3. Harley-Davidson Inc.	3. Aptargroup Inc.
4. Gentex Corp.	4. Arvinmeritor Inc.
5. Walgreen Co.	5. Automatic Data Processing
6. American Eagle Outfitters Inc.	6. Bed Bath & Beyond Inc.
7. Bed Bath & Beyond Inc.	7. Best Buy Co. Inc.
8. C. H. Robinson Worldwide Inc.	8. BJ's Wholesale Club Inc.
9. Outback Steakhouse Inc.	9. CEC Entertainment Inc.
10. Sysco Corp.	10. ChevronTexaco Corp.
11. Waters Corp.	11. Colgate-Palmolive Co.
12. Wal-Mart Stores	12. Devry Inc.
13. Ross Stores Inc.	13. Dollar General Corp.
14. Mylan Laboratories	14. Dollar Tree Stores Inc.
15. Anheuser-Busch Cos. Inc.	15. EOG Resources Inc.
16. Tiffany & Co.	16. Ethan Allen Interiors Inc.
17. Lincare Holdings Inc.	17. Family Dollar Stores
18. Omnicom Group	18. Gentex Corp.
19. Paccar Inc.	19. Home Depot Inc.
20. Brinker Intl. Inc.	20. Jack In The Box Inc.
21. Automatic Data Processing	21. La-Z-Boy Inc.
22. Best Buy Co. Inc.	22. Leggett & Platt Inc.
23. Ruby Tuesday Inc.	23. Masco Corp.
	24. Molex Inc.
	25. Mylan Laboratories
	26. Nike Inc.
	27. Omnicom Group
	28. Outback Steakhouse Inc.
	29. Paccar Inc.
	30. Renal Care Group Inc.
	31. Stryker Corp.
	32. Sysco Corp.
	33. Teleflex Inc.
	34. Timberland Co.
	35. Total System Services Inc.
	36. Walgreen Co.
	37. Wal-Mart Stores
	38. Waters Corp.
	39. WellPoint Health Networks Inc.

Table 7.7. *Hall of Fame (companies on both the 2001 and 2002 Organic Growth Indices)*

1.	American Eagle Outfitters Inc.
2.	Automatic Data Processing
3.	Bed Bath & Beyond Inc.
4.	Best Buy Co. Inc.
5.	Family Dollar Stores
6.	Gentex Corp.
7.	Mylan Laboratories
8.	Omnicom Group
9.	Outback Steakhouse Inc.
10.	Paccar Inc.
11.	Sysco Corp.
12.	Walgreen Co.
13.	Wal-Mart Stores
14.	Waters Corp.

difference in its market capitalization between January 2, 1997 and December 31, 2002. If this ratio was $33\frac{1}{3}\%$ or greater we eliminated the company. Thirty-nine companies failed this screen and twenty-three passed.

Final rankings

The Organic Growth Index is presented as a rank-ordered grouping of companies. For each of the EVA/Capital, Sales & CFFO Growth, Core Earnings, Cash Realization, and Mergers & Acquisitions tests, the companies were ranked in order of best performance in each category. These rankings were then averaged to determine an overall ranking identifying the best performers.

References

Brewer, P. & Chandra, G. 1999. Economic value added (EVA): its uses and limitations. *SAM Advanced Management Journal*, 64(2): 4–11.

Delmar, F., Davidsson, P., & Gartner, W. 2003. Arriving at the high-growth firm. *Journal of Business Venturing*, 19: 189–216.

Harrington, A. 2004. Organic growth: big firms, big growth. *Fortune Magazine*, May: 1–3.

Nelson, M. W., Elliott, J. A., & Tarply, R. L. 2003. How are earnings managed? *Accounting Horizons*, Supplement, 17–35.

Schilit, H. M. 2003. *Financial Shenanigans*. New York: McGraw-Hill, 17–35.

8 The make or buy growth decision: strategic entrepreneurship versus acquisitions

MICHAEL A. HITT, R. DUANE IRELAND, AND CHRISTOPHER S. TUGGLE

> There hasn't been a business climate this brutal in decades. But forget growth strategies or novel accounting: The *Business Week* top 50 rankings this year go to companies that have made themselves indispensable to customers – by extending inventive new services.
>
> *Business Week*, March 25, 2003

ALTHOUGH this quote downplays "growth strategies," the article from which this comment is taken actually reports that the *Business Week* Top 50 grew substantially during the focal time-period (Foust, Jespersen, Katzenberg, Barrett, & Crickett, 2003). Analysts characterized the companies included in the 2003 Top 50 list as "nimble," capable of making "quick turnarounds," and committed to placing an "emphasis on innovation." These companies, which appear to have the learning-oriented skills required to strategically innovate (Govindarajan & Trimble, 2004), were able to excel despite a stagnating economy and skeptical investors.

Google Inc.'s strategic and entrepreneurial actions demonstrate successful corporate growth. At a time when many businesses consider being able to maintain current revenues as an indicator of strong performance, Google Inc. appears to be an antidote to mediocrity and perhaps should be considered to be a model for smart or strategic innovation during challenging times. Google's commitment to hiring highly talented human capital results in crucial flexibility for the firm – flexibility through which the company is able to experiment, simultaneously pursuing multiple growth avenues while doing so (Hammonds, 2003). Skeptics may respond that Google, a relatively young company in a dynamic industry, shares few similarities with and is not comparable to most companies. However, we suggest that companies' responsibilities to shareholders are remarkably similar. While shareholders have an array of risk preferences (from high to low) that are shown by their investment decisions, maximization of the return on each of their individual investments is a common objective. To satisfy investors' expectation relative to returns on their investments, firms must develop and successfully use the skills required for leveraging existing competencies (for current returns) while continually developing new competencies (for future returns). Effectively balancing the competing demands associated with "exploiting" in the present while "exploring" for the future is the foundation of profitable firm growth and shareholder satisfaction. However, developing the skills necessary to achieve this balance challenges many firms and their decision-makers.

Firms grow profitably when they are able to further leverage their current value-creating skills (i.e. exploitation) or by developing new skills that add value to the organization's current products (goods or services) and contribute to the ability to offer completely new products in the future (i.e. exploration) that create value for customers. To distinguish between these types of growth, we label the former "leveraged growth" and the latter "entrepreneurial growth." *Leveraged growth* may be thought of as extrapolating existing competencies or capabilities (e.g. incremental innovations to the firm's goods, services, and processes or expanding the firm's market geographically within the same country). *Entrepreneurial growth* (referred to by some as organic growth) involves developing new competencies and capabilities that have the potential to create value in the future.

As illustrated in Figure 8.1, we suggest that strategic entrepreneurship is a helpful way to conceptualize the method of acquisition or internal development to use leveraged and/or entrepreneurial growth strategies. Strategic actions are the primary source of leveraged growth while entrepreneurial actions are the bedrock of entrepreneurial growth. We describe and discuss these two types of actions later in this chapter. While both actions are required to achieve either type of growth, their respective emphases that are depicted in Figure 8.1 are critical to the firm's efforts to achieve either leveraged or entrepreneurial growth.

Below, we explain the concept of strategic entrepreneurship and the benefits and costs of each growth method. First, however, we describe

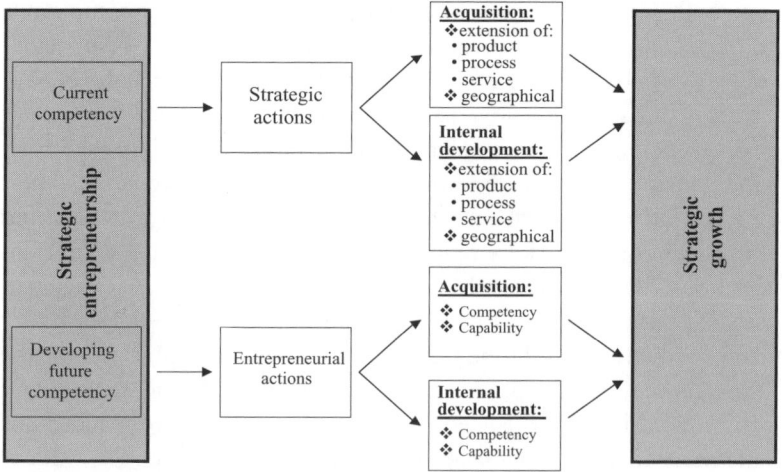

Figure 8.1. The make or buy growth decision.

the imperative of entrepreneurial growth and the general relationships scholars have found between firm size and growth.

The importance of entrepreneurial growth

It is widely understood that any organization that is not continually developing, acquiring, or adapting new technology has, *de facto*, made a decision to fail within five to ten years (Merrifield, 1991). Indeed, effectively coping with successive shifts in both the dominant technology within an industry and market requirements or preferences for a company's products is one of the main long-term competitive challenges facing firms of all types. To sustain and prosper from such shifts, a firm needs to seek (explore) and be prepared to develop new opportunities (building new competencies for future exploitation purposes) while simultaneously leveraging existing competencies. Thus, a firm's decision-makers must be flexible, willing to be entrepreneurial, and continually committed to reinventing the firm, as necessary.

Considering the "opportunity environment" of the firm, we explore the alternative strategic options for pursuing leveraged growth and entrepreneurial growth. These options can generally be categorized as internal development versus the external acquisition of perceived opportunities (see Figure 8.1). While each means of opportunity development may be effective, we suggest that the existing and future desired cultural atmospheres of the firm are crucial in determining the method of growth that will be appropriate for a particular organization at a particular point in time.

Organizational size and growth

Profitable growth is an expectation held by virtually all, if not all, investors. Thus, a major goal of most CEOs is to maximize organizational growth without sacrificing profits (Markman & Gartner, 2002). Though it may sometimes mask organizational inefficiencies, growth can benefit an organization by creating value through:

- strategic learning and increased firm knowledge (Kuwada, 1998);
- entrepreneurial behavior or innovation (Pettus, 2001); and,
- further utilization of its resources and capabilities (Ghoshal, Hahn, & Morton, 2000; Sirmon, Hitt, & Ireland, 2004).

Perhaps somewhat surprisingly, research does not find a positive relationship between growth and profits for young, small firms. Additionally, evidence suggests that, on average, young firms are more profitable than older ones (Markman & Gartner, 2002) while large, established companies are more likely to grow than small firms (Delmar, Davidsson, & Gartner, 2003; Orser, Hogarth-Scott, & Riding, 2000). These findings seem intuitive, as young firms typically have less overhead, generate and operate on the basis of new ideas, and, at least in the short run, tend to compete in less mature industries (e.g. Google). As industries and firms mature and greater efficiency evolves, firms become more competitive, meaning that new markets, leveraged or entrepreneurial, must be sought for organizational viability and profitability.

Additional research suggests that large established firms have more resources, making it easier for them to pursue growth through several means (Fishman & Rob, 2003). However, the larger established firms that use acquisitions to achieve growth often experience reduced profits (Hitt, Harrison, & Ireland, 2001). Even so, acquisitions can provide a needed infusion of ideas, knowledge, competencies, etc., for the firm seeking to grow. The critical issues related to acquisitions include (1) the cost of the acquisition (e.g. how high a premium is paid), and (2) the value-creating nature and transferability of the assets, both tangible and intangible. Obviously, these are difficult issues to evaluate accurately before completing an acquisition. Growth-seeking firms operating in hostile environments often must take bold, aggressive actions (Covin & Slevin, 1997), which perhaps offers at least a partial explanation of the reduced profitability researchers have found to be associated with acquisitions.

Growth can be achieved by natural (organic) or unnatural (acquisition) means. Both methods have been extensively used, often by the same organization. Below, we explore the advantages and disadvantages of each method. We begin by exploring strategic entrepreneurship and how it encourages organic growth. Later in the chapter, we investigate the evidence regarding acquisition as a growth strategy.

Organic growth through strategic entrepreneurship

Strategic entrepreneurship details the strategic discipline through which exploration is used to identify entrepreneurial opportunities while exploitation is concerned with the actions used to take advantage of those opportunities to create firm wealth (Hitt, Ireland, Camp, & Sexton, 2002). Thus, strategic entrepreneurship facilitates firms' efforts to identify the best opportunities (matched to their resources and with the highest potential returns) and to exploit these opportunities with the discipline imposed by effectively designed and executed strategic actions. Strategic entrepreneurship's goal is continually to identify entrepreneurial opportunities and subsequently create competitive advantages that lead to maximum wealth creation. Strategic entrepreneurship is critically important for use in the dynamic competitive landscape in which most organizations now compete (Hitt, Ireland, Camp, & Sexton, 2002).

"Strategic entrepreneurship" is based on two types of actions. *Strategic actions* are those through which companies concentrate on developing and exploiting current competitive advantages while supporting related and dedicated entrepreneurial initiatives (e.g. incremental innovations to existing products, processes, or services). Through *entrepreneurial actions*, companies identify and then exploit entrepreneurial opportunities that rivals have not noticed or fully exploited (e.g. radical innovation that will revolutionize an industry) (Hitt, Ireland, Camp, & Sexton, 2002; Ireland, Hitt, Camp, & Sexton, 2001). Newer and smaller firms are entrepreneurial, but less frequently strategic. In contrast, larger established firms are often strategic, but much less entrepreneurial.

Entrepreneurial opportunities are external conditions suggesting the viability of introducing and selling new products, services, raw materials, and organizing methods at prices exceeding their production costs (Casson, 1982; Shane & Venkataraman, 2000). Entrepreneurial opportunities exist because of information asymmetries through which different actors develop separate beliefs regarding the relative value of resources as well as the potential future value of those resources that follow from their transformation of inputs into outputs (Alvarez & Barney, 2002; Kirzner, 1973; Schumpeter, 1934; Shane & Venkataraman, 2000). Therefore, *strategic entrepreneurship* is the integration of opportunity-seeking actions with advantage-seeking actions for the purpose of designing and implementing initiatives to create firm wealth (Hitt, Ireland, Camp, & Sexton, 2001).

Entrepreneurial and strategic actions are complementary, but not interchangeable (McGrath & MacMillan, 2000; Meyer & Heppard, 2000). Entrepreneurial actions using a strategic perspective are helpful in identifying the most appropriate opportunities for a firm to pursue and in exploiting those opportunities through effective development and use of competitive advantages. Entrepreneurs may identify and exploit opportunities that create or establish temporary rather than sustainable competitive advantages. This occurs primarily when entrepreneurs fail to manage resources strategically, making it difficult to sustain the competitive advantages developed (Hitt, Ireland, Camp, & Sexton, 2001). Therefore, both opportunity-seeking (i.e. entrepreneurship) and advantage-seeking (i.e. strategic management) behaviors are necessary for wealth creation, yet neither alone is sufficient (Amit & Zott, 2001; Hitt & Ireland, 2000; Ireland, Hitt, & Sirmon, 2003; McGrath & MacMillan, 2000).

Organic growth, leveraged or entrepreneurial, may be important to an organization for many reasons. For example, the knowledge and information flows that the internal development process creates can have additional benefits to the organization as processes and procedures are implemented to perpetuate cycles of growth. Jeffery Immelt, chairman and CEO of General Electric, recently stated: "The world is closing the door on a decade that was about capital markets and acquiring things and opening the door on a new period that's more about developing things. The companies that know how to develop things are ultimately going to create the most shareholder value" (Buderi, 2003).

Applied organic growth

Forest Labs, which ranked #1 in *Business Week*'s Top 50 in 2003, is a nimble $2 billion firm that experienced a 39% increase in sales and a 25.2% increase in stock price in 2003. These outcomes suggest that the firm excels at the complementary tasks of leveraging its current advantages while simultaneously seeking new opportunities (strategic entrepreneurship). Historically, a key to Forest Labs' competitive success was the firm's identification of the following opportunity – foreign drug-makers with valuable products but without access to the lucrative US market. To capitalize on this opportunity, Forest Labs licensed promising drugs from mid-sized foreign pharmaceutical companies and introduced them to the US market (a market Forest Labs has a competency in serving). Celexa, an antidepressant, is a specific example of these actions. After licensing Celexa, Forest Labs negotiated a strategic alliance with Warner-Lambert for co-promotion. Identifying and then exploiting this opportunity resulted in sales of $1.4 billion.

Dimensions of strategic entrepreneurship

To enable the organic development that firms such as Google, GE, and Forest Labs have achieved, an organization must consider its internal environment and how its managers approach problems (and opportunities). An organizational environment that is conducive to strategic entrepreneurship (and thus, internally developed growth) requires planning and forethought and is based on several factors, all of which are critical to organic growth: an entrepreneurial mindset, entrepreneurial alertness, an entrepreneurial culture and leadership, the management of resources strategically, and creativity and innovation. Next, we briefly discuss each of these factors.

An entrepreneurial mindset

Opportunity recognition. To achieve growth through strategic entrepreneurship, an entrepreneurial focus must be diffused throughout an organization. Individuals within the company must actively seek to identify and take actions to exploit opportunities. Such an organizational mindset requires certain rules, policies, financial commitments, workers, managers, and so forth so that uncertainty can be embraced as the foundation for evaluating what often are first seen as unquantifiable possibilities. This set of actions begins with discovering possibilities.

Opportunity recognition is prompted from existing stocks of information that influence an individual's framework for interpreting new information. To recognize an opportunity, an individual must have prior information that is complementary to the new information, which in turn triggers an entrepreneurial idea (Kaish & Gilad, 1991). Opportunity recognition is at the heart of all entrepreneurial endeavors, as an opportunity can only be exploited to create value after it has been recognized. Thus, firms must actively seek to identify or discover entrepreneurial opportunities. Some scholars have suggested that prior knowledge and/or experience plays a role in opportunity identification (e.g. Shane, 2000; Simon, 1947). Others attribute entrepreneurial acumen to specific innate traits of individuals.

Some firms are able to identify opportunities, but unable to develop a sustainable competitive advantage. Other firms are able to build competitive advantages but lose their ability to identify valuable entrepreneurial opportunities. These two types of firms are unlikely to sustain competitive advantages, meaning that they are unable to continuously create significant amounts of wealth for shareholders. Therefore, as noted above, all firms, new and established, small and large, must engage in both opportunity-seeking and advantage-seeking behaviors (Ireland, Hitt, & Sirmon, 2003).

Entrepreneurial alertness

Entrepreneurial alertness is an entrepreneurial resource (Alvarez & Barney, 2002). In particular, it has been suggested that certain individuals, who are sometimes working for a corporation, often have "flashes of special insight" into potential market disequilibrium opportunities (Kirzner, 1973). Insight may be derived from an entrepreneur's, or an entrepreneurial firm's, acquired knowledge and experiences. Knowledge, which is justified true belief, is a critical intangible resource that helps firms identify and, especially, exploit opportunities and establish competitive advantages (von Krogh, Ichijo, & Nonaka, 2000). Sharma and Chrisman (1999) suggested that new knowledge is vital to organizational renewal. However, a delicate balance must be maintained between the equally important tasks of exploring (e.g. experimentation, discovery, and flexibility) for new knowledge and exploiting (e.g. efficiency, refinement, and execution) existing knowledge to create wealth (March, 1991).

Real options logic. Many academics and practicing managers recognize that various techniques (e.g. net present value and other discounted cash flow approaches to capital planning, project decision-making, and budgeting) provide valuable (i.e. necessary) but incomplete (i.e. insufficient) information and data for decision-makers. Indeed, techniques such as these, while important and valuable, do not capture the strategic flexibility associated with effective managerial decisions – decisions that are made in light of unexpected market opportunities and developments. Deriving his work from Merton's (1973) Nobel Prize winning option-pricing model, which made an important contribution to the Black–Scholes option-pricing theory in financial economics (Merton, 1998), Myers (1977) utilized this options lens to explore non-financial options, which he termed "growth options." He suggested that the options lens was a new way of thinking about discretionary investment opportunities. These "growth options" evolved in the finance literature and are now more often referred to as "real options." The approach to making such investment decisions is referred to as "real options reasoning."

In financial terms, a business strategy is more like a series of options than a series of static cash flows, meaning that the execution of a strategy is a product of a series of decisions. Some actions are taken immediately, while others are deliberately deferred, so managers can optimize the firm's competitive position in light of evolving circumstances. Strategy establishes the framework within which future decisions are to be made, but at the same time it allows for learning from ongoing developments and for discretion to act based on what is learned. Bowman and Hurry (1993) suggested that because real options reflect an organization's own sense-making (of its competitive environment and its perceived opportunities), they position the firm uniquely (compared to competitors with different sense-making). Options, teamed with resources currently employed by the firm, therefore, can form the inimitable capabilities that help an organization to sustain a competitive advantage and earn above-normal returns (Bowman & Hurry, 1993).

McGrath (1999) explores what she terms an anti-failure bias, which she suggests limits entrepreneurial processes. She defines real options as investment(s) in real assets that preserve the right to make a decision at some point in the future. Should conditions not prove favorable, resources can be withdrawn and redeployed elsewhere, at a loss only of the amount of the sunk cost invested in the business at the time. McGrath (1997) notes that the *ex ante* uncertainty is the important driver of real option value. If an option's present value is held constant, projects or ventures with greater variance of potential outcome have higher option value.

Many scholars and practitioners perceive the ultimate risk or consequence of uncertainty in an entrepreneurial venture to be the failure of that venture. However, McGrath (1999) suggested that the tendency to view failure as purely negative has introduced a pervasive bias in entrepreneurship theory and research. She utilizes the real options lens to demonstrate how an anti-failure bias can hinder understanding of the systemic relationship between success and failure, leading to unintended negative consequences. Real options reasoning suggests that the key issue is not of avoiding failure, but of managing the cost of failure by limiting exposure to the downside while preserving access to attractive opportunities and maximizing gains (McGrath, 1999).

An entrepreneurial culture and leadership

Creating an environment that is conducive to entrepreneurial actions and subsequent growth requires an organizational culture with certain characteristics. For example, such a culture should facilitate the development of new ideas, encourage risk-taking, tolerate failure, promote learning, and champion innovations and change (Ireland, Hitt, & Sirmon, 2003). For an entrepreneurial culture to create value, organizational leaders must support and foster it. Leadership can do this by nurturing entrepreneurial capability, protecting innovations that threaten the current business model, questioning the dominant logic, and revisiting the deceptively simple questions (Covin & Slevin, 2002). Leaders must also develop and implement systems that are designed to promote the design and implementation of creative actions and reward programs that provide incentives for people actively to take creative actions.

The management of resources strategically

An organization must leverage its existing capabilities to create value for customers in order to build a competitive advantage (Ghoshal,

Hahn, & Morton, 2000). At a minimum, these resources and capabilities include financial capital, human capital, and social capital (Florin, Lubatkin, & Schulze, 2003; Hitt & Ireland, 2002; Ireland, Hitt, & Sirmon, 2003). The firm's ability to effectively manage its resource portfolio affects its performance (Henderson & Cockburn, 1994; Ireland, Hitt, & Sirmon, 2003; Teece, Pisano, & Shuen, 1997; Zott, 2003). Dell Inc. and Wal-Mart effectively manage their resources and capabilities. Dell has a competitive advantage over rivals with its effective indirect sales model and superior service quality capability. While industry-wide sales fell by 9%, Dell's sales grew by 14% in 2003. In addition, Dell is further leveraging its competencies by moving into new geographic markets (e.g. China) and related product markets (e.g. printers, hand-held computers, and cash registers). Wal-Mart, ranked #1 in *Fortune*'s 2003 Most Admired Corporation survey, was highly evaluated in all categories – management, product and service quality, human capital, and innovation, suggesting that the firm is able effectively to integrate and manage its various resources.

Creativity and innovation

The factors we are considering interact to create the overall organizational atmosphere. In particular, though, the creativity and innovation factor and the entrepreneurial mindset factor are strongly related in that they apply to multiple levels of the firm – the entire organization, organizational teams and groups, and individuals. For example, the concept of *bisociation* is the combining of two previously unrelated matrices of information/knowledge (Koestler, 1964; Smith & Di Gregorio, 2002). Bisociation facilitates recognition of entrepreneurial opportunities, helps differentiate goods and services, and facilitates development of innovation. Insights resulting from bisociation may occur when certain combinations of people come together with divergent knowledge or when one person is exposed to different information or knowledge.

Innovation is the engine of growth (Klette & Griliches, 2000), suggesting that an innovative ability is synonymous with corporate success. However, innovation may not always be successful, in that a firm's innovative outputs must still create more value for customers compared to competitors' offerings. Innovation can be as incremental as a new use for an existing product or process, or can be radical, such as a new product that revolutionizes a market. A revolutionary, or disruptive, innovation may create new markets and new business models (Christensen, 1997). Sustaining innovations helps prolong competitive advantage and, subsequently, the firm's ability to earn returns greater than those earned by rivals (Christensen, Johnson, & Rigby, 2002). Thus, in a competitive dynamics context, the firm must carefully study its competitors' actions and reactions to fully understand the value-creating potential of its innovations relative to those being introduced by rivals.

Innovation is often assumed to be a small-firm phenomenon. However, 80% of the research and development (inherently entrepreneurially focused) conducted in developed nations occurs in large firms. Nevertheless, large firms account for less than half of recorded patents (Hoskisson & Busenitz, 2002). In fact, newer and smaller firms have developed approximately 95% of the radical innovations introduced in the United States since the 1940s. Furthermore, research supported by the National Science Foundation showed that smaller firms developed almost twenty-four times as many innovations for the dollars invested in R&D, as did large firms (Timmons, 2004). Therefore, while large firms allocate more resources towards entrepreneurial endeavors, they may be ineffective in terms of identifying and/or exploiting entrepreneurial opportunities. Some scholars suggest that larger established firms are producing, or certainly contributing to the production of, radical or "breakthrough" innovation much more than is recognized (Ahuja & Lampert, 2001). In fact, Ahuja and Lampert contend that large firms can, and at least some do, develop routines to foster the development of major innovations that represent significant technological breakthroughs.

Samsung, for example, is a large, yet innovative company. This firm recently completed a rapid turnaround by efficiently managing its resources and emphasizing innovation. Samsung is the Sony of the past. It has become the benchmark for excellence in making and marketing products that consumers want. For example, Samsung produces state-of-the-art mobile telephone headsets (one of its multiple products) ahead of many of its competitors.

United Parcel Service (UPS) is another company epitomizing innovation. UPS has become entrepreneurial by (1) implementing a new higher-margin service, (2) managing its customers' supply chains, and (3) providing financial services to small businesses. UPS is not only

developing competencies, but it is also leveraging its existing competencies via geographical expansion (e.g. to China). In 2003, despite only
a 3% increase in sales revenue, UPS had a 60% increase in deliveries
and an exceptional 34% increase in net income.

Unnatural growth through acquisitions

Despite the negative connotation of the term "unnatural," growth
through acquisitions is sometimes the most appropriate course of organizational action. We propose that the suitability of acquisition for
growth versus internal development for growth depends greatly on
the firm's internal structure and strategic goals. If an organization
is efficiency-seeking, internal development as a means of achieving
growth may challenge many of its alignment mechanisms. Growth,
especially entrepreneurial growth, involves substantial uncertainty,
which may confound an efficiency-based structure.

Organizational structure and growth

In their study of electronic firms, Burns and Stalker (1961) distinguished between mechanistic and organic organizations. They
classified organizations according to their patterns of adaptation to
technological and commercial change and suggested that mechanistic
organizations have lower complexity (hence, less specialization, lower
amounts of internal and external communication, and greater verti-
cal differentiation) than organic organizations. The key components
of the organic organizations as described by Burns and Stalker (1961)
provide guidelines for organizing that promote creativity and innovation. Research suggests that organizational characteristics that positively influence innovation are more similar to organic rather than
mechanistic structures/organizations.

Mechanistic and organic organizations are ideal types representing
separate ends of a continuum. Scholars have attempted to identify
the characteristics of intermediate types on this continuum (Hull &
Hage, 1982). One effort distinguishes organizational types on the basis
of innovativeness over time (Damanpour & Evan, 1984). In a population of organizations, some are continually innovative (organic),
some are continually non-innovative (mechanistic), while others are
intermittently innovative (intermediate). Organizations in each group

should have distinct characteristics. In many populations of organizations, highly adaptive, high-performance organizations could actually be members of the intermediate group. Past research has not adequately explored the characteristics of intermediate types (Damanpour, 1991). However, firms with more mechanistic structures may find growth easier to achieve through acquisitions than by internal development. In contrast, firms with more organic structures should be able to grow effectively through internally developed innovation. Firms with intermediate structures may use either method of growth or perhaps some combination of both internal development and acquisitions.

Risks of growth through acquisitions

Research suggests that acquisitions do not create value when (1) designed to achieve market power, (2) based on CEO hubris (Hayward & Hambrick, 1997), (3) too high a premium is paid (Sirower, 1997), and (4) the firm has difficulty achieving integration and/or is overdependent on debt for financing the acquisition (Hitt, Harrison, & Ireland, 2001). A study of 278 large acquisitions found 12 high performers, as measured by growth in sales, profits, and innovation (Hitt, Hoskisson, Ireland, & Harrison, 1991). Thus, in this particular sample, only 4.3% of the acquisitions were highly successful. Other acquisitions resulted in positive but normal returns while many others led to unsuccessful outcomes in terms of the performance measures used in the study.

Some firms are able to achieve more power in the market by acquiring competitors. However, they may experience higher costs than expected if they are unable to integrate the two companies successfully. Additionally, firms that acquire others to achieve market power often place too much emphasis on gaining efficiencies and lose, or are unable to develop, the capabilities required to be innovative (Hitt, Hoskisson, Johnson, & Moesel, 1996). When this occurs, entrepreneurial and more nimble competitors may introduce new products to the marketplace that eventually erode the focal firm's market share and market power.

Acquisitions driven by CEO hubris are more likely to be ineffective. Hubris-driven acquisitions are ones in which the CEO believes that "he" can manage the acquired firm much better than its previous managers and/or that "he" will be able to more easily integrate the acquired firm's operations into the acquiring company's routines. If the acquisition is a mistake, integration may be much more difficult and synergy may not be achieved. Additionally, when hubris is the basis for an acquisition decision, the acquiring firm is more likely to pay a higher premium for the target firm.

Premiums are paid based on the expectation of creating synergy from the integration of the two firms such that the value of the output (or of the combined assets) is greater than the value of the output generated by independent use of the individual firms' assets. Premiums have averaged between 30% and 40% (and sometimes more) over various recent time-periods (Hitt, Harrison, & Ireland, 2001). Sirower (1997) argued that any premium greater than 25% is excessive and unlikely to be recovered because synergy is difficult to achieve. He suggested that to recoup a 50% premium, the acquiring firm must increase its return on equity by 12% each year through the ninth year following the year of the acquisition. Given this evidence, we conclude that it is unlikely that firms will earn a desired return on their investment from an acquisition if too high a premium is paid to complete the transaction. Thus, while the firm achieves growth in this case, it is not "profitable" growth.

Commonly, high premiums cause the acquiring firm to access significant amounts of capital to finance the acquisition. In such cases, firms may use substantial debt capital to do this. Large amounts of debt can be costly and when firms are highly leveraged, they often have to pay high interest rates because of debt-holders' financial risk. Furthermore, the interest charges pose opportunity costs. Hoskisson and Hitt (1994) found that firms with high debt costs invested less in R&D. As a result, highly leveraged firms engage in less internal development. Also, debt limits future acquisitions as well as the strategic flexibility the firm needs to cope successfully with unexpected environmental opportunities and threats. As a result, leverage can be useful to finance growth, especially growth by acquisitions, but it may significantly limit the flexibility required to pursue future growth by any means (Hitt, Harrison, & Ireland, 2001).

One of the major barriers to successful acquisition is the difficulty in integrating the two firms. The net effect of integration difficulties is to reduce the probability the newly created firm will attain the expected or desired synergy (Haspeslagh & Jemison, 1991). It is not uncommon, for example, for the two firms to have different organizational cultures. These differences contribute to resistance by employees of the acquired firm to adopting the style and value set of the acquiring firm. Additionally, different information systems and operating systems and policies greatly complicate the ability of the two firms to integrate their operations. Without integration, it is more difficult for the merged firm to achieve the economies of scale desired and synergy needed for the firm to produce returns above the premium paid and to offset the other costs of the merger (e.g. debt costs, costs of layoffs). For example, many analysts believed that the Daimler-Benz acquisition of the Chrysler Corporation to create DaimlerChrysler had much potential to create synergy. However, the substantial differences in organizational culture and operating styles in the two firms led to significant conflicts, resulting in a loss of much of Chrysler's human capital. This loss contributed to an ineffective integration of the formerly independent firms, at least in the short to medium time-frame, for the newly created company. Indeed, DaimlerChrysler has struggled since the acquisition to grow profitably. Although the firm's performance has improved, DaimlerChrysler has not, after several years, achieved the synergy once expected or the level of performance of which it seems capable using the complementary capabilities that once existed in the formerly independent organizational entities (Hitt, Harrison, & Ireland, 2001).

These multiple barriers limit the ability of acquisitions to produce profitable growth. The large number of difficulties involved in making successful acquisitions is the reason we refer to this form of growth as "unnatural." A recent meta-analysis supports this conclusion. King, Dalton, Daily, and Covin (2004) found that in general, and on average, the research evidence suggests that acquisitions produce small negative returns. Yet, as we discuss next, acquisitions can be successful and create profitable growth under certain conditions (Hitt, Harrison, Ireland, & Best, 1998).

Creating value through acquisition of growth

Acquisitions provide a rapid means of achieving significant growth. Attempting to grow through acquisitions may produce a number of positive outcomes, including (1) learning (Barkema & Vermeulen, 1998), (2) synergy, and/or (3) economies of scale. Often, mergers between highly related firms create opportunities to reduce overall costs through economies of scale. However, these economies are rarely enough to offset the acquisition's costs (Hitt, Harrison, & Ireland, 2001), causing us to focus on the other two means of creating profitable growth through acquisitions.

Barkema and Vermeulen (1998) and Vermeulen and Barkema (2001) found that acquiring firms can benefit from learning new capabilities when they purchase other companies. Thus, there are two general types of learning that can occur – learning new capabilities for enhancing operational effectiveness of the merged firm and learning skills to enhance the effectiveness of acquisitions. For example, a large pharmaceutical firm could reenergize its R&D operations with new research skills learned from an acquired biotech firm's research processes and knowledge (Rothaermel, 2001). Alternatively, managers in the acquiring firm can learn from their experiences in making acquisitions. In so doing, they can enhance their capabilities in negotiation, financing, integration, and assimilation. Enriching their skills in these areas should increase the probability that they will make more effective acquisitions in the future (Hitt, Harrison, & Ireland, 2001).

Synergy is possible when the firm acquired has resources and capabilities that are complementary to those held by the acquiring firm. To realize the benefits of complementarity, firms' resources must be integrated so that they work together to generate synergy. Research has shown that when complementary assets are integrated effectively, firm innovation can be enhanced (Ahuja & Katila, 2001). Such integration usually requires substantial cooperation between employees from the acquiring and acquired firms. Hitt, Harrison, and Ireland (2001) argued that friendly acquisitions (as opposed to hostile acquisitions) usually foster cooperation between the two firms. The process of managing integration frequently begins before the acquisition is consummated and continues for months or perhaps a year, or sometimes even longer, after the merger begins. Many firms have begun using merger teams composed of key personnel from the acquiring and acquired firms to foster the integration. Cisco Systems, which historically achieved significant growth through acquisitions, has a permanent acquisition team and has a policy that no employee in the acquired firm can be laid off after the merger unless the CEO from the acquired firm (Cisco always tries to retain the CEO) and the CEO of Cisco agree. In this way, employees from the acquired firm feel more secure, resulting in fewer losses of the valuable human capital that Cisco obtained in the acquisition (Killick, Rawoot, & Stockport, 2003).

The evidence discussed above allows us to conclude that although challenging, acquisitions can lead to profitable firm growth. Multiple barriers allow the path between acquisitions and profitable growth to be thought of as "unnatural." Thus, to create firm growth and positive returns for stakeholders, acquisitions must be carefully planned and managed (Hitt, Harrison, & Ireland, 2001).

Conclusion

Entrepreneurship is important for a number of organizational outcomes, including survival, profitability, growth, and renewal (Zahra, 1996). In prior corporate entrepreneurship research, scholars have explored the mere presence of the "corporate entrepreneurship" construct and performance, top management teams, inside/outside directors, etc. However, the causal nature of these associations has typically remained unexplained. It is suggested that the perception of opportunity influences a firm's decision-makers to invest limited resources towards the development of new competencies, invariably at the expense of existing competencies. If opportunities lead to the investments and actions that constitute "corporate entrepreneurship," why do some firms, compared to their rivals, for example, excel at identifying and subsequently exploiting entrepreneurial opportunities?

We assert that firms should engage in strategic entrepreneurship to identify and exploit opportunities and simultaneously seek to establish and sustain, over time, a competitive advantage in the process of doing so. This process usually produces organic (and natural) growth that strengthens the firm's capabilities, while producing advantages that are relatively sustainable over the long term. Firms can also grow through acquisitions. But, unless they learn and internalize new capabilities and are able to integrate complementary capabilities, the problems associated with acquisitions delimit or may even prevent the attainment of profitable growth as the foundation for the earning of above-average returns. In our view, these problems suggest that acquisitions can be properly viewed as an "unnatural" path to profitable/effective organizational growth. However, even in light of the problems with acquisitions, as explained herein, acquisitions, when well planned and managed, can help firms build new capabilities and create synergy that results in positive returns. When this happens, acquisitions lead to more natural and successful organizational growth.

142   *Michael A. Hitt, R. Duane Ireland, and Christopher S. Tuggle*

References

Ahuja, G. & Katila, R. 2001. Technological acquisitions and the innovation performance of acquiring firms: a longitudinal study. *Strategic Management Journal*, 22: 197–220.

Ahuja, G. & Lampert, C. M. 2001. Entrepreneurship in the large corporation: a longitudinal study of how established firms create breakthrough inventions. *Strategic Management Journal*, 22 (Special Issue): 521–543.

Alvarez, S. A. & Barney, J. B. 2002. Resource-based theory and the entrepreneurial firm. In M. A. Hitt, R. D. Ireland, S. M. Camp, & D. L. Sexton (eds.), *Strategic Entrepreneurship*. Oxford: Blackwell.

Amit, R. & Zott, C. 2001. Value creation in e-business. *Strategic Management Journal*, 22 (Special Issue): 493–520.

Barkema, H. G. & Vermeulen, F. 1998. International expansion through start-up or acquisition: a learning perspective. *Academy of Management Journal*, 41: 7–26.

Bowman, E. H. & Hurry, D. 1993. Strategy through the option lens – an integrated view of resource investments and the incremental-choice process. *Academy of Management Review*, 18: 760–782.

Buderi, R. 2003. GE finds its inner Edison. *Technology Review*, 106: 46.

Burns, T. & Stalker, G. M. 1961. *The Management of Innovation*, 2nd edn. London: Tavistock Institute.

Casson, M. 1982. *The Entrepreneur: An Economic Theory*. Totowa, NJ: Barnes & Noble.

Christensen, C. 1997. *The Innovator's Dilemma*. Cambridge, MA: Harvard Business School Press.

Christensen, C. M., Johnson, M. W., & Rigby, D. K. 2002. Foundations for growth – how to identify and build disruptive new businesses. *MIT Sloan Management Review*, 43(3): 22–31.

Covin, J. G. & Slevin, D. P. (eds.) 1997. *High Growth Transitions: Theoretical Perspectives and Suggested Directions*. Chicago: Upstart.

Covin, J. G. & Slevin, D. P. 2002. The entrepreneurial imperatives of strategic leadership. In M. A. Hitt, R. D. Ireland, S. M. Camp, & D. L. Sexton (eds.), *Strategic Entrepreneurship: Creating a New Mindset*. Oxford: Blackwell.

Damanpour, F. 1991. Organizational innovation: a meta-analysis of effects of determinants and moderators. *Academy of Management Journal*, 34: 555–590.

Damanpour, F. & Evan, W. M. 1984. Organizational innovation and performance – the problem of organizational lag. *Administrative Science Quarterly*, 29: 392–409.

Delmar, F., Davidsson, P., & Gartner, W. B. 2003. Arriving at the high-growth firm. *Journal of Business Venturing*, 18: 189–216.

Fishman, A. & Rob, R. 2003. Consumer inertia, firm growth and industry dynamics. *Journal of Economic Theory*, 109: 24–38.

Florin, J., Lubatkin, M., & Schulze, W. 2003. A social capital model of high-growth ventures. *Academy of Management Journal*, 46: 374–384.

Foust, D., Jespersen, F. F., Katzenberg, F., Barrett, A., & Crickett, R. O. 2003. The Business Week 50: the best performers, *Business Week*, March, 25: 34.

Ghoshal, S., Hahn, M., & Morton, P. 2000. Organizing for firm growth: the interaction between resource-accumulating and organizing processes. In N. J. Foss & V. Mahnke (eds.), *Competence, Governance and Entrepreneurship: Advances in Economic Strategy Research*. New York: Oxford University Press.

Govindarajan, V. & Trimble, C. 2004. Strategic innovation and the science of learning. *MIT Sloan Management Review*, 45(2): 67–75.

Hammonds, K. H. 2003. Growth search. *Fast Company*, April: 74–81.

Haspeslagh, P. & Jemison, D. B. 1991. *Managing Acquisitions*. New York: The Free Press.

Hayward, M. L. A. & Hambrick, D. C. 1997. Explaining the premiums paid for large acquisitions: evidence of CEO hubris. *Administrative Science Quarterly*, 42: 103–127.

Henderson, R. & Cockburn, I. 1994. Measuring competence – exploring firm effects in pharmaceutical research. *Strategic Management Journal*, 15: 63–84.

Hitt, M. A., Harrison, J. S., & Ireland, R. D. 2001. *Mergers and Acquisitions: A Guide to Creating Value for Stakeholders*. New York: Oxford University Press.

Hitt, M. A., Harrison, J. S., Ireland, R. D., & Best, A. 1998. Attributes of successful and unsuccessful acquisitions of U.S. firms. *British Journal of Management*, 9: 91–114.

Hitt, M. A., Hoskisson, R. E., Ireland, R. D., & Harrison, J. S. 1991. Effects of acquisitions on research-and-development inputs and outputs. *Academy of Management Journal*, 34: 693–706.

Hitt, M. A., Hoskisson, R. E., Johnson, R. A., & Moesel, D. D. 1996. The market for corporate control and firm innovation. *Academy of Management Journal*, 39: 1084–1119.

Hitt, M. A. & Ireland, R. D. 2000. The intersection of entrepreneurship and strategic management research. In D. L. Sexton & H. Landstrom (eds.), *Handbook of Entrepreneurship*. Oxford: Blackwell.

2002. The essence of strategic leadership: managing human and social capital. *Journal of Leadership and Organizational Studies*, 9(1): 3–15.

Hitt, M. A., Ireland, R. D., Camp, S. M., & Sexton, D. L. 2001. Guest editors' introduction to the Special Issue "Strategic entrepreneurship: entrepreneurial strategies for wealth creation." *Strategic Management Journal*, 22 (Special Issue): 479–491.

—— 2002. Strategic entrepreneurship: integrating entrepreneurial and strategic management perspectives. In M. A. Hitt, R. D. Ireland, S. M. Camp, & D. L. Sexton (eds.), *Strategic Entrepreneurship: Creating a New Mindset*. Oxford: Blackwell.

Hoskisson, R. E. & Busenitz, L. W. 2002. Market uncertainty and learning distance in corporate entrepreneurship entry mode choice. In M. A. Hitt, R. D. Ireland, S. M. Camp, & D. L. Sexton (eds.), *Strategic Entrepreneurship: Creating a New Mindset*. Oxford: Blackwell.

Hoskisson, R. E. & Hitt, M. A. 1994. *Downscoping: How to Tame the Diversified Firm*. New York: Oxford University Press.

Hull, F. & Hage, J. 1982. Organizing for innovation – beyond Burns and Stalker organic type. *Sociology: The Journal of the British Sociological Association*, 16: 564–577.

Ireland, R. D., Hitt, M. A., Camp, S. M., & Sexton, D. L. 2001. Integrating entrepreneurship and strategic management actions to create firm wealth. *Academy of Management Executive*, 15(1): 49–63.

Ireland, R. D., Hitt, M. A., & Sirmon, D. G. 2003. A model of strategic entrepreneurship: the construct and its dimensions. *Journal of Management*, 29: 963–989.

Kaish, S. & Gilad, B. 1991. Characteristics of opportunities search of entrepreneurs versus executives – sources, interests, general alertness. *Journal of Business Venturing*, 6: 45–61.

Killick, M., Rawoot, I., & Stockport, G. J. 2003. Cisco Systems Inc. – growth through acquisitions. In M. A. Hitt, R. D. Ireland, & R. E. Hoskisson (eds.), *Strategic Management: Competitiveness and Globalization*, 5th edn. Cincinnati: South-Western Publishing.

King, D. R., Dalton, D. R., Daily, C. M., & Covin, J. G. 2004. Meta-analyses of post-acquisition performance: indications of unidentified moderators. *Strategic Management Journal*, 25: 187–200.

Kirzner, I. 1973. *Competition and Entrepreneurship*. Chicago: University of Chicago Press.

Klette, T. J. & Griliches, Z. 2000. Empirical patterns of firm growth and R&D investment: a quality ladder model interpretation. *Economic Journal*, 110(463): 363–387.

Koestler, A. 1964. *The Act of Creation*. New York: Dell.

Kuwada, K. 1998. Strategic learning: the continuous side of discontinuous strategic change. *Organization Science*, 9: 719–736.

March, J. G. 1991. Exploration and exploitation in organizational learning. *Organization Science*, 2: 71–87.

Markman, G. D. & Gartner, W. B. 2002. Is extraordinary growth profitable? A study of Inc. 500 high-growth companies. *Entrepreneurship Theory and Practice*, 27(1): 65–75.

McGrath, R. G. 1997. A real options logic for initiating technology positioning investments. *Academy of Management Review*, 22: 974–996.

1999. Falling forward: real options reasoning and entrepreneurial failure. *Academy of Management Review*, 24: 13–30.

McGrath, R. G. & MacMillan, I. C. 2000. *The Entrepreneurial Mindset: Strategies for Continuously Creating Opportunity in an Age of Uncertainty*. Boston: Harvard Business School Press.

Merrifield, D. B. 1991. Value-added: the dominant factor in industrial competitiveness. *International Journal of Technology Management*, Special Publication on the Role of Technology in Corporate Policy: 226–235.

Merton, R. C. 1973. Theory of rational option pricing. *Bell Journal of Economics*, 4: 141–183.

1998. Applications of option-pricing theory: twenty-five years later. *American Economic Review*, 88: 323–349.

Meyer, G. D. & Heppard, K. A. 2000. *Entrepreneurship as Strategy: Competing on the Entrepreneurial Edge*. Thousand Oaks, CA: Sage Publications.

Myers, S. C. 1977. Determinants of corporate borrowing. *Journal of Financial Economics*, 5: 147–175.

Orser, B. J., Hogarth-Scott, S., & Riding, A. L. 2000. Performance, firm size, and management problem solving. *Journal of Small Business Management*, 38(4): 42–58.

Pettus, N. L. 2001. The resource-based view as a developmental growth process: evidence from the deregulated trucking industry. *Academy of Management Journal*, 44: 878–896.

Rothaermel, F. 2001. Incumbent's advantage through exploiting complementary assets via interfirm cooperation. *Strategic Management Journal*, 22 (Special Issue): 687–699.

Schumpeter, J. A. 1934. *The Theory of Economic Development*. Cambridge, MA: Harvard University Press.

Shane, S. 2000. Prior knowledge and the discovery of entrepreneurial opportunities. *Organization Science*, 11: 448–469.

Shane, S. & Venkataraman, S. 2000. The promise of entrepreneurship as a field of research. *Academy of Management Review*, 25: 217–226.

Sharma, P. & Chrisman, J. J. 1999. Toward a reconciliation of the definitional issues in the field of corporate entrepreneurship. *Entrepreneurship Theory and Practice*, 23(3): 11.

Simon, H. A. 1947. *Administrative Behavior.: A Study of Decision-Making Processes in Administrative Organizations.* Chicago: Macmillan.

Sirmon, D. G., Hitt, M. A., & Ireland, R. D. 2004. Dynamically managing firm resources for value creation. Arizona State University, unpublished working paper.

Sirower, M. L. 1997. *The Synergy Trap: How Companies Lose the Acquisition Game.* New York: The Free Press.

Smith, K. G. & Di Gregorio, D. 2002. Bisociation, discovery, and the role of entrepreneurial action. In M. A. Hitt, R. D. Ireland, S. M. Camp, & D. L. Sexton (eds.), *Strategic Entrepreneurship: Creating a New Mindset.* Oxford: Blackwell.

Teece, D. J., Pisano, G., & Shuen, A. 1997. Dynamic capabilities and strategic management. *Strategic Management Journal,* 18: 509–533.

Timmons, J. A. 2004. Opportunity recognition. In W. D Bygrave and A. Zacharakis (eds.), *The Portable MBA in Entrepreneurship.* Hoboken, NJ: Wiley.

Vermeulen, F. & Barkema, H. 2001. Learning through acquisition. *Academy of Management Journal,* 44: 457–476.

von Krogh, G., Ichijo, K., & Nonaka, I. 2000. *Enabling Knowledge Creation: How to Unlock the Mystery of Tacit Knowledge and Release the Power of Innovation.* New York: Oxford University Press.

Zahra, S. A. 1996. Governance, ownership, and corporate entrepreneurship: the moderating impact of industry technological opportunities. *Academy of Management Journal,* 39: 1713–1735.

Zott, C. 2003. Dynamic capabilities and the emergence of intraindustry differential firm performance: insights from a simulation study. *Strategic Management Journal,* 24: 97–125.

9 The misunderstood role of the middle manager in driving successful growth programs

RITA McGRATH

Organic growth: more rare than you think

Growth. The term has become a mantra in business. As the other chapters in this volume suggest, driving organic growth for the leaders of established companies is essential, urgent, and critical. As the other chapters also suggest, it is also extraordinarily difficult.

To get a sense of just how hard it is, let us consider some recent evidence. We created a sample of publicly traded firms (drawing from the Factiva database) with market capitalizations in 2004 of over $1 billion. We then established reasonable criteria for what a healthy, growing firm might look like (using revenue/sales growth). We thought a modest target of 5% a year would be fairly conservative, and thus selected firms with three-year average growth rates (from the 2001–2004 period) of 15% or five-year average growth rates of 25% (in the United States), and a three-year average growth rate of 15% and a four-year average growth rate of 20% (for non-US firms). Of this population, 583 of the US firms met the three-year growth cutoff, and 248 also met the five-year cutoff. Of the non-US firms, 348 met the three-year growth target, while 179 also met the four-year growth target. This yielded a population within the world's highest market capitialized firms of 427 that were able to achieve a sustained growth rate in the early 2000s of at least 5% a year.

So far, so good. We were really interested, however, in which firms were growing not by acquisition, merger, or other maneuvers relevant to corporate control, but organically. These results surprised us. Of the US population that had grown steadily over the five-year period, only thirty-five had done so without significant acquisitions. Of the non-US sample that had enjoyed at least four years of steady growth, only twenty-four firms had done so without significant acquisition activity. What this suggests is that of the sample of large companies we examined, organic growth companies represent in the neighborhood of 6%

Table 9.1. *Growth without major acquisition*

	US-based firms	Non US-based firms
Companies with sustained growth	583	348
Primarily organic growth	35	24
Percentage	6	6.9

Notes: Population: companies with market capitalization > US$1 billion. Three- and five-year growth of 5%/year for US companies; three- and four-year growth of 5%/year for non-US companies.

of all companies who were growing at even a modest rate overall. Table 9.1 summarizes our results.

What are we to conclude from these data? One interpretation is that acquisition activity as a source of growth may be far more prevalent than popular mythology suggests – indeed, moving the pieces of companies around through ownership exchanges seemed to be far more popular than creating growing businesses within the firm. This leads to something of a puzzle.

New wealth creation is often associated with the ability of corporations to create new businesses within the firm. Yet, relatively few companies appear to rely on internal development as their primary vehicle for growth. This explains, perhaps, why the long-term track record of most corporations in providing sustained, above-average performance is uninspiring (Foster & Kaplan, 2001). Although acquisition is certainly one viable option for creating new growth platforms, share price dilution for the acquirers, integration difficulties, and mythical synergies are well-documented issues, to the extent that only around 4% of large-scale acquisitions have been found to be highly successful (Hitt, Hoskisson, Ireland, & Harrison, 1991).

As other chapters in this book document, senior leadership, strategy, effective internal entrepreneurship, and other factors have a role to play in the organic growth process. But when we contrasted interview responses between firms that had successfully initiated growth and firms that struggled, one theme stood out starkly. This was that the tasks of knitting together the existing business and the new business, of articulating how projects with uncertain payback periods and unpredictable outcomes were still worth doing, and of managing the internal power struggles and politics of venturing were often not handled well, or even worse, not handled at all. These missing tasks – which those we interviewed recognized as critical, and yet which were nobody's specific "job" – are one key factor leading to stalled or non-existent growth programs.

In this chapter, therefore, I should like to turn the spotlight on a somewhat neglected set of players in the growth process: the middle managers, who play a pivotal role in the ability of the modern corporation to turn ideas into strategies and concepts into growth vehicles. My underlying assumption is that the conundrum of rare organic growth can be partially explained by a lack of understanding of the specific tasks that fall to middle managers in the growth process; and a lack of organizational adeptness at developing managers competent to perform these tasks.

One more time: what do middle managers do?

In classic management thinking, middle managers are seen as "linking pins" (Likert, 1961) who tie together the strategies formulated by more senior managers with the operational activities required to execute those strategies by subordinates. Formally, managers at successive levels of authority (from division to business unit to area to front-line supervision) are expected to translate broad corporate goals into increasingly specific tasks relevant to their levels of authority until the goals become manifest in specific transactions across the boundaries of the firm, with customers, suppliers, and the like. At their best, they save senior managers the cognitive burden of day-to-day operations. At their worst, they are expensive bureaucrats feeding off bloated corporate hierarchies and are best eliminated (or so the thinking goes).

In the classic model, the discretion afforded middle managers is limited, and the leadership they are expected to display is confined to the scope of their more-or-less hierarchical jobs. Be a good "company man" and implement; that's the job.

But if your company is chock-a-block with middle managers just doing the job of implementing, be worried. Be very worried. Because our research suggests that if you wish to seek growth (or even if you wish to maintain current performance) in a turbulent environment, a good chunk of your middle management talent needs to be engaged in innovative and strategic activities, not just doing the implementation job. And we are not alone (Huy, 2001; Kanter, 1982).

I have picked out four groups of such activities around which to structure this chapter, discussed some practices observed in recent fieldwork examining high-growth companies (McGrath & MacMillan, 2005), and provided a checklist that might help you understand whether your company is effectively deploying middle management talent. The activities are: (1) creating a growth mindset; (2) opportunity identification; (3) establishment of growth projects; and (4) managing the transition from a project to a grown-up business (MacMillan & McGrath, 2004; MacMillan & McGrath, 2005). Although each of these areas also require activities on the part of senior leaders and venture-level leaders, here I shall focus on the challenge of the players in the middle.

Creating a growth mindset

It has been fashionable for some time for companies to adopt technologies and practices that ruthlessly squeeze out variety and inconsistency in their behavior. Remember reengineering? Business Process Redesign? Total Quality and its current descendants, such as Six Sigma? And what about all that investment companies have been making in enterprise resource systems, such as SAP? It is not that there is anything inherently wrong with ensuring consistency in processes (and consistency is of course essential for cost leadership and global alignment). The problem is that when the whole middle management group is driven to reduce variability, the skills that are essential for adaptation and innovation can be squeezed out as well, with negative consequences in situations requiring adaptation or when a company seeks innovative growth (Benner & Tushman, 2002).

To manage across multiple product life cycles and to sustain growth initiatives while at the same time engaging in the sets of activities that are essential to sustain a profitable and healthy core business requires that your middle managers develop a different set of skills than you will see in a classic textbook. It requires actions that are, to be blunt, somewhat schizophrenic – simultaneously holding teams supporting the core business accountable for profits, costs, and delivery as promised while imposing an entirely different set of requirements on teams working on new businesses (O'Reilly & Tushman, 2004). The key challenge is creating a mindset in the operating parts of the organization that recognizes the different and inconsistent roles played by these teams, and is able to assess and reward their activities appropriately.

We found three specific practices to be associated with the creation of the right mindset within an organization's operating units. The first has to do with making it clear to peers and subordinates that different disciplines are appropriate for higher uncertainty activities (such as innovation) and lower uncertainty activities (such as changing the packaging of an existing product). The second has to do with helping people cope with the risk and uncertainty of exploring new territory. The final practice is learning to think of the activities of the organization in terms of a portfolio arrayed across different dimensions of uncertainty.

Different disciplines

As my colleagues and I have emphasized elsewhere, growth projects typically involve the organization in more uncertain situations than projects to extend the existing business. The core difference is that the assumption to knowledge ratio is much higher when you are probing new territory than when you are exploiting knowledge you already have (McGrath & MacMillan, 1995). Recognizing that there is a difference is the starting point for establishing differential management processes within the group being led by a middle manager. Effective leaders of growth deploy *different* disciplines for the new stuff.

In an established business, it should be pretty straightforward to meet your projections, anticipate operational issues, stick to your budget, and otherwise do what you thought you would. As the level of uncertainty in an initiative increases, these things become more difficult. The level of new learning needed goes up, the importance of sensemaking, feedback, and data-generation increases, and predictions become less reliable. This suggests the need for different criteria for performance and accompanying management behaviors in the one situation as opposed to the other.

Failing to meet objectives, a form of failure, should not be tolerated easily in the core business because it suggests ignorance of facts that could be known if the relevant leader were sufficiently diligent. In a new business, on the other hand, failing to meet objectives is almost inevitable, and thus is not a good indicator of performance. What matters instead is whether resources are conserved, learning is enhanced, and the new knowledge generated is used in a productive way.

Absorbing uncertainty

For people who have learned to operate as managers in the relatively predictable context of an established business, the uncertainty of pursuing a new initiative can be paralyzing. Because performance is unpredictable, such initiatives can appear to be riskier than the established business. Because data do not exist, or are hard to interpret, it is hard to know how to answer questions about the project, and difficult to anticipate what will happen next. Facts are not available; assumptions are.

The middle manager's role in situations like this involves absorbing risks. An effective practice is to help people anticipate the likely next steps in a particular project. For instance, if a prototype is first going to be given to a target customer, it is quite normal for a number of new problems with design to be revealed. Preparing people for these future issues can help them avoid being disoriented by unpleasant surprises. Absorbing risks can include helping people define a set of operating, "roughly right" assumptions that the group will agree to live with until more information is revealed, particularly if the manager in question is prepared to take personal responsibility for the assumptions so that the operating individuals do not feel exposed to being wrong on their own.

Managing portfolios

A final practice that in our experience helps middle managers create the right mindset with respect to growth is to take a portfolio approach to initiatives. There are a number of alternative models that have been used to think in terms of sets of activities, including the McKinsey "three-horizon" model (Baghai, Coley, & White, 1999) and our own "Opportunity Map" (McGrath & MacMillan, 2000). The key points of implementing portfolio-style thinking are, first, to make sure that projects with differing levels of certainty are treated differently; and, secondly, to make sure that there is clarity and alignment with respect to the strategic purposes played by different kinds of projects. For instance, in developing an R&D portfolio, there might be certain projects whose main purpose is to preserve an opportunity or to act as a hedge (which we have called "positioning"). These serve a different purpose than projects whose primary purpose is to develop insight about market demand (which we call "scouting") (MacMillan & McGrath, 2002).

Opportunity identification

Having an organization that is prepared to act on growth concepts is a great start. An accompanying issue is to create the conditions under which new opportunities are identified and figure out which ones are worth pursuing.

Although from the perspective of someone who has spent most of their career in a mainstream business this might sound heretical, we find that for most firms the problem is not one of finding new opportunities – in fact, they are everywhere. As we have documented in a recent book (McGrath & MacMillan, 2005), they can come from bettering the customer's experience, changing something about products or services, changing key metrics, anticipating industry trends, or creating entirely new markets. What makes the difference between companies that act effectively on opportunities and those that let them lie fallow seems to be the firms' orientation to a few practices that lead to opportunities being recognized, captured in some way, reviewed, and provided with resources.

Managing agenda and paying attention

The first thing you will notice about a company whose middle management is oriented towards growth is that new opportunities are quite literally on the agenda. They are discussed frequently, both in formal meetings and in informal asides. People realize that finding new opportunities is an activity that everyone in the company can engage in, and are actively encouraged, up and down the organization, to consider what is new. In fact, best-practice companies actively involve people who come into contact with the customer in their quest for opportunities, unlike many companies in which these people are seldom consulted. When was the last time you asked a customer service representative what three things could be done to improve significantly a customer's experience?

My general rule of thumb is that if an organization is serious about finding new growth opportunities, topics relevant to this challenge will be item #1, #2, or #3 on the agenda at every significant management meeting. So, paying attention is the first place to start thinking about making your middle managers more entrepreneurial. At General Electric, for instance, CEO Jeff Immelt holds regular "Commercial Council" sessions, in which growth proposals are reviewed and assessed. Leaders are required to submit at least three "Imagination Breakthrough" proposals per year which go before the Council for discussion, and compensation is in part linked to coming up with new ideas (Brady, 2005).

Creating an inventory of opportunities

Beyond talking about growth opportunities, some firms go a step further and keep what we have called an "opportunity register" which they regularly review. This register is like an inventory of ideas that might or might not be worth pursuing at some point in the future. It is one way of making sure that you never run out of new things to think about. The process of developing such a register is described in *The Entrepreneurial Mindset* (McGrath & MacMillan, 2000) in which we suggested that you collect basic information about opportunities, and then regularly revisit these ideas. Often, an idea that is not quite ready at one point in time can become an intriguing opportunity later on.

Screening

Once you have a good inventory of ideas, a critical middle management task is to translate the corporate-level strategy of your company into parameters that will allow you to select among the different proposals for further development. For instance, if the "corporate" strategy has to do with moving into service businesses, how would this be relevant to the activities of a foreign subsidiary? To a production operation? Answering this question is a key middle management job.

We have found that one excellent way to make the translation tangible is to establish what we call "screening" criteria. Working with a

Table 9.2. *Checklist: Supporting a growth mindset*

Do I utilize different practices for high-uncertainty projects than I do for low-uncertainty projects?

In high-uncertainty projects, am I known to tolerate failures provided that their cost to the organization is low and they have high learning potential?

Have I thought about the perceived risks people engaging in growth projects face and put into place mechanisms to absorb these risks?

Do I actively manage a portfolio of projects for my areas of responsibility that distinguishes between projects of varying levels of uncertainty?

team, the middle managers can identify specific elements that would make a particular opportunity more or less attractive for the unit under consideration. We break these screening elements into two categories, as in the example listed here. The first category consists of aspects that would make a project a candidate for immediate rejection. Typical "screen out" criteria would include generic statements, such as "this project can't be successfully developed without incurring a risk to our ethical or safety standards." Other statements might be company-specific. One of our clients, for example, might refuse to fund projects which involve a direct medical intervention for a customer, citing concerns about medical liability.

The second category of screening statement are "screen ins" which give a weighting to those aspects of a project that would make it more or less attractive to the corporation. Again, some of these are generic while others are idiosyncratic. The scoring system depicted in Table 9.3 was adopted from a technique deployed by our colleague, Robert Cooper, at DuPont, drawn from the skewed scores that are utilized in Six Sigma projects. Your screening system works together with the portfolio approach to determine which projects will be "in" and which projects should be rejected or postponed, given the corporate-level objectives for the group.

Part 1: Screen-outs

What are the few criteria that would cause us to reject a proposal out of hand unless they can be successfully addressed? Typical issues would

Table 9.3. *Screening score card template*

Dimension	Exceptional if …	Acceptable if …	Unfavorable if …	Score totals
Strategic intent	The initiative takes us exactly where we want to go in terms of our strategy. 9	The initiative is not inconsistent with our strategy, but offers no engine to drive it. 3	The initiative, even if successful, is inconsistent with our strategy. 1	
Builds competitive advantage	The program builds both short-term revenue streams and long-term competitive advantage. 9	The program has either long- or short-term benefits, but not both. 3	The program provides only short-term benefits and may interfere with a long-term opportunity. 1	
Spillover / cross-sell potential	The program generates major opportunities to cross-sell to other clients or companies or geographies. 9	The program offers some cross-selling potential, but the opportunities are relatively narrow. 3	It is hard to imagine cross-selling opportunities emerging from this program. 1	
Our expertise	The program requires knowledge that is a strength of our people and which we wish to develop further. 9	The program requires knowledge that we can assemble, but is not a strength. 3	The program does not draw on any of our expertise – we would have to go outside for most of the content. 1	
"Wow" factor	This is such a fascinating opportunity that we are all falling over ourselves to work on it. 9	This would be OK – I would not mind working on it. 3	OMDB Over my dead body ("you do it"; "no, you do it"; "no, I did the last one! . . ."). 1	

Table 9.4. *Checklist: Opportunity identification*

When I audit my meeting agendas, are growth opportunities receiving regular
priority? Am I personally paying attention and spending time on growth?
Am I bringing diverse voices and experiences into the search for new
opportunities? How am I engaging every level of the organization to
provide insights about potential opportunities?
Am I cataloging and revisiting opportunities in a systematic way?
Do I have a transparent, well-understood mechanism in place to screen
opportunities?

---

be a lack of fit with ethics, safety, or quality standards, or an offering
that is relevant only to one part of the business.

Part 2: Screen-ins

A score card can be developed that weights positive features/attributes
of a proposal to determine which are the most attractive of those we
have to assess. Example items are shown in Table 9.3.

A checklist for opportunity identification is given in Table 9.4.

Establishment of growth projects

So far so good – you have come up with an interesting, innovative
growth idea and vetted it through some kind of systematic screening process. The next key middle management task has to do with
getting the right resources, creating the right kind of organizational
entity, and establishing the right networks that will allow the concept to realize its promise. This is tricky work – if a project is set
up far away from the existing business, it is apt to be rejected later
on, even if it is commercially successful. Indeed, in some of my early
research, I found only a 0.4 correlation between a construct that
measured the extent to which a venture had gained market acceptance and the extent to which it was supported by other parts of
the organization (McGrath, MacMillan, & Venkataraman, 1992). If
a new business is set up too close to existing operations, particularly in cases in which they have radically different business models,
the existing groups can smother the upstart (Christensen & Raynor,
2003).

Table 9.5. Mini-case: Leading from the middle

The implementation of discovery driven planning at Air Products

Ron Pierantozzi is Director of New Business Development at Air Products and Chemicals, Inc., a $7.4 billion revenue provider of industrial gases and chemical products, currently enjoying double-digit growth despite being active in many mature industries. The company entrusted Pierantozzi with the creation of a New Business Development group in 2002, and set out two objectives: (1) provide the right environment for incubating new businesses; and (2) foster a more innovative environment. Pierantozzi brought extensive experience in developing and implementing new technologies to the job, but realized that he would need to develop additional capabilities if his insights into new technologies were going to translate to the issue of business creation.

His first step was to attend an executive education seminar focused on the challenge of building growth businesses, where he was introduced to the concept of "discovery driven planning." Intrigued by the idea, he followed up by having Ian MacMillan, one of the originators of the concept, present it to an informal discussion group, the "Innovation Roundtable" as well as discuss it with new business development leaders. The concept was well received, and on the basis of this reaction, Pierantozzi decided to move forward towards implementing it in Air Products.

He could have initiated a visionary-sounding corporate initiative; he could have written memos to senior leaders asking for endorsement; he could have paid expensive consultants; and he could have waited for someone to make it an official corporate policy. He did none of those things – in a textbook case of leading as a middle manager, he instead orchestrated the conditions under which the new concept could be accepted.

He moved next on two fronts: first, sending additional people to the same executive education course that he attended; and then creating the conditions under which the effectiveness of discovery driven planning (DDP) could be demonstrated in practice. The project managers who attended the course were encouraged to use the tool as a pilot for projects on which they were working. Three of them, Kerri Friedl, Nancy Easterbrook, and Jeff DePinto, began not only to use it for business-building projects, but to show the technique to others in the company. Air Products people began to hear about it. Managers liked the way in which both financial and business targets were captured in the plans, but in such a way that they were consistent with the learning challenges of a new venture.

The first three demonstration projects helped build demand for Pierantozzi's next move, namely creating a critical mass of supporters for the concept. He arranged to have MacMillan and co-author Rita McGrath (with colleagues) create in-house seminars at Air Products facilities in both Allentown and London to reach a broader audience. His success at creating "buzz" for the concept can be seen in that the first course was fully subscribed within hours of being posted as available! The full course ran in three modules, with two days per module to minimize the disruption of attendees to their normal working life (the courses also involved additional innovation concepts). This began the next phase of adoption – a cohort of people who knew about and could use the tool.

During this phase, Pierantozzi tried to seed the utilization of DDP in projects with enough variety that it would be accepted as an improvement in the way Air Products routinely manages innovation. Both new business and new technology projects were thus developed using the tool, and it was even applied to challenges that were quite close to the existing business. For instance, one group used DDP to gain insight into a supplier's cost structure in order to facilitate more effective price negotiations. Another applied it to the entry of a mature business into the Chinese market.

The next evolutionary phase was the engagement of more senior leaders in the process, but not through any kind of formal approach. Instead, senior people were introduced to the new methodology by their own people, as they worked through project plans and resource allocation choices. When first one, then another, then another, then many, discovery driven plans were presented, senior people gradually found themselves understanding and finally embracing the approach. In effect, the process which started in the middle spread "upward" by becoming embedded in real work. A side benefit was that it provided a consistent method for discussing different types of projects – such as those emerging from the more technologically focused areas and those with a pure business focus. Previously, it had been difficult to talk of the two types in the same terms.

As of this writing, Pierantozzi is working with the most senior level of the company, with Paul Huck, the company's CFO. With the broad acceptance of discovery driven planning behind them, the two are exploring other kinds of new thinking that might benefit Air Products, such as the utilization of options reasoning and alternative measurement systems for uncertain projects. The major recognition spurring these efforts is that "we need different tools for different types of projects," as Pierantozzi observed (Pierantozzi, 2005).

Obtaining resources while maximizing flexibility

Resource strategies for new businesses should be long on flexibility and short on specific commitments until enough key assumptions are vetted that confidence in making further resource investments is warranted. Unfortunately, middle managers, particularly those used to conventional budgeting and planning processes, are prone to predictable errors in acquiring resources.

First is the tendency to over-promise in order to "sell" a proposal to their seniors. This usually sets in place a vicious cycle. The venture gets too visible, too early, and may actually receive more resources than it really needs. When, as typically happens, things do not go as planned, the venture team gets charged with failure to deliver results and the idea is often abandoned, while the whole team loses credibility. Secondly, managers accustomed to conventional planning tend to place an excessive emphasis on meeting plan as opposed to learning. Finally, managers using a mental model of the existing business on which to base a new business tend to distort its economics – either by deploying overhead costs that are excessive or by fixing too early on activities that might cover ambitious revenue-generating goals to the long-term strategic detriment of the concept.

Using alternative practices requires both the recognition that planning for new businesses is and should be different, and the political savvy to persuade others of the correctness of this approach. One useful framework for capturing these differences is embedded in a methodology termed "discovery driven planning" (McGrath & MacMillan, 1995), in which the entire planning system has to do with spending as little as possible to learn as much as possible, preserving flexibility and redirecting ventures as new information becomes available.

Deploying the discovery driven approach, however, requires the agreement of those in control of resources and who review the plans to live with the "different" disciplines of this approach, as opposed to those of conventional planning. A critical middle management task is thus to create a receptive community for the discovery driven approach among a coalition of powerful people. At Air Products and Chemicals, Inc., for example, Ron Pierantozzi, the Director of New Business Development, spent considerable time orchestrating the acceptance of the discovery driven approach (see the mini-case in Table 9.5).

Finding an organizational home for the venture

A key concept, although one that often gets lost in endless discussions about formal structures and the extent of relatedness of a venture, is that of a "charter" for a new business unit (Galunic & Eisenhardt, 2001). A "charter" refers to the match between the resources of a given line of business (for example, a division), the markets it seeks to serve, and the products and services it offers. In contrast to the conventional view of structuring for innovation in which the structures are seen as more or less fixed once initial design decisions are made, Galunic and Eisenhardt's research finds instead that charters can move between various parts of an organization with some fluidity.

Groups might lose a charter for three reasons: (1) because they had failed to deliver or because other groups competed away their resources; (2) because they were so successful that certain charters were deemed eventually to be distracting; or (3) because existing charters failed to adapt to changing market conditions and needed to be "shed" (Galunic & Eisenhardt, 1996). Groups might gain a charter for three different reasons: (1) because the new charter promises to strengthen a weak group; (2) because a new charter is temporarily "orphaned" and needs a "foster home"; or (3) as the result of victory in a "charter war" in which different groups within the company vie for the right to manage the charter (Galunic & Eisenhardt, 2001).

Three points are worth noting. First, as Block and MacMillan pointed out, any venture is likely to have knowledge and capability gaps, whether these are relevant to the offerings of a business, to technologies and capabilities, or to the markets it serves (Block & MacMillan, 1993). Thus, one goal for finding the initial location of a new venture is to locate it where those in the venture can learn from the corporate parent. However, this learning can go too far, particularly if the business model or processes in the housing unit have an excessive influence on the activities of the venture.

A key middle management role is thus identifying whether and when charter moves will best facilitate the venture's chances. At telecommunications provider Nokia, for instance, charters are managed proactively in a milestone-oriented discovery approach. Ideas that were incubated in their new ventures organization might make the transition to an established line of business. Conversely, sometimes the company will pull charters out of existing lines of business, combine them with new ventures, and form entirely different divisions, as occurred recently with the formation of their Enterprise Solutions group.

Although middle managers conduct the negotiations that influence where a charter goes, this is seldom an explicitly defined task for which support or training are provided – nor is it likely to be explicitly rewarded. A key mentoring role is thus helping those involved in charter negotiations to do so effectively (and mediating the inevitable disputes that arise). Nokia, for instance, has a series of training and mentoring initiatives, the purpose of which is to build skills at creating new combinations of charters and capabilities deep in the organization, facilitated by a unique organizational structure which the company refers to as its "operating model" (http://www.nokia.com/nokia/0,,33080,00.html).

Third, charters can be malleable, resulting in the diffusion of ideas and technologies represented by a charter to different parts of the organization. While certain corporate-wide practices (such as common budgeting forms and procedures) facilitate charter movement, charter negotiations require time, energy, and influencing skills. This suggests that the more explicitly middle managers understand the task of horse-trading charters, and the greater the linkage of charter movement is to the overall strategy of the corporation, the more effective structural and organizing outcomes will be.

Creating and sustaining networks

A final critical aspect of developing growth projects with high potential is creating networks – both within and external to the organization. Much has been written about the importance of networking, particularly in the context of innovations. We have learned a lot; for instance, that middle managers should seek to maintain networks of both strong and weak ties; and that powerful positions in a network are often developed when an individual bridges a "structural hole" between other networks – in other words, when they have a unique ability to connect two networks that are otherwise unrelated (Burt, 1992). Networking and the deployment of social capital have been shown to be critical to the resource acquisition strategies for new ventures (Starr & MacMillan, 1990). These activities, however, operate at a more or less individual level. What might an organization-wide approach to the creation of networks that facilitate growth look like?

At an organizational level, the IBM "Emerging Business Opportunity" (EBO) structure is a fascinating study of how an organization deliberately harnessed cross-division networking to create new growth opportunities. First, IBM capitalized on the success of those respected middle managers who had already run large, established businesses by formally putting them in charge of an EBO area, often tearing them away from high-profile jobs with huge budgets and staff counts. Next, resources for each EBO were kept deliberately slim, forcing the newly anointed leader to create new networks – often across traditional lines of business – to obtain resources, test the concepts, and validate assumptions. The pattern is very similar to the "real options" investment pattern often advocated as a sensible way to allocate funds to new ventures (McGrath, 1997).

This dependence on others for resources created inexorable pressure to go beyond conventional authority lines to create networks and engage supporters. As one EBO leader was recently quoted as saying, "We wanted to be Tom Sawyer getting the rest of the company to paint our fence" (Deutschman, 2005). If early trials of an EBO concept proved successful, the initial informal networks were followed by more formal structures, often including the reorganization of entire business divisions, as recently occurred in IBM's Life Sciences division.

In parallel with the efforts of the EBO leader, IBM also has a managerial superstructure that provides support, ring-fences resources, and acts as a sounding board, under the direction of J. Bruce Harreld, IBM's senior vice-president for strategy. This sort of arrangement is also common to innovative firms, in which internal venture boards or other loosely organized entities interact with multiple ventures and weigh in on critical venturing decisions.

A checklist for the establishment of growth projects is given in Table 9.6.

The transition from a project to a grown-up business

Ironically, it is frighteningly common for a growth venture to stumble when it seems to be on the brink of its greatest success (Hambrick & Crozier, 1985). One root cause is that the very skills and capabilities that were highly valuable during the earlier piloting and start-up stages of a venture can become liabilities when its primary challenges

Table 9.6. *Checklist: Growth projects*

Do I clearly understand the differences between conventional business
    planning and the discipline appropriate to new, uncertain businesses?
Have I thought through my political strategy for building a coalition of
    support for a different discipline for new businesses?
Can I demonstrate a solid early success using more discovery driven
    approaches?
Do I understand what organizational home would best facilitate the learning
    required in my venture? Am I clear on the early warnings that might suggest
    that my charter might need to move elsewhere? Have I thought through my
    influence strategy for getting the best organizational setup for my venture?
Have I created a context (or found a context) that facilitates cross-business
    networking, protects key resources, and offers a chance to pilot new ideas
    before they consume significant resources?

are no longer those of a start-up, but of a more mature business. Author
Geoffrey Moore goes so far as to assert that the advantages a company
garners in one stage of the technology adoption life cycle become out-
right liabilities at the next (Moore, 2000). Other, organizational factors
also emerge in response to the success of a new venture, as jealousy,
turf battles, and competition for increasingly scarce resources increase
the political tensions surrounding the business. And eventually, robust
and reliable processes that will ensure the health of ongoing operations
need to be implemented.

Managing transitions in skills and capabilities

It is well known in the world of independent ventures that there often
comes a point at which the founding team needs to be replaced by
managers with different qualities. Indeed, one of the ways in which
venture capitalists claim they add value is in provoking these transitions and helping locate relevant managerial talent. The same applies
to many key people working within a corporate venture: those with
the right skills to function well when the task is discovery and creation are not necessarily able to make the transition to the tasks of
enhancement and operational excellence. Moore (1991) terms this
transition the transition from "pioneers" to "settlers." As he describes
(1991, p. 199):

pioneers . . . do not institutionalize. They do not like to create infrastructure. They don't even like to document. They want to do great deeds, and when there are no more great deeds to be done, they want to move on . . . once you have crossed the chasm, these people can become a potential liability.

Yet, for a venture to become a multi-million or multi-billion enterprise, management systems and processes need to be reliable, standards need to be adopted and adhered to, and consistency and predictability become important. The challenge for middle managers bears some similarity to that of those tasked with integrating an acquired company with a different culture than one's own. Yet, just as with integrating acquisitions, such a crucial process is often not handled very systematically.

Ideally, consideration of the actions necessary to manage skill and capability transitions will be started before they become necessary – experienced middle managers, for instance, will already be looking for process and procedure experts before they are needed – and consideration of where their "pioneers" might go will be made before their shortcomings in a more mature business trip them up. In the midst of the transition, all the practices of effective change management come into play as new jobs emerge, old ones disappear, and the core team on the venture changes. Compensation, similarly, needs to shift, from an emphasis on starting new things to rewards for developing and maintaining ongoing streams of business.

Managing political pressures

As a new growth initiative becomes a substantive contributor to the core business, it also needs to become a good citizen. At the project championing level, this can feel like the imposition of adult supervision on a rowdy adolescent. The growth initiative now has to begin abiding by the corporate rules. Rules about corporate overhead and transfer payments, rules about human resource policies, and rules about harmonization with centralized systems begin to become important. Targets need to be met more consistently, and accountability for performance starts to matter. The middle manager takes on a diplomatic role now, mediating between the venture and the rest of the corporation.

In addition to diplomacy, hard-core political work is often necessary as well. Successful new ventures can be intensely threatening to other parts of the organization. For one thing, they often suck up valuable resources as they grow. For another, they often represent fundamental changes in underlying company capabilities that can endanger the skills and competencies that managers in other parts of the business have painstakingly developed. At IBM, for instance, the cross-cutting businesses represented by the EBO program had to overcome the political challenges of changing power structures embedded in the former product-centric operating model of the company.

Middle managers are not always able to overcome these challenges on their own. For that reason, many companies have established cross-organizational, counterbalancing structures that can neutralize the political challenges. IBM, for instance, separates out EBO funding and ensures that a very senior person is in charge of those resources. At other companies (such as Nokia) a venturing board performs a similar function, in addition to assessing resource outlays to ventures at key milestones. Sometimes, the need to quell internal competition can result in a wholesale corporate reorganization. Companies such as DuPont and 3M, for instance, have moved away from treating individual businesses as individual profit centers, instead operating in groups of "platforms" in which businesses with common customers, technologies, or other capabilities report in to the same organizational authority structure.

Institutionalizing venturing

As some ventures develop into businesses, they begin to face the same challenge facing the core business before them – where is the next major growth opportunity going to come from? Acting on this insight requires the last practice we shall review here, which some authors have termed developing an ability to cope with the "ambidextrous" quality in middle managers (O'Reilly & Tushman, 2004). The term is meant to capture the necessity of dual focus: on reliable and efficient operations excellence in those parts of the business that have achieved a stable track record while continuously seeking opportunity for business expansion and new business development. Middle managers, more than any other actors within the corporation, need to have both goals firmly before them.

Backing them up can be corporate practices that avoid a unidimensional focus on one or the other objective. Thus, some companies allocate a specific portion of resources to new businesses, while contin-uing to support existing businesses at competitive levels. Others adopt an approach to budgeting that allows middle managers to steer towards future markets, rather than driving budgets from what was done (and even worse, what was spent) the previous year (Hope & Fraser, 2003). Still others insist on variety in the types of businesses they pursue, with the explicit goal of being prepared to cope with changes in the mar-ket that cannot be anticipated. Among the most important practices appear to be compensation systems that not only reward those in more mature businesses with benefits stemming from the new businesses but also provide incentives to those in new businesses based on the perfor-mance of the existing ones.

One of the most challenging roles of the middle manager has to do with terminating those projects that do not look promising. The dilemma here is that this judgment is exactly that – a judgment. Indeed, corporate venturing lore is replete with examples of projects that were given up for dead and yet came roaring back to save their parent firms from decline. The 3M Post-It is one of the best known.

The challenges of managing disappointment are many, including how one properly rewards people who tried and failed, and how to make the distinction between bad luck and bad management. Learn-ing from disappointment and being able to admit when things did not go as planned are key to developing a culture that is capable of growth. Indeed, CEOs at both IBM and GE have been quoted as observing that improving the way disappointments are managed is key to their growth strategies.

A critical concern, however, lies in what the academics call "escala-tion of commitment to a failing course of action." This involves a case in which good people get sucked into supporting projects well past the point at which it is pretty clear that they are simply not working. Royer (2003) goes so far as to advocate a specialist middle management role to help companies avoid this temptation, the "stopping champion." This individual, typically someone who is not embroiled in the day-to-day operations of the growth business, is responsible for providing more or less dispassionate oversight and recommending when he or she believes a venture has too little promise to proceed.

Stopping champions aside, Montealegre and Keil (2000) have sug-gested a list of ways in which the context for de-escalation of commit-ment can occur:

Table 9.7. *Checklist: From a project to a business*

Have I consciously anticipated the shifts that will be required in skills and
preferences for the business to succeed?

Do I have a transition plan for my "pioneers"? And a recruitment plan for
my "settlers"?

Have I adjusted my compensation system to account for both obtaining new
business and ensuring ongoing customer loyalty?

Am I helping the people in the business conform to necessary corporate rules
and structures?

Do I have a political plan to manage the inevitable tensions between a
rapid-growth venture and the rest of the corporation?

Have I been proactive in terminating businesses or projects that are not
making sufficiently good progress? Can I recycle the valuable talent and
lessons learned elsewhere in my organization?

Am I alert to and actively avoiding escalation of commitment to a failing
course of action?

- changes in top management or project championship
- publicly stated limits on expenditure
- availability of alternative internal investments
- setting minimum target levels for achievement
- making negative outcomes less threatening
- engaging in regular evaluation
- separation of responsibility for initiating and evaluating projects
- appeals to stakeholders from externally affected parties
- external pressure on the organization
- unambiguously negative feedback
- visibility of project costs.

Putting these forces to work in stopping unproductive projects is as
important as getting good ones started.

A checklist for the transition from a project to a grown-up business
is given in Table 9.7.

Some closing thoughts

Middle managers have been blamed for any number of organizational ills. Critics have accused them of adding unnecessary bureaucracy to organizations, increasing costs and decreasing the ability of

organizations to respond to external challenges. Obviously, in this chapter I have taken a different view. I have argued instead that what is needed in the pursuit of growth is not the elimination of the middle management job. Rather, middle managers perform a series of absolutely essential, yet relatively obscure tasks. Because these tasks are often poorly understood, organizations mismanage them, to the ultimate detriment of their growth efforts.

What I have attempted to do here is to outline some of the essential activities performed by middle managers through the course of a growth process. My belief is that by making these activities more explicit, organizations can improve their effectiveness at driving growth on a consistent basis. The middle management job can be a lot more productive, a lot more fun, and ultimately provide an engine for corporate revitalization.

References

Baghai, M., Coley, S., & White, D. 1999. *The Alchemy of Growth: Practical Insights for Building the Enduring Enterprise*. New York: Perseus.

Benner, M. J. & Tushman, M. 2002. Process management and technological innovation: a longitudinal study of the photography and paint industries. *Administrative Science Quarterly*, 47(4): 676.

Block, Z. & MacMillan, I. C. 1993. *Corporate Venturing: Creating New Businesses Within the Firm*. Boston: Harvard Business School Press.

Brady, D. 2005. The Immelt revolution, *Business Week*, no. 3926: 64–73.

Burt, R. S. 1992. *Structural Holes: The Social Structure of Competition*. Cambridge, MA: Harvard University Press.

Christensen, C. M. & Raynor, M. E. 2003. *The Innovator's Solution: Creating and Sustaining Successful Growth*. Boston: Harvard Business School Press.

Deutschman, A. 2005. Building a better skunk work. *Fast Company*, 92: 68–69.

Foster, R. & Kaplan, S. 2001. *Creative Destruction: Why Companies that are Built to Last Underperform the Market – and How to Successfully Transform Them*. New York: Doubleday.

Galunic, D. C. & Eisenhardt, K. M. 1996. The evolution of intracorporate domains: divisional charter losses in high-technology, multidivisional corporations. *Organization Science*, 7(3): 255.

2001. Architectural innovation and modular organizational forms. *Academy of Management Journal*, Special Research Forum on New and Evolving Organizational Forms, 44(6): 1229–1249.

Hambrick, D. C. & Crozier, L. M. 1985. Stumblers and stars in the management of rapid growth. _Journal of Business Venturing_, 1(1): 31–45.

Hitt, M. A., Hoskisson, R. E., Ireland, R. D., & Harrison, J. S. 1991. Effects of acquisitions on R&D inputs and outputs. _Academy of Management Journal_, 34(3): 693.

Hope, J. & Fraser, R. 2003. _Beyond Budgeting: How Managers Can Break Free from the Annual Performance Trap_. Boston: Harvard Business School Press.

Huy, Q. N. 2001. In praise of middle managers. _Harvard Business Review_, 79(8): 73.

Kanter, R. M. 1982. The middle manager as innovator. _Harvard Business Review_, 60(4): 95–105.

Likert, R. 1961. _New Patterns of Management_. New York: McGraw-Hill.

MacMillan, I. C. & McGrath, R. G. 2002. Crafting R&D project portfolios. _Research-Technology Management_, 45(5): 48–59.

2004. Nine new roles for technology managers. _Research-Technology Management_, 47(3): 16–26.

2005. For sustained growth of your bottom line, WYDIWYG – what you DO is what you get. The Wharton School, University of Pennsylvania, unpublished working paper.

McGrath, R. G. 1997. A real options logic for initiating technology positioning investments. _Academy of Management Review_, 22(4): 974–996.

McGrath, R. G. & MacMillan, I. C. 1995. Discovery driven planning. _Harvard Business Review_, 73(4): 44–54.

2000. _The Entrepreneurial Mindset: Strategies for Continuously Creating Opportunity in an Age of Uncertainty_. Boston: Harvard Business School Press.

2005. _MarketBusters: 40 Strategic Moves that Drive Exceptional Business Growth_. Boston: Harvard Business School Press.

McGrath, R. G., MacMillan, I. C., & Venkataraman, S. 1992. Measuring outcomes in corporate venturing: an alternative perspective. Paper presented at the Academy of Management Best Paper Proceedings.

Montealegre, R. & Keil, M. 2000. De-escalating information technology projects: lessons from the Denver International Airport. _MIS Quarterly_, 24(3): 417–447.

Moore, G. A. 1991. _Crossing the Chasm: Marketing and Selling High-Tech Products to Mainstream Customers_. New York: HarperCollins.

2000. _Living on the Fault Line: Managing for Shareholder Value in the Age of the Internet_. New York: Harper Business.

O'Reilly, C. A. & Tushman, M. L. 2004. The ambidextrous organization. _Harvard Business Review_, 82(4): 74.

Pierantozzi, R. 2005. Implementing discovery driven planning at Air Products and Chemicals, Inc. Personal communication.

Royer, I. 2003. Why bad projects are so hard to kill. *Harvard Business Review*, 81(2): 49–56.

Starr, J. A. & MacMillan, I. C. 1990. Resource cooptation and social contracting: resource acquisition strategies for new ventures. *Strategic Management Journal*, 11: 79–92.

10 | Organic growth through internal corporate ventures

PHILIP ANDERSON

W HAT options are open to a corporation when it "hits the wall" and its growth plateaus? One alternative is to revitalize and renew its core businesses (e.g. Waterman, 1987; Zook, 2001). Another is to acquire other companies, despite considerable evidence that the majority of acquisitions probably destroy economic value. A third alternative is to grow organically by extending today's businesses.

Along this third growth path, one choice is to extend an organization's geographic footprint. For example, after the fall of the Berlin Wall, HeidelbergCement was one of the first major cement manufacturers to enter the Polish market, which became a springboard for expansion into other Eastern European countries. From 1990 to 2004, HeidelbergCement built a network of plants covering every key geography in Central and Eastern Europe, and by 2004 it had the #1 market share in the region, although it is #4 in worldwide market share. Today, the key growth challenge for HeidelbergCement as for others in the industry is building market share in China.

Another possibility is expanding into new roles along existing value chains. For example, Apple Computer ignited a new wave of growth with its phenomenally successful iPod MP3 music player. To drive more sales of iPods, Apple launched its iTunes MP3-format music downloading service in April 2003. Apple's move into the distribution part of the music value chain created a new stream of revenues. Similarly, once manufacturers reach a certain size, they commonly establish financial services subsidiaries that start by financing equipment purchases. Sometimes (as in the case of GE Credit), the financial services division ultimately becomes the most profitable wing of the parent company (Slater, 1992).

A third way to grow organically is to create new lines of business through internal corporate ventures. For example, Sony's growth for ten years was heavily influenced by the introduction of its Playstation video game console in 1994. Sony's entry into electronic gaming grew out of a project of Nintendo and Sony with the goal of developing a CD-ROM system for Nintendo's game console (Asakura, 2000). Sony produced a prototype by May 1990, but a year later, Nintendo abandoned its arrangement with Sony in favor of a new joint development agreement with Philips. For twelve months, Sony and Nintendo were deadlocked in negotiations, until in June 1992, Sony president Norio Ohga approved a project to develop a new game machine that would challenge Nintendo's dominance. Under the leadership of Ken Kutaragi (who was in turn guided by Shigeo Maruyama, head of Sony's Epic records subsidiary), Sony engineers developed a next-generation gaming system based on innovative three-dimensional graphics technology. Teruhisa Tokunaka, an expert in mergers and business development, crafted a business plan for the Playstation, and in November 1993, the company established a new division, Sony Computer Entertainment Inc. (SCEI), to develop and market game machines and software. Introduced in December 1994, the Sony Playstation was a huge hit, and SCEI became one of Sony's fastest-growing and most profitable business units.

Growth through internal corporate ventures has gone into and out of fashion several times. Gifford Pinchot generated a wave of interest in the mid-1980s with his book *Intrapreneuring* (Pinchot, 1985), which illustrated how companies such as 3M and Convergent Technologies grew by sponsoring entrepreneurs inside their organizations. The growth of "dotcom" entrepreneurial organizations in the late 1990s spawned another wave of interest in internal entrepreneurship, as corporations fought to keep their most talented people from leaving for start-ups. Advised to set up quasi-independent organizations in order to cope with disruptive technologies (Christensen, 1997), many companies set up their own "internal dotcoms," either terminating them or bringing them back into the parent organization after the NASDAQ crash of April 2000 diminished the perceived threat of disruption through e-commerce. For example, General Motors, Ford, and DaimlerChrysler sponsored Covisint as a pilot project to build an online platform for supply chain collaboration and parts purchasing. Covisint was set up as an independent corporation in 2000, but the three automotive manufacturers withdrew their funding in 2002, and Covisint ceased operations in 2004.

At the height of the dotcom boom, Gary Hamel urged corporations to "bring Silicon Valley inside," funding and nurturing innovative internal growth projects by emulating practices borrowed from venture capitalists (Hamel, 1999). A number of corporations set up "venture business offices" to encourage, fund, and incubate internal ventures aimed at creating significant innovations (see Mason & Rohner, 2002 for a thorough description). But long before, Thermo Electron showed how a corporation can be structured as a collection of quasi-independent entrepreneurial subsidiaries, spun off from a parent. Thermo Electron took public eight subsidiaries between 1983 and 1990, retaining majority control of each (Kahalas & Suchon, 1995). As a result, each business unit could tie measures and incentives to feedback from the stock market. Thermo Electron was more than a holding company; it continued to develop new lines of business internally and take public only those with a solid business plan and management that it thought would be well received by public markets.

Bringing the vibrancy of the venture capital world into a corporation is an attractive, compelling vision; most senior executives in fast-moving sectors immediately grasp why this might be useful. However, a corporate venture is not the same as a start-up venture, and there are limits to the analogy between the new companies and new corporate lines of business. This chapter highlights one of these key differences, the problem of sustaining a venture whose growth path ends up having little to do with its business plan. How can a corporation get the most out of internal growth ventures whose success often depends on pursuing unforeseen directions that may be loosely linked or even contrary to the overall corporate strategy? The chapter then discusses one approach to this problem: allowing ventures to emerge from a self-organizing system within an enterprise. The concept is illustrated by a description of corporate venturing at Singapore Technologies.

Internal corporate ventures contrasted with start-ups

In many ways, the challenge of allocating resources to and creating new lines of business internally is similar to the challenge of fostering innovation through R&D (see Bower, 1970; Helfat, 1988). However, the purpose of R&D is to sponsor innovations; the purpose of a corporate venture is to create a new *business* inside the firm (Block & MacMillan, 1993). Most new business units are innovative, but many innovations are brought to market by a firm's existing sub-units. Corporate entrepreneurship arises when an existing organization spawns a new business unit internally. A corporate venture is not the same as a spinoff (a business that becomes an independent entity outside the firm) and corporate venturing is not the same as corporate venture capital (taking equity stakes in independent entrepreneurial ventures).

New businesses inside existing companies start off with many advantages compared to newly founded independent enterprises. The biggest problem many new ventures face initially is getting stakeholders to believe in them; they constantly must address the question, "Why should I do business with you if you might not be around tomorrow?" In contrast, ventures inside established firms gain an umbrella benefit from the legitimacy, social capital, reputation, and brands of their parents. Typically, corporate ventures also inherit systems, routines, trusted relationships between employees, and financial stability from the enterprises that created them.

On the other hand, corporate ventures also must deal with serious constraints that independent ventures do not face. A new venture can align itself so that all aspects of its organization design fit its task environment. In contrast, when a corporate venture inherits people, structures, processes, and culture from its parent, its organizational design usually fits the environment the parent faces (Nadler, Tushman, & Nadler, 1997). Unless the environments are quite similar, there is usually a misalignment that requires the corporate venture to manage strategic change at the same time it is trying to launch a business (Tushman & Anderson, 2004).

Perhaps even more crucially, a corporate venture tends to be more restricted in its choice of domain than a start-up. First, its choices are limited by the need to fit its parent's dominant logic, which delineates its positioning and source of competitive advantage (Prahalad, 2004). Secondly, is can be constrained by its parent's brand image and brand equity. Thirdly, the incumbent divisions of the parent may jealously guard what they regard as their turf, opposing potential cannibalization of their revenues by a venture (Govindarajan & Kopalle, 2004).

Such constraints can impose severe burdens on corporate entrepreneurs, because ventures often engage in extensive exploration before settling on a domain, identity, and business model. The purpose of a business plan is to impose discipline on a venture, even though both the entrepreneurs and their stakeholders are aware that most ventures depart considerably from their business plans (McGrath & MacMillan, 2000). A business plan is a point of departure, a way to legitimate a business and help it attract resources. As entrepreneurs search for paying customers and react to what they perceive as the voice of the market, start-up ventures often morph into forms that are barely recognizable as descendants of the initial idea (Bhide, 2000).

For example, serial entrepreneurs Rajesh Reddy and Ashok Narasimhan, both Indians who had built successful businesses in Silicon Valley, launched a new venture in January 2002 called July Systems. Their original idea was to build a software platform that would allow corporations to deploy their existing enterprise applications to employees using mobile devices on cellular data networks. They believed corporations would pay to ensure that employees could access the same applications with the same rights and privileges when on the road as they had when in an office attached to the corporate network. On the strength of this idea, they raised $5.5 million in venture capital in April 2002, and hired fifty engineers based in Bangalore, India to build their system.

Within a year, it became clear that the market for this software platform would not materialize soon enough; enterprises were deploying applications to mobile data networks more slowly than had been predicted. However, sales of digital "infotainment" to mobile subscribers were growing much more rapidly than had been forecast. Consumers were reluctant to pay for content delivered via the Internet to personal computers, but they seemed quite willing to pay for alert services, Java games, and ringtones for their mobile telephones. In fact, sales of ringtones exceeded sales of recorded music in many markets by 2003. Consequently, July Systems repositioned its platform, which made its debut in 2003, as infrastructure for retailing digital content to mobile users.

Initially, the company targeted mobile telecommunications operators, expecting them to buy a platform that made it simple to pipe in content from various publishers, format it for the bewildering variety of handsets and standards on the market, manage promotions (e.g. one free trial before paying) and pricing, and output charges to the operator's billing system. However, mobile operators proved unable to acquire content or manage promotions, so by 2004, July Systems changed its offering to a managed service. July offered to provide operators with a complete end-to-end solution, from acquiring content to managing promotions.

When mobile operators still proved slow to adopt the solution, July changed its direction once again. It opened its own retail store on AT&T Wireless's mMode mobile portal, offering a catalog of games for sale so that when subscribers bought the package, they received one free playing session for each game in the bundle. At the same time, it put together and delivered complete promotional campaigns for new movies, and operated a game tournament service on a portal in the UK that reached across four different carriers. By 2005, July Systems' business looked nothing like the concept that was the basis of its first-round financing, but despite the twists and turns, it raised another $10 million in venture capital in August 2004. July completely changed its positioning, identity, target customer, and revenue model without ever losing the faith of its initial investors, all of whom contributed to the second round of financing.

Network365, founded in 1999 with headquarters in Ireland, illustrates the same idea. Its founder, serial entrepreneur Raomal Perera, raised €2.5 million in seed financing in February 2000 to build an e-commerce platform. As Perera narrates the story:

I went to Enterprise Ireland, an Irish government body that funds entrepreneurs and that has offices in thirty-five countries. We had to do a business plan to get money from them, but I was still thinking about what was the right thing to do. The lady who was the development advisor asked me about the business plan, saying, "Is this accurate?" I looked at her and said, "I can only tell you that none of that is accurate." She said to me, "You can't say things like that, Raomal!" I replied that in two years' time, we wouldn't be doing what the business plan said; we'd have to evolve the thing. I wasn't too sure exactly what we had to do.

A friend of a friend introduced Perera to Digifone, one of Ireland's leading mobile operators. Digifone paid Network365 to build a mobile commerce payment and shopping platform, and on the strength of this contract, the start-up shifted its efforts and identity from e-commerce to m-commerce software. Perera comments, "The business plan was all changed so that it looked as if we had been developing mobile commerce software since the day we were born. Now we were positioned as a mobile commerce company." With a reference customer in hand, Network365 raised €15 million in venture capital.

Enterprise Ireland then introduced Perera to Hong Kong CSL ("Create a Simple Life"), a wholly owned subsidiary of Telstra and the second-largest mobile operator in Hong Kong. CSL was only interested in one part of the platform that Network365 had built for Digifone: mobile wallet software that simplified payments for goods purchased via a mobile phone. This deal helped Network365 acquire a contract to build a secure mobile payments platform from a large Hong Kong operator, and on the strength of that reference customer, Network365 won a contract to build a complete mobile payment and financial services system for Japan's DoCoMo, the world leader in mobile commerce, thanks to its innovative iMode service.

By 2003, Network365 was positioned as a leader in payment software for mobile commerce. But Raomal Perera realized that with the rise of digital infotainment sales on mobile networks, the market for software to support micropayments (charges too small to merit billing them through a credit card) would grow much faster outside Japan and Korea. In November 2003, Network365 merged with iPIN, a California-based leader in micropayment software that was available at an attractive price because it had run out of money. The two software systems were combined into a single platform renamed Payments Plus, and the merged entity was renamed Valista. In April 2004, Valista signed a landmark deal with America Online (AOL), which agreed to use Valista's software to process payments for AOL content and services. Unlike Network365, which focused on mobile payments, Valista's market now extended beyond mobile operators to Internet service providers, telecommunications companies, and banks. Like July Systems, Valista morphed within a few years into a company whose identity, product, target customers, and business model were completely different from those the founder initially envisioned.

The stories of July Systems and Valista illustrate how severely domain restrictions can impact corporate ventures. Could a new business inside a large company ever have survived so many twists and turns? Could it ever have strayed so far from the strategic concept that won it the initial blessing of senior management?

Typically, within large, multidivisional corporations, individual business units are given charters to look after particular business areas, defining each division's turf (Galunic & Eisenhardt, 1996). The market for new charters is competitive, and divisions starting up new businesses can lose their charters to other divisions if the initial results of their efforts are not favorable. Divisions can also lose charters for peripheral businesses when their core business areas are growing rapidly, and they can lose charters for core businesses when the maturing of the sector they occupy leads to a misfit between their skills and the demands of the competitive environment. Galunic and Eisenhardt's research demonstrates that a multidivisional company is not a stable entity with a fixed division of labor between business units. Rather, it is an arena where environmental change and jostling between subunits creates a landscape of turf struggles and shifting divisional charters.

Corporate venture units must cope with this fluid arena. At any time, their right to pursue a particular opportunity may be denied, and powerful political forces can be marshaled against them to bar them from domains that look promising. Start-ups, such as July Systems and Valista, can explore with relative freedom, adapting as they reinterpret what the marketplace wants. Corporate ventures seldom have such luxury. For example, in 1976, Ken Kutaragi, the future inventor of the Playstation, was a new Sony employee whose first invention was a prototype for a liquid crystal display (LCD) projector (Asakura, 2000). However, he was never able to develop it into a product, much less a business, because of a power struggle between Sony subunits that were developing rival display technologies (electroluminescence and plasma). Instead, Epson introduced the first LCD projector for video in 1989, and with Epson's introduction of projectors that could display data output in 1994, a multi-billion dollar market for "beamers" that could display presentations from personal computers grew up rapidly, with Sony languishing as an also-ran.

Battling to carve out a niche as the aspirations of existing divisions clash, a corporate venture must legitimate itself within the firm, win its fair share of resource allocation battles, and overcome resistance and inertia (Block & MacMillan, 1993). Entrepreneurs who start companies and the venture capitalists who support them are used to coping with market risk, technology risk, management risk, and execution risk. Those who build organizations inside existing firms may be advantaged on some of these dimensions, but they face an additional threat: political risk. Often, the primary challenge for key executives in start-ups is legitimating their organization's existence in the eyes of key stakeholders. For executives building new lines of business within corporations, it is usually legitimating continuing exploration that can stray far from the corporate venture's original charter.

Managing political risk can be complex for those building companies inside existing enterprises because large organizations demand
reliability (Hannan & Freeman, 1989). A July Systems or a Valista
wins the continued backing of sponsors by reliably pursuing what
they construct and reconstruct as the market's "sweet spot." As has
been illustrated, this can lead to a change in a start-up's product concept, target customer, business model, and even its very identity: the
way it describes who it is, what it does, and with whom it competes.
A corporate venture must maneuver to retain the charter its parent
originally awarded, in a landscape of competition between existing
divisions over who is permitted to do what. As it learns about the
market and plots a course towards profitable growth, it must sustain
the impression that it is reliable, ever vulnerable to charges that it
has spun out of control and violated the charter that legitimates its
existence.

How can a corporation that wants to grow organically through
internal ventures overcome the innate tendency of organizations to
confine ventures, limit their ability to explore, and demand that start-
ups adhere to something like their original charters even though such
expectations are unrealistic? How can it minimize the political risk
with which ventures must cope? One approach builds on the theory of
self-organizing systems, which suggests that *collective entities* can be
reliable even if their individual elements appear to be out of control.

The self-organizing systems alternative

In recent years, scholars have attempted to apply insights from the
emerging area of complexity theory to the study of organizations (see
Anderson, 1999 for an overview). Complexity theory explains why in
many systems interactions among a network of interconnected agents
lead to the emergence of patterns that are reinforced. Structure mate-
rializes from initially random configurations, without any coordinator
guiding it.

In a self-organizing system, agents pursue individual courses that are
unpredictable. Reliable, reproducible structures emerge at the *collective* level from the interactions of those agents. Individual agents are
literally out of control, but the system as a whole produces relatively
stable results (see Kelly, 1994 for many interesting applications of this
concept to economic life).

One way to reduce political risk is for an organization to set up an architecture around corporate ventures that produces reliable collective results, even though individual corporate ventures can appear as chaotic and loosely coupled to their charters as July Systems or Valista. Such an organization has its own charter which, instead of allocating it a specific domain, sets forth a set of rules or principles for governing corporate ventures. Individual ventures may remain subject to domain challenges, as these seem to be an inescapable part of corporate life, but they are free to explore within a collective governance structure. Corporate ventures are managed as part of a network, and order is an emergent property of the network, not any one venture.

This abstract idea is best understood through a concrete example. In 2000, Singapore Technologies launched Incubators@Work!, an effort to encourage innovation and keep talented people from leaving the company during the dotcom boom. Incubators@Work! was established and managed in an original and intriguing fashion as a self-organizing system. It is too early to tell whether this concept will produce great returns or growth for Singapore Technologies, but it provides much food for thought.

Corporate ventures at Singapore Technologies

Singapore Technologies (ST) is a highly diversified conglomerate that includes many of the most important technology-based companies in Singapore. The organization is a private company 100% owned by Temasek Holdings, the investment holding company of the government of Singapore. Fourteen of ST's companies are publicly traded; the parent's stake in each company varies, but always exceeds 50%.

ST is one of the most important government-linked companies[1] (GLCs) in Singapore. With increasing vigor since the Asian financial crisis of 1997, the government has sought ways to increase the number of entrepreneurial companies founded in Singapore and develop the entrepreneurial spirit of the Singaporean people. Historically, the GLCs have created many new subsidiaries, and the government sees

---

[1] See John Burton, Government-linked companies, *Financial Times*, April 12, 2003 for an overview of this institution (available at http://www.singapore-window.org/sw02/020412f5.htm).

them as a source of "institutionalized entrepreneurship." Additionally, ST's senior management felt a responsibility to help promote the formation of independent entrepreneurial ventures in Singapore.

The genesis of Incubators@Work!

Consequently, in 2000, Singapore Technologies created three investment clubs, unofficially called "Tortoise Clubs." The corporate human resources department tapped approximately thirty executives from various parts of ST and asked them to form three different venture investment clubs. The mission of each was to manage a fund that would invest in companies founded by ST staff. One was Neo Kok Beng,[2] an engineer who joined Singapore Technologies' computer subsidiary and had worked in a variety of technical and business development positions. He comments:

At that time, around the world, we were seeing a lot of new start-ups that could create value, so we decided to invest in our own people who were enterprising enough to run their own business. There weren't many guidelines – we were told that how we funded entrepreneurs and what methodology we used to choose investments would be up to us. The three funds were allowed to operate independently, and ended up hardly consulting with each other, so that there would be several different approaches.

One of the investment groups included senior executives at the vice-president level from different arms of Singapore Technologies. Another included primarily young engineers, many fresh out of school. The third was a group of people who had been with Singapore Technologies for a few years (typically three or four); it was thought that they had been with the company long enough to understand its culture and operations, but not so long as to have deeply ingrained thinking patterns. This was the group that Neo joined.

When Neo joined the group of younger employees with experience, he did not know any of the other members personally. All the participants had been chosen by the corporate human resources department, and in a firm as large and diverse as ST, it was not surprising that the others were not personal acquaintances. He comments:

---

[2] Neo is his family name, Kok Beng his given name.

I had faith in the selection process; I knew that whoever was selected for this project would be motivated. I believed we could work together and expected everyone to have his own ideas and contribute actively to the group, without being encumbered by any one mindset. I have no problem going into a totally foreign environment and working something out. I don't like to work in a fixed setting; I prefer having more room to stretch and maneuver.

The eleven members of the nascent investment club staged their first get-together and started to become acquainted. As the most experienced member of the team, Neo took an active role in shaping the group's approach to investing its venture fund. "We got to know each other, and I shared my ideas about what we could do and how we might want to do it," he says. "We came to a consensus about our objective, and then set targets." Neo and two others volunteered to write a plan for the fund, which was approved at the team's next meeting. The team chose the name "Incubators@Work!," and moved forward to implement the plan.

Crafting and implementing a five-year plan

ST corporate headquarters had provided Incubators@Work! (http://www.incubators.com.sg/home.htm) with $10 million (Singapore) to fund ST staff who wanted to strike out on their own as entrepreneurs and start new companies. The venture team set an objective of funding six companies per year for the first three years. It also established a target of 25% average gross return on investment over a five-year fund life. The members further agreed that as a matter of policy, Incubators@Work! would not hold a majority stake in any of its portfolio companies, and would ensure that its stake was always less than that of the founders. Says Neo, "We preferred a venture capital model; we want the entrepreneurs to be enterprising and know they are responsible, so we thought the management team as a whole should hold a majority of the shares."

Having established a basic investment framework, the Incubators@Work! team developed a five-year implementation schedule, broken into four phases. First, the team planned to spend two years creating entrepreneurial awareness within Singapore Technologies. It used corporate newsletters and events to publicize Incubators@Work!;

conducted a series of road shows around the corporation; and visited dozens of managers to talk about the mechanics of how it funded ventures. It also developed a course for entrepreneurs, explaining (for example) how to write a business plan, how to value a start-up enterprise, and how to negotiate an investment term sheet. By 2002, Incubators@Work! offered a monthly newsletter and an annual entrepreneurs' workshop, advertising these to as wide an audience as possible within Singapore Technologies via its own database of contacts in the firm and through the corporate human resources department.

In parallel, the team built up an entrepreneurial infrastructure, consisting of an intellectual property network, a venture capital network, and a business network. The intellectual property network was designed to provide a steady flow of technologies and products that could serve as the basis of an enterprise. Says Neo:

We don't see Singapore Technologies as the monopoly provider of ideas and innovation. We recognize that staff may have ideas, but not have the technologies to implement them, or the time to develop those technologies. As long as our people develop the business plan and set up the business, we're willing to fund a good idea. We do a lot of matching, finding interesting prototypes and introducing them to staff who approach us with an interest in running a business. We set up a memorandum of understanding with all the universities in Singapore to tap into their technologies and prototypes, and we encourage people to license intellectual property from these sources or ST, then set up a business.

Incubators@Work! also built a set of relationships with independent venture capital firms. It positioned itself as a source of early-stage financing that would introduce portfolio companies to venture capitalists when they had built a product and needed growth capital. Finally, it built a network of operational executives within ST's various operating companies. Says Neo, "When our start-up companies have a product, we help them find their first customer within a Singapore Technologies company. The first customer is always the most difficult to get, and some of our internal customers are listed on the NASDAQ or Singapore Exchange (SGX), so they are very good reference sites."

In 2003, Incubators@Work! began implementing the third phase of its five-year plan, aimed at encouraging a culture of proactive entrepreneurship. Says Neo:

We have entrepreneurs in residence who believe in certain things enough to take positive steps now, instead of waiting until things are ready. We encourage prospective entrepreneurs to come to us for help developing their business plans. We saw cases of ST employees who took unpaid leave, enrolled in a technopreneurship program at Nanyang Technological University [in Singapore], and developed a business plan. We are working with one person who quit his job and is working on a business plan without pay; we stand ready to fund him when his business plan is ready. We aren't targeting lots of people. We are providing an alternative path for enterprising people, who want to work in ST for a while and then decide whether to climb the corporate ladder or start a new business.

Incubators@Work!: 2002–2003

By the end of 2001, Incubators@Work! had made five investments, all in software companies. These companies targeted applications such as knowledge management; building e-business systems based on Enterprise Resource Planning back-end systems; accelerating the delivery of content from web servers; and tools for building 3D environments that can be viewed via a web browser. As the dotcom boom ground to a halt, however, the original target of six investments per year began to appear too aggressive.

Although it had five portfolio companies and continued to seek new investment opportunities, Incubators@Work! operated like a corporate task force. Each of its members held a full-time job in ST, and the group only met periodically to review investment opportunities and plot strategy. At the end of 2001, the team hired one full-time employee, Thia Sim Peng. She started out at ST, where she met Neo, as an engineer, and was with SingTel's (Singapore's national telecommunications company) mergers and acquisitions group before she joined Incubators@Work!. She joined Incubators@Work! for the experience of working with portfolio companies, on the understanding that after two years, she and Neo would review whether this job might lead to a viable career path within ST.

Thia began to handle the day-to-day work of building awareness within ST, reviewing business plans and working with prospective entrepreneurs. For the first time in 2002, Incubators@Work! conducted an Entrepreneurs Day, broadly advertised throughout ST, which significantly increased its visibility. Thia notes, "The new CEO agreed to give the opening speech for the event, which helped increase our exposure throughout the group." By the second half of 2002, despite the end of the dotcom boom, a small but steady stream of prospective entrepreneurs was contacting Incubators@Work!, usually at a very early stage in the process of conceptualizing a venture. Says Thia:

Because we provide seed funding for start-ups, lots of people come to us with a one-page business idea, or even one that is still in their heads. I talked to about two different prospective business founders a week on average, often via an informal chat or phone call. Many would-be entrepreneurs never made it past this stage, either because they had already left ST and did not qualify, or because they were not willing to quit their jobs – they wanted a stake in their own business without risking unemployment.

Thia spearheaded the next level of investigation into prospective entrepreneurs who got past the initial stage, using three criteria established by the Incubators@Work! team. First, at least one member of the founding team had to be an ST employee who was willing to quit his job, spend 100% of his or her time working for the new venture, and put his or her own money into the start-up. Secondly, Thia examined whether the founders had some intellectual property, a proprietary technology that would give them an edge and differentiate them. Thirdly, Thia performed a rough market assessment, looking for businesses that had growth potential. She explains: "We want a business with a solid technology that can scale. Many people came to us with software ideas that were clearly not scalable, like building a niche application sitting on an SAP server. It is most likely that something like that will end up as a small consulting business."

Most of those who passed these initial screens still dropped out before launching a company. According to Thia, perhaps 40–50% of people with promising ideas would balk when it came time to quit their jobs and put their own money on the table. In other cases, ventures that initially looked promising turned out not to have a solid intellectual property asset. Incubators@Work! preferred to work with those who had invented a technology or could secure exclusive rights to one (perhaps with assistance from the incubator). In several cases, it turned out that would-be founders had nothing more than a non-exclusive license from the owner of proprietary technology.

Incubators@Work! not only responded to inquiries from ST staff, but also tried proactively to develop new enterprises based on its intellectual property network. Thia explains:

A lot of people who have approached us want to do their own thing, but do not have their own original ideas. Many Singapore Technologies employees are trained engineers but are working in marketing or business development, so they are not developing their own technologies. There are limits to the amount of proprietary technology that our staff can come up with on their own, and we want to generate as many feasible start-ups as we can. Therefore, we worked actively with universities and university-based inventors to see whether we could exploit patents they owned or were assigned.

One way in which Incubators@Work! tried to match university-developed technology with prospective ST entrepreneurs was to cooperate with the National University of Singapore (NUS) on a business plan workshop. In collaboration with Professor Wong Poh Kam, who spearheads entrepreneurship research and teaching at NUS, they selected ten technologies for which NUS had a patent, and presented them to workshop participants. The workshop members had to choose a technology, write a business plan around it, and present their plan. According to Thia, in three cases Incubators@Work! came close to investing in companies that would have used intellectual property from universities, but none of these deals had yet panned out by the end of 2003.

Ultimately, Incubators@Work! made three investments during 2002–2003. Tunity Technologies (http://www.tunitytech.com/) focuses on developing, integrating, and marketing contact-less identification products, solutions, and services that rely on wireless technologies such as radio frequency identification. The founders came out of CET, a subsidiary of ST Electronics that provides solutions for customers in communications, electronics, and intelligent transportation. CET recognized that its radio frequency technology unit had valuable technology, but thought it had more growth potential as an independent company, so it approached Incubators@Work!, asking if it wanted to participate in a spinoff.

A second investment, Vientity (http://www.vientity.com/), is a procurement software company that reached Incubators@Work! via word of mouth. A senior manager from ST Technologies had a friend who was looking for funding, and because one founder was an ST staff member, he referred the deal to Incubators@Work!.

The third investment, Scalable Systems (http://www.scalablesys. com/), came to Incubators@Work! via the incubator's internal business plan competition, which was started in 2000. The competition was open to any venture that had at least one person presently on the staff of an ST company, and the prize for the winner was guaranteed seed funding of S$500,000 from Incubators@Work! if the business was launched. The competition regularly attracted 15–20 entries per year, but Scalable Systems was the first entrant that ended up in the Incubators@Work! portfolio. Thia comments:

We would typically attract perhaps 15–20 initial one-page descriptions, and most people would follow through and write a full business plan. However, a majority of these plans were very academic. You would get a beautifully prepared plan for a business with a market potential of S$100 million within five years, but you could tell that management did not have the domain expertise to follow through. They didn't have the experience needed to execute the plan, and didn't have a clear idea how to reach their revenue objectives.

Summary

It is too early to judge whether Incubators@Work! or the other two "Tortoise Clubs" produced superior returns, or whether any of the portfolio companies will ultimately become the basis for new lines of business within Singapore Technologies. The point of this example is that Singapore Technologies pioneered a novel approach to promoting the entrepreneurial spirit within a large, diverse corporation. Some elements of its design may fit other companies; others may not. The illustration is meant to be thought-provoking and showcase the self-organizing approach to corporate venturing.

One of the key choices Singapore Technologies made was to fund three different entities deliberately designed to be different from one another demographically, so that each would tap into a different social network. Each club was allowed to establish its own policies and was not asked to coordinate with the others, to promote diverse approaches. Incubators@Work! chose to take a minority stake in ventures that would be incubated outside the parent, but it could have selected different policies had it wished. Its purpose was to catalyze innovation by serving as the hub of a self-organizing network. Its primary function was matchmaking, fostering novel interconnections between prospective entrepreneurs and between the firm and the outside world through its intellectual property network, venture capital network, and business network with one employee cross-pollinating and nurturing these linkages. Through its educational efforts, Incubators@Work! focused on creating a culture of entrepreneurship and an educated body of prospective entrepreneurs.

Corporate support for Incubators@Work! was not withdrawn as the technology bubble burst, because Incubators@Work! as a collective entity reliably produced outputs such as education, social connections, and role models. This left individual entities such as Tunity Technologies, Vientity, and Scalable Systems free to search for viable niches, disciplined by the need to win external sources of funding.

Incubators@Work! is an innovative approach to the abstract idea of "bringing Silicon Valley inside" an enterprise. Its design mitigates many of the political risks that the ventures it supports would otherwise have to face by nicely balancing order at the collective level with freedom at the level of the individual venture. It is only one of many ways a firm might address the challenges of corporate venturing, but it suggests that a self-organizing system can stimulate innovation with surprisingly low overhead and risk, as long as it has the support of senior management.

Conclusion

When firms hit growth plateaux, growing new lines of business organically can be an attractive alternative to acquisitions or strategic change efforts. Yet internal entrepreneurs who try to foster corporate growth in this way face unique challenges, because multidivisional organizations are dynamic entities where subunits vie to win and retain charters. Entrepreneurs usually succeed for reasons that have little to do with their original business plans; they win because they adapt successfully, not because they have superior foresight into an uncertain future. Consequently, the political risks that corporate ventures face may be greater than any of the usual risks with which entrepreneurs must cope.

Faced with pressures to behave reliably and challenges to their legitimacy should they stray too far from their original charters, corporate ventures may face severe competitive disadvantages *vis-à-vis* start-ups that enjoy more liberty to explore. One way to address such difficulties is to design a self-organizing system to govern corporate ventures, generating collective reliability and emergent order even though individual ventures may appear out of control to the parent corporation. Such an approach suggests that the way to understand organic growth through internal corporate ventures is to focus on the *network* that supports them collectively, not each venture in isolation.

References

Anderson, P. 1999. Complexity theory and organization science. *Organization Science*, 10: 216–232.

Asakura, R. 2000. Revolutionaries at Sony: the making of the Sony PlayStation and the visionaries who conquered the world of video games. In A. Bhide (ed.), *The Origin and Evolution of New Businesses*. New York: Oxford University Press.

Bhide, A. (ed.) 2000. *The Origin and Evolution of New Businesses*. New York: Oxford University Press.

Block, Z. & MacMillan, I. 1993. Corporate venturing: creating new businesses within the firm. In J. Bower (ed.), *Managing the Resource Allocation Process*. Boston: Harvard Business School Press.

Bower, J. (ed.) 1970. *Managing the Resource Allocation Process*. Boston: Harvard Business School Press.

Christensen, C. 1997. *The Innovator's Dilemma: When New Technologies Cause Great Firms to Fail*. Boston: Harvard Business School Press.

Galunic, D. C. & Eisenhardt, K. 1996. The evolution of intra-corporate domains: divisional charter losses in high-technology, multi-divisional corporations. *Organization Science*, 7: 255–282.

Govindarajan, V. & Kopalle, P. 2004. How legacy firms can introduce radical and disruptive innovations: theoretical and empirical analyses. *Academy of Management Proceedings*, pp. A1–A7.

Hamel, Gary. 1999. Bringing Silicon Valley inside. *Harvard Business Review*, 77(5): 70–84.

Hannan, M. & Freeman, J. 1989. *Organizational Ecology*. Cambridge, MA: Harvard University Press.

Helfat, C. 1988. *Investment Choices in Industry*. Cambridge, MA: MIT Press.

Kahalas, H. & Suchon, K. 1995. Managing a perpetual idea machine: inside the creator's mind. *Academy of Management Executive*, 9(2): 57–66.

Kelly, K. 1994. *Out of Control: The Rise of Neo-Biological Civilization*. Reading, MA: Addison-Wesley.

Mason, H. & Rohner, T. 2002. *The Venture Imperative: A New Model for Corporate Innovation*. Boston: Harvard Business School Press.

McGrath, R. G. & MacMillan, I. 2000. *The Entrepreneurial Mindset*. Boston: Harvard Business School Press.

Nadler, D., Tushman, M., & Nadler, M. 1997. *Competing by Design: The Power of Organizational Architecture*. New York: Oxford University Press.

Pinchot, G. 1985. *Intrapreneuring*. New York: Harper & Row.

Prahalad, C. K. 2004. The blinders of dominant logic. *Long Range Planning*, 37: 171–180.

Slater, R. 1992. *The New GE: How Jack Welch Revived an American Institution*. New York: McGraw-Hill.

Tushman, M. & Anderson, P. 2004. *Managing Strategic Innovation and Change*, 2nd edn. New York: Oxford University Press.

Waterman, R. 1987. *The Renewal Factor: How the Best Get and Keep the Competitive Edge*. New York: Bantam.

Zook, C. 2001. *Profit from the Core: Growth Strategy in an Era of Turbulence*. Boston: Harvard Business School Press.

11 | Linking customer management efforts to growth and profitability

DOUGLAS BOWMAN AND DAS NARAYANDAS

As firms search for ways to achieve profitable growth, it is natural for them to consider seeking more business with the customers they presently serve. Customer management pundits often propose that it is easier and less costly for firms to gain incremental sales from existing customers than to prospect for, and develop, customers with whom they currently do not do business. Yet, as Anderson and Narus (2003) argue, most firms struggle to devise or implement anything but the most sales-oriented growth strategies and tactics.

A particular challenge is how to link resource investments, especially those deployed at the customer or segment level (versus market level), with customer-level sales and profitability (Libai, Narayandas, & Humby, 2002). Profit chain-of-effects or cascading frameworks represent an intuitively appealing way to achieve this objective. They link resource inputs under the control of managers to customer-level sales and profitability. Consider, for example, Heskett, Jones, Loveman, Sasser, and Schlesinger's (1994) Service–Profit Chain (SPC). Working backwards, customer profitability is largely based on customer loyalty. Supporting arguments that have been advanced include loyal customers being less costly to serve, less price-sensitive and hence willing to pay higher prices, and more likely to be advocates who generate sales via positive word-of-mouth, to name a few. Further, the widespread adoption of loyalty programs can only be assumed to be due in part to their (assumed) positive impact on profits.

Customer loyalty, in turn, is driven by customer satisfaction. This relationship has similar intuitive appeal; if customers are satisfied with a vendor's products and services, then it is only natural that loyalty should follow. Anecdotal support abounds, such as Xerox's finding that top-box customers in a satisfaction survey are six times more likely to repurchase than those responding with four out of five (Heskett, *et al.*, 1994).

The antecedent linkages also seem straightforward: satisfaction is driven by vendor performance; and vendor performance on important attributes results from the vendor's effort or resource investments. Vendors who perform well on important attributes should make a customer more satisfied, and customer management effort appropriately expended should lead to better performance.

The result is a parsimonious framework with intuitive appeal that supports investments in customer satisfaction programs and customer loyalty programs. To counter-balance the linkages discussed above, the cost impact of the vendor's customer management effort can be implicitly (e.g. Heskett, *et al.*, 1994) or explicitly (e.g. Bowman & Narayandas, 2004; Kamakura, Mittal, de Rose, & Mazzon, 2002) accounted for.

Pairwise analyses of profit-chain variables

While sequentially linking resource inputs through to customer profitability has intuitive appeal in that it ties together resource investments, customer satisfaction, customer loyalty, and profitability into a single framework, more common in practice is a focus on pairs of variables (in isolation). For example, an analyst may be interested in assessing, for a given firm, the strength of the relationship between customer satisfaction and customer loyalty, with an eye towards supporting future investments in customer satisfaction initiatives aimed at building customer loyalty. A sample of customers is drawn, a measure of customer loyalty (attitudinal or behavioral) is defined and data are compiled, customer satisfaction is taken from a recent survey, and the two variables are related. A visual representation such as a scatter plot is prepared or a quantitative measure such as correlation is computed.

Rather than providing support for the existence of a profit chain-of-effects framework, and the investments in customer satisfaction and customer loyalty programs that rely on it, simple pairwise analyses of profit-chain variables almost always provide results that raise doubt about its underlying assumptions. Three examples follow.

Example 1 – Customer loyalty and customer profitability. Investments made in customer loyalty initiatives are largely justified by an assumed positive influence on profitability. The empirical results of Reinartz and Kumar (2002), however, challenge the assumption that higher loyalty is associated with increased profits. They examine the dynamics of customer loyalty using four customer databases from different industries: a high-technology corporate service provider, a large US mail-order house, a French retail food business, and a German direct brokerage house. Collectively they compare the behavior, revenue, and profitability of over 16,000 individual and corporate customers over a four-year period. For the four companies studied, they find a correlation coefficient between customer longevity (their measure of loyalty) and profits of 0.45 for the grocery retailer, 0.30 for the corporate service provider, 0.29 for the direct brokerage firm, and just 0.20 for the mail-order company. They interpret these results as providing evidence that the customer loyalty–customer profitability link is weak at best: "What we've found is that the relationship between loyalty and profitability is much weaker, and subtler, than the proponents of loyalty programs claim."

Example 2 – Resource inputs and customer profitability. Firms invest resources in a customer relationship with the objective of earning a return on that investment. Consistent with this goal, Shapiro, Rangan, Moriarty, and Ross (1987) develop the price versus cost-to-serve (which includes pre-sale, order-related, distribution, and post-sale service costs) framework, which links vendor investments to the returns from each customer relationship. This relationship, however, is not a simple one; efforts to find a strong correlation between vendor investments in a relationship (as measured by cost-to-serve) and returns (i.e. price paid by the customer) typically fail. Shapiro, Rangan, Moriarty, and Ross (1987) interpret this as evidence that "high income does not necessarily mean high cost-to-serve." And nor does low income necessarily mean low cost-to-serve.

Example 3 – Customer satisfaction and customer loyalty. A basic operating assumption that firms use to justify investments in customer satisfaction programs is their assumed strong linkage with customer loyalty; more satisfied customers should be more loyal. However, when firms seek to relate satisfaction and loyalty by customer using a linear model such as correlation analysis, they often fail to find a clear relationship. The lack of a clear, positive relationship between customer satisfaction and customer loyalty, regardless of what measures are used, is viewed as disturbing and suggestive that the firm's customer satisfaction programs are not working as planned.

The lack of a clear, universal relationship is consistent with data compiled by Jones and Sasser (1995), who found high variance in the customer satisfaction–customer loyalty relationship across five industries: local telephone, airlines, hospitals, personal computers, and automobiles. It is also consistent with the field interviews summarized in Bowman and Narayandas (2004), who report managers questioning the customer satisfaction–customer loyalty link with statements such as, "We have numerous examples where satisfaction scores are similar, but customer loyalty and customer profitability are quite different."

In summary, it is more common to examine pairs of variables from a profit chain-of-effects model rather than the profit chain in its entirety. A scatter plot or correlation analysis of a pair of profit-chain variables (e.g. satisfaction and loyalty) almost always indicates a weak correlation. The weak correlation is typically interpreted as suggesting a crisis whereby the implied profit chain-of-effects or cascading model is not supported.

Why simple approaches can fail

Regardless of the methodology used, scatter plot or correlation, each of the above examples misinterprets the lack of a positive, linear relationship between two chain-of-effects variables to mean lack of association. However, a lack of correlation does not necessarily mean lack of association.

There are a number of reasons why simple approaches such as a correlation analysis can fail to find an association. First, a correlation or related analysis assumes a linear relationship between the two variables of interest. An assumption of linearity constrains the relationship such that a one unit change in the antecedent variable (e.g. satisfaction) leads to the same change in the criterion variable (e.g. loyalty) regardless of where on the scale the firm is currently operating. In reality, the relationship between pairs of variables from profit chain-of-effects models such as satisfaction and loyalty is more often nonlinear. Agustin and Singh (2005) find this in their study of antecedents of customer loyalty intentions in two service industries, retail clothing purchases and non-business airline travel. Customer satisfaction has a decreasing incremental (i.e. nonlinear) effect on loyalty intentions in their retail clothing industry sample. In both samples, trust in the service provider has an increasing incremental (increasing returns) effect on loyalty intentions.

Turning to the relationship between attribute performance and customer satisfaction, analysts often engage in a search for attributes
where the relationship exhibits increasing returns; changes in performance at the upper end of the performance scale are more consequential
than the same change at the lower end. These are often called "surprise"
or "delight" attributes, and depict the underlying relationship implied
when analysts stress the importance of being rated in the "top box"
on a Likert scale performance assessment.

Second, links can be asymmetric. That is, the impact of a change
of one unit for an antecedent variable (e.g. the impact of customer
satisfaction on customer loyalty) can vary depending on whether the
change is an increase or decrease, and/or depending on whether the
vendor firm currently operates above or below a specific scale point
or reference point. Reference points arise when customers evaluate
performance on the basis of relative performance and not absolute
performance (Mittal, Ross, & Baldasare, 1998).

In some instances, an S-shaped relationship that captures both asymmetry and decreasing returns is proposed for the impact of attribute
performance on customer satisfaction. Decreasing returns imply that
the impact of changes in attribute performance on customer satisfaction
is more consequential at the middle of the scale than at the extremes.
And, because the impact of a change in performance at the lower end
of the performance scale is thought to be more consequential than the
same change at the upper end of the performance scale, an asymmetry
exists. Anderson and Mittal (2000) define attributes that exhibit this
relationship as "satisfaction maintaining." In competitive industries,
these attributes are the "table stakes" or the minimum a firm needs to
provide to be even considered as a viable option by customers.

Third, simple approaches constrain the relationship to be the same
for all contexts. Jones and Sasser (1995) find that the customer
satisfaction–customer loyalty relationship varies by industry, possibly because of differences in competitive environment. Bowman and
Narayandas (2001, 2004) find that customer-specific factors such as
the competitive context at a given customer account can occasion differential responsiveness. Accounting for heterogeneity in customer relationships and customer response to a vendor's strategies and tactics is
a key theme of much recent research in management science.

Fourth, for variables conceptualized as having multiple antecedents,
interactions involving them may exist. For example, if product/service

value is influenced largely by, say, two factors, reliability and responsiveness, each has a main effect on product/service value and there can also be a synergistic effect beyond that that needs to be explained to fully understand these variables' full impact.

In summary, simple approaches based on scatter plots or correlation analyses can lead to an erroneous conclusion that the profit chain does not hold in practice. However, a lack of correlation does not necessarily mean a lack of association.

An example from business marketing

Virtually all published chain-link or cascading models linking vendor resource inputs with customer-level profits share roots in Heskett, *et al.*'s (1994) Service–Profit Chain (SPC). Examples include its derivatives (e.g. Kamakura, Mittal, de Rose, & Mazzon, 2002; Loveman, 1998; Soteriou & Zenios, 1999), the return-on-quality (ROQ) framework (Rust, Zahorik, & Keiningham, 1995), and the general satisfaction–profit chain (Anderson & Mittal, 2000). Further, with one exception (Bowman & Narayandas, 2004), all are developed in a consumer setting.

In many ways, business markets may be more conducive than consumer markets to the customer-level strategies and tactics that follow from profit-chain frameworks. Complex decision-making units and decision-making processes necessitate customer-level plans. Customers typically choose a portfolio of vendors in a planned, strategic manner whereas, in consumer markets, brand-switching can often be opportunistic or for reasons related to variety-seeking behavior. In business markets, resources are typically allocated at the level of an individual customer (versus a market). The distribution of business across customers is highly skewed; over 90% of a vendor's volume can come from less than 10% of its customers. Consider a firm like paper products manufacturer Kimberly-Clark. In their diapers business, demand from a heavy user can be a few times that of a light user. But in their industrial markets, demand from a heavy user is many, many multiples of that of a light user. Table 11.1 summarizes these and many of the other key differences between business and consumer markets that support applying profit-chain frameworks to best understand the drivers of profitable growth in business markets.

Table 11.1. *Typology of marketing in business-to-business and business-to-consumer contexts*

Business-to-business (B2B)	Business-to-consumer (B2C)
1. Complex DMU/DMP	1. Simple DMU/DMP; heuristics
2. Choosing a portfolio of suppliers: strategic decision	2. Brand-switching: unplanned, tactical, opportunistic, variety
3. Disciplined customer selection: customer-level resource allocation	3. Mass market; transactions; segment level resource allocation
4. Direct sales	4. Sales support
5. 10/90 rule	5. More even distribution
6. Effort planned and targeted at customer level	6. Mass-market planning; mass-market communication
7. Potential for collaboration and opportunism	7. Arms-length relationships
8. Price negotiations	8. Posted prices
9. Product/service bundle	9. Product
10. Intuition	10. Information
11. Customer profitability	11. Market share

Figure 11.1, taken from Bowman and Narayandas (2004), depicts the service–profit chain for business markets. Customer management effort (customer-specific and segment- or market-level) is manifested in the form of a product/solution offering. Customers assess vendor performance on both tangible (such as product quality) and intangible (such as trust in the vendor's account management team) attributes. This assessment is made by multiple members who constitute the customer's purchase decision-making unit. The various attribute-level performance assessments then drive overall satisfaction with the vendor's performance which is assessed, again, by each member of the customer's purchase decision-making unit. Key observable outputs include sales volume and customer loyalty measures such as share of customer wallet (SCW). These are inputs to customer-level profitability – total contribution and contribution margin. Countering these positive effects are the costs associated with the customer management effort. This is important to consider because a cost-benefit analysis is what enables vendor firms to assess the return to their customer management

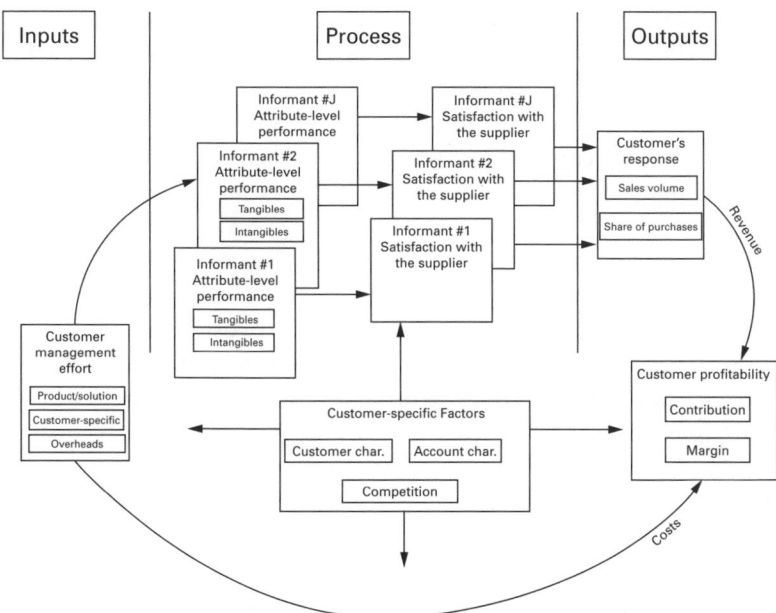

Figure 11.1. The service–profit chain for business markets.

effort. Finally, each linkage can be affected by customer-specific factors: customer characteristics, account-specific factors, and the competitive context at a given account.

Data

Our example uses the data from Bowman and Narayandas (2004). The customer firms are more than 300 industrial customers of firms that provide metal processing, fabrication, and distribution services. The customer firms are in industries that include manufacturing, construction, transportation, aerospace, and electrical. As a group, these customers use over sixty different vendors. A sponsoring vendor firm provided financial data and details of its efforts at the customer account level, enabling us to link vendor resource commitments to vendor performance and customer profitability.

A market research firm administered by telephone, to each customer in the sample, a questionnaire. Interviewers introduced themselves as calling to solicit participation in a study of processed metal vendors.

The sponsoring firm was not identified. The survey comprised three sections. The first recorded the identity of and purchasing data for the respondent's top two metal products vendors. The second section collected vendor performance ratings at the level of each performance attribute and overall vendor performance. The third section collected demographic information on the respondent firms.

Descriptive analyses

The data show a general pattern of satisfied customers: fully 90% report some degree of satisfaction with their primary vendor and 80% with their secondary vendor whereas 6% of respondents reported being dissatisfied with their primary vendor and 7% with their secondary vendor. While these statistics indicating satisfaction might appear to be high at first sight, they are in line with anecdotal evidence we have observed across a variety of mature, commoditized industrial product categories.

On average, the primary vendor received 79% of a customer's business, and the secondary vendor 20%, with 34% of customers reporting using only a single (primary) vendor. When more than one vendor is used, consistent with recent studies of industrial purchasing (e.g. Bowman, Farley, & Schmittlein, 2000) the top two vendors are extremely important. Ninety-nine percent of firms in the sample allocated 75% or more of their business to their top two vendors. In his study of purchasing behavior for industrial components, Wind (1970) defined industrial source loyalty as 50% or more of purchases from a primary vendor. Eighty-four percent of the primary vendors in our data received more than 50% of a buyer's business. Six percent of firms in our sample reported the same share of purchases from their primary and secondary vendors. Sales to individual customers range from less than $1,000 to nearly $13 million. The data are highly skewed: 20% of customers provide 64%, the largest 5% of customers 27%, of the total sales revenue.

Operating profit varied greatly across customers, ranging from, on average, $56,000 for a given customer to nearly $800,000 from the firm's most profitable relationship. Interestingly, 31% of the relationships recorded a negative operating profit, although more than 62% of those losses were less than $10,000, and 90% less than $55,000. Mulhern (1999), in his study of physician profitability for a major

Table 11.2. *Correlations of SPC variables*

	Pearson correlations					Rank correlations				
	1	2	3	4	5	1	2	3	4	5
1 Satisfaction	1					1				
2 Share of customer wallet (%)	.28	1				.33	1			
3 Sales ($)	−.03	.14	1			−.07	.17	1		
4 Operating profit ($)	−.01	.09	.68	1		.07	.21	.51	1	
5 Operating margin (%)	.09	.09	.03	.31	1	.10	.09	.09	.73	1

Significant correlations ($p < .05$) in bold

pharmaceutical manufacturer, also reports "customers" with negative profits albeit with lower incidence than in our data. Niraj, Gupta, and Narasimhan (2001) report that 32% of a regional supermarket grocery products distributor's customers are unprofitable.

We next examined the correlations of the important SPC variables (Table 11.2). The results are similar if the sample is restricted to only customers with a positive operating profit, or to customers who provide more than 50% of the business to the focal vendor, or if we examine nonlinear (that is, take the log) relationships. We find a positive correlation between satisfaction and share of customer wallet; in general, higher satisfaction is associated with higher retention. Interestingly, we do not find a significant correlation between satisfaction and operating margin or between share of customer wallet and operating margin. Although satisfaction and retention are hypothesized to be antecedents of customer profitability, no simple relationship exists, as one can see from the correlations.

Table 11.3 presents summary descriptive statistics for those relationships for which financial data were available. Descriptive statistics are provided for sales revenue, operating profit, operating margin, concentration of purchases with the top two vendors, share of purchases with the largest alternative vendor, and overall satisfaction with the largest alternative vendor. Again, to protect confidentiality, contribution margin is not disclosed.

The first row-block compares descriptive statistics for customers grouped into three sales revenue groups. Moderately sized accounts, defined for exposition as those with purchases of between $0.5 million

Table 11.3. Descriptive statistics by respondent categories given availability of financial data

	Proportion of the sample (%)	Overall satisfaction	Share of customer purchases (%)	Sales revenue ($m)	Operating profit ($k)	Operating margin (%)
		Mean : Median	Mean : Median	Mean : Median	Mean : Median	Mean : Median
Sales revenue (n=168)						
>$2 million	17	4.41 : 5	62 : 65	4.1 : 3.9	236 : 205	5.9 : 5.1
$0.5–1.999 million	33	4.18 : 4.4	60 : 55	1.1 : 1.1	37 : 31	3.3 : 3.6
$0–499k	50	4.42 : 5	56 : 68	0.2 : 0.1	8 : 1	4.4 : 3.5
Operating profit (n=168)						
>51k	29	4.38 : 5	59 : 50	2.7 : 2.1	204 : 143	8.7 : 8.6
$0–50k	41	4.42 : 5	60 : 70	0.5 : 0.4	16 : 10	8.3 : 5.1
<0	30	4.19 : 4	56 : 60	0.7 : 0.2	−26 : −5	−5.2 : −3.4
Operating margin (n=168)						
>5%	42	4.35 : 5	53 : 50	1.3 : 0.5	125 : 49	12.2 : 9.7
0–5%	27	4.48 : 5	69 : 75	1.6 : 1.0	43 : 18	2.6 : 3.0
<0%	30	4.19 : 4	56 : 60	0.7 : 0.2	−27 : −5	−5.0 : −3.3
Share of purchases from the top two vendors (n=113)						
>95%	58	4.41 : 4.8	67 : 80	1.3 : 0.6	66 : 4	3.2 : 3.5
86–95%	22	4.33 : 4.6	58 : 65	0.8 : 0.4	20 : 8	3.7 : 4.4
0–85%	19	3.90 : 4	33 : 30	1.1 : 0.7	36 : 5	3.3 : 1.3
Share of purchases from the largest alternative vendor (n=113)						
>25%	48	4.09 : 4	36 : 40	0.9 : 0.4	31 : 2	2.3 : 2.0
11–25%	25	4.38 : 4.8	64 : 73	1.1 : 0.5	65 : 15	4.0 : 2.8
1–10%	27	4.55 : 4	92 : 90	1.4 : 0.8	69 : 8	4.6 : 3.5
Overall satisfaction with the largest alternative vendor						
5	42	4.42 : 5	45 : 50	0.9 : 0.5	40 : 1	3.2 : 2.8
4	39	4.41 : 4.5	73 : 80	1.1 : 0.4	34 : 4	2.5 : 2.4
1, 2, 3	19	3.89 : 4	61 : 50	1.6 : 0.9	89 : 38	5.3 : 4.4

and $2 million, seem to be the most competitive. On average, these customers report lower overall satisfaction with vendors and operating margins are lower. The second and third row-blocks report descriptive statistics for operating profit and operating margin, respectively. Aggressive pricing is not necessarily associated with higher satisfaction; that customers, on average, report significantly lower satisfaction when operating profit is negative (4.2) versus positive (4.4) demonstrates the importance of non-price factors on overall satisfaction. Among relationships with positive operating profit, overall satisfaction is, on average, lower for more profitable relationships.

On average, customers who concentrate their business with one or two top vendors report higher overall satisfaction with those vendors (4.4) than customers who spread their business around (3.9). Either the presence of viable alternative vendors could make customers more demanding or dissatisfaction with the top two vendors prompts customers to spread their purchases across more vendors.

The performance of the closest alternative vendor is important. The presence of an alternative vendor that receives a large share of a customer's purchases, defined for exposition as greater than 25% (fifth row-block), is associated with lower customer satisfaction and lower profitability (operating margin). A neutral or dissatisfied rating for the closest alternative vendor is, on average, associated with a higher operating margin. It is also associated with lower overall satisfaction for the focal vendor, suggesting that low satisfaction ratings might be a response style or indicative of a more demanding customer. We do not find such an association for satisfaction ratings above neutral.

High customer satisfaction should lead to current customers' increased loyalty. We find a significant positive correlation for overall satisfaction and share of customer wallet ($\rho = 0.27$; $p < .01$). Interestingly, 15% of customers report higher overall satisfaction with their secondary than with their primary vendors. We do not find in these instances, compared with the rest of the sample, significant differences in share of purchases, sales, and operating profit for the primary vendor, although the secondary vendor, on average, fares better, receiving a larger share of purchases ($t = 2.25$; $p < .05$). We find as expected a positive, although not significant, correlation for overall satisfaction and operating margin ($\rho = 0.09$; $p < .23$). Factors other than overall satisfaction contribute to higher margins.

Table 11.4. *Analysis using the price versus cost-to-serve matrix*

Price	Cost-to-serve	Supplier rank	Share of customer wallet (SCW)	Overall satisf.	Satisf. with competition	Operating margin	Total sales ($k)	Share costs	Competitor share costs
Low	Low	1.12	0.60	4.23	4.23	−0.020	749.1	4.15	3.44
Low	High	1.17	0.61	4.34	4.21	−0.028	1,241.0	3.67	3.52
High	Low	*1.34*	*0.43*	4.38	*4.12*	*0.097*	*765.6*[a]	*3.85*	3.72
High	High	1.12	0.68	4.39	4.06	0.101	1,975.0	3.93	3.72

Notes:

1 Splitting the total sample on each variable at the median value created the subsamples.

2 For each variable of interest we first conducted an ANOVA analysis and in all cases found that some subsample means were significantly different from one another. Next, given that the distributions of the subsample populations were normal and the variances not different, we conducted the Tukey multiple comparison test to identify the pairs that were significantly different from one another. For ease of analysis and readability, we report in italics means that are significantly different from the corresponding mean of the Low-Low subsample. Means that are emboldened and italicized are significantly different from both the Low-Low and Low-High subsamples. All tests were at the 5% level.

[a] Significantly less than the low-price, high cost-to-serve subsample mean.

Finally, we examine descriptive statistics that relate attribute-level performance scores and share of customer wallet. Although in general we find a positive correlation between attribute performance scores and share of customer wallet, case-by-case examination reveals exceptions.

Descriptive analysis – price versus cost-to-serve

Shapiro, Rangan, Moriarty, and Ross (1987), Rangan, Moriarty, Gordon, and Swartz (1992), and others conceptualize industrial buying behavior segmentation in mature markets as based on price and cost-to-serve. This framework permits the linking of a vendor's customer management effort (value creation) with ability to extract customer value (prices).[1]

To utilize the framework with our data, we first classified each customer's price (high versus low) and cost-to-serve (high versus low) using median splits. We compared the means across the resulting four groups on customer profitability, size, share of wallet, satisfaction with vendor performance, satisfaction with competitor performance, and propensity to share costs. The results are provided in Table 11.4.

A number of interesting conclusions can be drawn from this analysis. Comparing high- versus low-price customers, we find, as expected, high-price customers to be more profitable. These customers are also more satisfied with their primary vendor's and less satisfied with other vendors' performance than low-price customers. Customers are willing to pay a higher price with increasing differences in their satisfaction

---

[1] Rangan, Moriarty, Gordon, and Swartz (1992) point out that it would be preferable to use actual price and cost information in this analysis. But, recognizing the difficulty of obtaining actual pricing and cost-to-serve data, they recommend the use of perceptual data. We were able to use actual data. For each customer, we observed sales and costs aggregated over a twelve-month observation period. Given the product mix, volume, and revenues, we can observe operating margin, which can then be expressed as:

$$\text{OpMargin} = \frac{(\text{Sales} - \text{OpCosts})}{\text{Sales}} = \frac{(\text{Price} - \text{UnitOpCosts})(\text{Volume})}{(\text{Price})(\text{Volume})}$$

$$= 1 - \frac{\text{UnitOpCosts}}{\text{Price}}$$

We have no evidence to suggest that unit operating costs for similar products should vary across customers for a given vendor. Hence, controlling for vendor (which we do), price is inversely proportional to operating margins.

between the primary and secondary vendors. Such customers also might be less expensive to serve, leading to higher profits for the primary vendor.

Comparing high versus low cost-to-serve customers, we find high cost-to-serve customers to be larger. Moving to differences across quadrants, we find secondary vendors more likely to be present in the high-price, low cost-to-serve quadrant, a result consistent with Rangan, Moriarty, Gordon, and Swartz (1992), who find that customers are likely to use secondary vendors as insurance and are, therefore, less price-sensitive given the significantly smaller volume of business transacted.

We also find that customers in the low-price, low cost-to-serve quadrant, although typically not the largest ones, are most likely to share costs. They are also the most difficult to satisfy, are equally satisfied with their other vendors' performances, and are unprofitable. It is possible that these customers share costs with vendors and jointly work with them to reduce the overall procurement costs. But rather than mutually share the gains from cost reductions, it appears that these customers might squeeze margins beyond the cost reductions that accrue to the vendors.

Finally, customers in the low-price, high cost-to-serve quadrant, being larger, are able to use their buying power to extract greater concessions from vendors. These are the focal vendor's most unprofitable customers. Customers in the high-price, high cost-to-serve quadrant are the most interesting, being not only the largest, but also more likely to share costs, buy most of their total requirements from their primary vendor, and be most satisfied with vendor performance. Most important, these are the focal vendor's most profitable customers. They are likely to be interested in making their relationships mutually beneficial and to view their vendors not just as targets of cost reduction, but also as a source of added value (Kalwani & Narayandas, 1995).

In summary, these descriptive results support our basic thesis that the impact of satisfaction and customer loyalty on customer profitability is moderated by situation-specific factors encountered by the vendor.

Chain-link model of customer profitability

In Bowman and Narayandas (2004), we present a chain-link model of customer profitability using these data. The results from this study may be summarized as follows. Strong nonlinear and asymmetric effects exist in each link of the profit chain. In particular, we find decreasing returns for (a) the effect of customer management effort on firm product/service performance, and (b) customer loyalty (share of customer wallet) on customer margin. We find increasing returns or a "delight" effect for the impact of customer satisfaction on customer loyalty (SCW). We also find that competition acts as a benchmark in the case of this firm, when its customers evaluate its attribute-level importance.

Our results demonstrate the importance of accounting for customer-specific effects. We find differential responsiveness occasioned by (a) competitor factors (e.g. competitor performance), (b) customer factors (e.g. firm size), (c) company factors (e.g. account team tenure), and (d) relationship factors (e.g. sharing information). Readers are referred to the paper for more complete discussion of the results.

Conclusion

Understanding factors that influence individual customer sales and profitability (or margin) can help managers more effectively allocate marketing effort across customers and better target high-potential customers. No longer is it enough to allocate effort at market level and manage market-level response. The time has come for business marketers to focus more on managing individual customers for profits.

Customer profitability is particularly important in business markets, where, compared to say consumer packaged goods contexts, vendors tend to allocate a greater proportion of their marketing resources at the level of the individual customer. Industrial marketers' emphasis on customer profitability is further driven by (1) the difficulty of obtaining timely and accurate information on share, (2) the presence of very large customers, and (3) an often-skewed distribution of business across customers (see, for example, Shapiro, Rangan, Moriarty, & Ross, 1987). Yet customer profitability as it links to customer management effort has been little studied, especially outside the domain of consumer services (see, for example, Rust, Zahorik, & Keiningham, 1995), in an effort to understand how it is linked to a vendor's customer management efforts.

In this chapter, we have discussed how to link returns to customer management effort reflected in customer profitability, specifically in industrial markets. Empirical research to date has emphasized the study of antecedents of customer profitability. Examples from industrial marketing contexts include sales revenue (e.g. Ittner and Larcker, 1998), share of purchases from a primary supplier (e.g. Wind, 1970), strength of preference for a vendor (e.g. Gensch, 1984), and a plethora of studies of customer satisfaction. It is not clear how these metrics relate to customer profitability since the few studies that link customer attitude (or behavior) to profitability are mostly aggregate firm-level investigations in which the objective is to test for a positive relationship between, say, aggregate customer satisfaction and firm profitability, not to understand the process by which a firm can increase profitability through satisfaction at the individual customer level. Prior efforts to link marketing actions with profitability, particularly in industrial contexts, have also typically been at the firm level (e.g. PIMS studies; Kalwani & Narayandas, 1995).

Research to date set in industrial marketing contexts has largely examined (a) antecedents of customer profitability, or (b) customer profitability indirectly. Wind (1970) (share of purchases), Gensch (1984) (strength of preference), Ittner and Larcker (1998) (sales revenue), and Bowman, Farley, and Schmittlein (2000) (supplier rank) are examples of the former; Rangan, Moriarty, Gordon, and Swartz (1992) an example of the latter. Rangan, Moriarty, Gordon, and Swartz (1992) use account managers' perceptions to segment a vendor's customers according to the (relative) prices they pay and their (relative) cost-to-serve (Shapiro, Rangan, Moriarty, & Ross, 1987) (which together relate to customer profitability), and include descriptors such as customer characteristics.

In this chapter, we suggest that vendors that attempt to manage individual customers for profit should not fail to focus on a variety of situation-specific (or customer account-specific) factors. We also urge vendors to go beyond just a descriptive tack focusing on the means of these variables, and to study their impact on response coefficients that reflect customer behavior sensitivity to instruments under managerial control. Only then will vendors make appropriate short- and long-term investment decisions in their customer management effort that will lead not only to more effective individual account management but also to improved customer profitability.

References

Agustin, C. & Singh, J. 2005. Curvilinear effects of consumer loyalty determinants in relational exchange. *Journal of Marketing Research*, 42(1): 96–108.

Anderson, E. W. & Mittal, V. 2000. Strengthening the satisfaction profit chain. *Journal of Service Research*, 3(2): 107–120.

Anderson, J. C. & Narus J. A. 2003. Selectively pursuing more of your customer's business. *Sloan Management Review*, 44(3): 4436.

Bowman, D., Farley, J. U., & Schmittlein, D. C. 2000. Cross-national empirical generalization in business services buying behavior. *Journal of International Business Studies*, 31(4): 667–685.

Bowman, D. & Narayandas, D. 2001. Managing customer-initiated contacts with manufacturers: the impact on share of category requirements and word-of-mouth behavior. *Journal of Marketing Research*, 38(3): 281–297.

2004. Linking customer management effort to customer profitability in business markets. *Journal of Marketing Research*, 41(4): 433–447.

Gensch, D. H. 1984. Targeting the switchable industrial customer. *Marketing Science*, 3(1): 41–54.

Heskett, J. L., Jones, T. O., Loveman, G. W., Sasser, E., Jr., & Schlesinger, L. A. 1994. Putting the service profit-chain to work. *Harvard Business Review*, 72(2): 164–174.

Ittner, C. & Larcker, D. F. 1998. Are nonfinancial measures leading indicators of financial performance? An analysis of customer satisfaction. *Journal of Accounting Research*, 36 (Supplement): 1–35.

Jones, T. O. & Sasser, W. E., Jr. 1995. Why satisfied customers defect. *Harvard Business Review*, 73(6): 88–99.

Kalwani, M. U. & Narayandas, D. 1995. Long-term manufacturer–supplier relationships: do they pay off for supplier firms? *Journal of Marketing*, 59(1): 1–16.

Kamakura, W. A., Mittal, V., de Rose, F., & Mazzon, J. A. 2002. Assessing the service–profit chain, *Marketing Science*, 21(3): 294–317.

Libai, B., Narayandas, D., & Humby, C. 2002. Toward an individual customer profitability model. *Journal of Service Research*, 5(1): 69–76.

Loveman, G. W. 1998. Employee satisfaction, customer loyalty, and financial performance: an empirical examination of the service profit chain in retail banking. *Journal of Service Research*, 2(2): 138–144.

Mittal, V., Ross, W. T., & Baldasare, P. M. 1998. The asymmetric impact of negative and positive attribute-level performance on overall satisfaction and repurchase intentions. *Journal of Marketing*, 62(1): 33–47.

Mulhern, F. J. 1999. Customer profitability analysis: measurement, concentration, and research directions. *Journal of Interactive Marketing*, 13(1): 25–40.

Narayandas, D. 1998. Measuring and managing the benefits of customer retention. *Journal of Service Research*, 1(2): 108–128.

Narayandas, D. & Rangan, V. K. 2004. Building and sustaining buyer–seller relationships in mature industrial markets. *Journal of Marketing*, 68(3): 63–77.

Niraj, R., Gupta, M., & Narasimhan, C. 2001. Customer profitability in a supply chain. *Journal of Marketing*, 65(3): 1–16.

Rangan, V. K., Moriarty, R. T., Gordon, S., & Swartz, G. S. 1992. Segmenting customers in mature industrial markets. *Journal of Marketing*, 56(4): 72–82.

Reinartz, W. J. & Kumar, V. 2002. The mismanagement of customer loyalty. *Harvard Business Review*, 80(7): 86–92.

Rust, R. T., Zahorik, A. J., & Keiningham, T. L. 1995. Return on quality (ROQ): making service quality financially accountable. *Journal of Marketing*, 59(2): 58–70.

Shapiro, B. P., Rangan, V. K., Moriarty, R., Jr., & Ross, E. B. 1987. Manage customers for profits (not just sales). *Harvard Business Review*, September–October, Reprint 87513.

Soteriou, A. & Zenios, S. A. 1999. Operations, quality, and profitability in the provision of banking services. *Management Science*, 45(9): 1221–1238.

Wind, Y. 1970 Industrial source loyalty. *Journal of Marketing Research*, 7(4): 450–457.

12 | Harnessing knowledge resources for increasing returns: scalable structuration at Infosys Technologies

RAGHU GARUD, ARUN
KUMARASWAMY, AND VALLABH
SAMBAMURTHY

P RACTITIONERS and researchers increasingly view knowledge as being a strategic resource (Winter, 1987). With rapid advances being made in information-based technologies, we are witnessing nothing short of another industrial revolution – one in which artisans are "using their heads and not their hands" (*Fortune*, 1991). Echoing the sentiments of a growing number of scholars and practitioners, an article in *Business Week* (1992) suggested "competitive advantage no longer belongs to the biggest or those blessed with abundant natural resources or the most capital. In the global economy, knowledge is king."

Although knowledge is now gaining the recognition that it rightfully deserves, it has always played a key role in the functioning of modern firms. Penrose's (1995) work is illustrative in this regard. She pointed out that a firm is a bundle of resources possessing only an unrealized potential to yield different services. Eventually, it is the firm's managerial capacity to identify and realize productive services from these resources that yields competitive advantage.

Since Penrose's time, a key shift has occurred in the nature of resources that firms harness. Specifically, a firm's productive resources are no longer inert but, instead, infused with knowledge. This shift has profound implications for processes associated with knowledge production and use. Arthur (1991), for instance, pointed out that knowledge-infused resources have properties that are different from traditional resources such as land, labor, and financial capital. Rather than the diminishing returns that can set in with the use of such traditional resources, knowledge-infused resources have the potential to yield increasing returns. That is, returns from knowledge-infused resources can increase with use, not at a diminishing rate, but at an increasing rate.

It is possible to realize increasing returns from knowledge-infused resources for several reasons. One reason is that the very application of existing knowledge produces new knowledge. Not only do knowledge workers learn to accomplish tasks better (Argote, 1999; Arrow, 1962; Dutton and Thomas, 1985), but they also gain new insights as they deploy existing knowledge (Giddens, 1986; Schon, 1983; Zuboff, 1984). This new knowledge can be reused over time, not only by the creator, but also by others (Alavi & Leidner, 2001). Moreover, such knowledge can be combined with a firm's accumulated knowledge to yield deeper insights and better ways to function.

The creation of knowledge during the very deployment of knowledge, to us, represents *scalable structuration*. Structuration captures the duality between structure and action (Barley, 1986; Giddens, 1986; Orlikowski, 1992). In the context of knowledge, structures that emerge are both the medium and the outcome of action. Specifically, the new knowledge that emerges because of the deployment of existing knowledge has the potential to change the firm's existing knowledge. It does so not just in a cumulative manner, but also in a manner that is transformative. Old and new knowledge vectors combine to transform the frameworks within which knowledge is created and deployed (Garud & Nayyar, 1994; Kogut & Zander, 1992).

Scalability implies an ability to use the very resources that generate services in the present as platforms for future growth. Using terminology offered by March (1991), scalability represents structures and processes wherein exploration occurs as a byproduct of exploitation. Thereby, it reduces considerably the costs that a firm incurs in reconciling once separated forces for exploration with exploitation (Christensen & Raynor, 2003; Thompson, 1967). Indeed, in dynamic environments, the flexibility, speed, and scope of operations required of a firm can be accomplished only if a balance can be generated between exploration and exploitation (Brown & Eisenhardt, 1998; March, 1991; Tushman, Smith, Wood, Westerman, & O'Reilly, 2004).

How might a firm induce scalable structuration for sustained growth? The processes a firm employs to harness inert resources are clearly inadequate to induce scalable structuration. A different set of organizational structures, systems, and processes is required (Galbraith

& Kazanjian, 1986). Scalable structuration requires techniques to explore even as one exploits; the incentives and culture to contribute emerging knowledge to a larger collective through codification, sharing, and reuse; and the wherewithal to leverage existing knowledge to create a new future. These are the critical elements that must be addressed to design organizations for emergence (Drazin & Sandelands, 1992).

This chapter attempts to identify mechanisms that firms might employ to induce scalable structuration. It begins with a summary of the literature on resources and capabilities. This sets the stage for developing an understanding of the nature of change that post-modern corporations confront. We then highlight possibilities for structuration to occur, first at the point of contact where knowledge resources are deployed, and then at other levels of the firm. To understand what it means to induce scalable structuration, we examine practices followed by one exemplary firm, Infosys Technologies.

Harnessing knowledge resources

Organizing, at its core, is a knowledge-generating and knowledge-utilizing activity. March and Simon (1958) argued many years ago that organizations are inherently information-processing entities consisting of embedded routines through which information is stored and enacted. Conceptualized this way, organizing involves all of a firm's systems and structures – in other words, its organizational capabilities.

The importance of organizational capabilities begs the question as to how they emerge in the first place. Penrose's work is very useful in this regard. She pointed out that a firm is "a collection of productive resources the disposal of which between different uses and over time is determined by administrative decision" (Penrose, 1995: 24). In other words, resources such as plant, equipment, land, and natural resources by themselves are inert, possessing only an unrealized potential to yield different services. Critical to determining the productive uses to which resources can be deployed is a firm's managerial capacity. This managerial capacity involves knowledge not only of the resources themselves, but of the external opportunities they can service.

Penrose suggested that a firm's managerial capacity set a limit to its growth in any given period. However, this capacity itself changes over time. As managerial capacity is deployed, it expands through experience, and as this happens, "valuable productive services from a firm's resources will also tend to change" (Penrose, 1995: 76). Based on these observations, she concluded, "there is a close connection between the type of knowledge possessed by the personnel of the firm and the services obtainable from its material resources" (1995: 76).

This early work spawned research in the resource-based-view tradition (Mahoney & Pandian, 1992; Wernerfelt, 1984). Penrose's description of how managerial capacity emerged through interactions with other resources set the stage for thinking of firms as unique bundles of resources and distinguishing between resource "stocks" and "flows" (Dierickx & Cool, 1989). Subsequent work (e.g. Barney, 1991; Collis & Montgomery, 1997; Petaraf, 1993) has explored what characteristics made resources "valuable" and how firms may leverage these valuable resources to create and sustain competitive advantage.

These developments served as the precursor to research on firm capabilities (cf. Foss and Robertson, 2000). For instance, Metcalfe and James (2000: 41) suggested that capabilities are "Penrosian bundles of productive services, derived from resources, and articulated by routines in specific organizational contexts." The concept of routines is well established in the literature on evolutionary organizational change (cf. Dosi & Marengo, 1994; Nelson & Winter, 1982). Routines are decision rules that provide a template or the instructions for action according to prevailing circumstances. If organizational memory resides in a set of stored action programs, then organizational learning is the continual evolution of these programs in response to environmental constraints and conditions. Scholars have thus been concerned with developing a grammar to describe the nature of organizational routines (e.g. Feldman & Pentland, 2003), understanding the interdependence of routines in complex task situations (e.g. Cohen & Bacdayan, 1994), and adapting routines to environmental variation and change (e.g. Barley, 1986; Levinthal, 1997).

As Metcalfe and James (2000: 45) highlighted, it is important for us to distinguish between "those capabilities which generate the current rents and those which develop that rent-earning capacity." Using the terminology offered by March (1991), one set represents exploitation of the past whereas the other represents an exploration of future possibilities. March pointed out that processes that underlie exploitation are inimical to processes that are required for exploration. Moreover, a firm that is organized to exploit may become trapped by the very resources and capabilities that it is harnessing. That is, the firm's core capabilities could become core rigidities (Leonard-Barton, 1992) or competency traps (Levitt & March, 1988).

Recent work has attempted to address this tension. For instance, Lei, Hitt, and Bettis (1996) suggested that firms operating in turbulent environments develop dynamic core competences based on meta-learning. Similarly, Teece, Pisano, and Shuen (1997: 270) offered the notion of dynamic capabilities as "the subset of the competencies/capabilities which allow the firm to create new products and processes, and respond to changing market circumstances." In other words, dynamic capabilities and dynamic core competences are concerned with exploration and are very different from the Nelson and Winter (1982) characterization of routines as means for effective exploitation. Subsequently, Eisenhardt and Martin (2000) broadened the concept of dynamic capabilities to include any specific process – not just new product or process development – that allows managers to learn and, in the process, redefine their very resource base. They argued that dynamic capabilities are much more than just routines to learn routines, especially in high-velocity environments. More recently, Zollo and Winter (2002) have explored how dynamic capabilities and, in turn, operating routines evolve through experiential learning and the codification of such learning.

Changing nature of resources

Even as our understanding of firm resources and capabilities has grown, the nature and functioning of firms themselves have changed. This change has occurred because of the infusion of information technologies into the work place and the emergence of knowledge workers (Zuboff, 1984). Knowledge workers are no longer passive instruments engaging with inert material artifacts. Instead, these workers and the artifacts they use are infused with knowledge.

As Zuboff (1984) pointed out, these knowledge workers can no longer be just "responsible" to someone else. They also have to be "responsive" to the continual flow of information because they are the first to encounter this information and possess the power to utilize or ignore it. After all, the knowledge worker is the "man on the spot" (Hayek, 1945) with local knowledge of the situation.

This shift to viewing firms as bundles of knowledge-infused resources instead of bundles of inert resources is subtle but significant, because it brings with it several important implications. First, the capacity to identify the useful purposes to which these resources can be deployed is endogenized in the resources themselves. Therefore, the knowledge to harness these resources cannot be centralized in a few managers, but must lie distributed (cf. Grant, 1996). As Tsoukas (1996: 22) pointed out, "The key to achieving coordinated action does not so much depend on those 'higher up' collecting more and more knowledge, as on those 'lower down' finding more and more way of getting connected and interrelating the knowledge each one has." Second, it means that these bundles of knowledge-infused resources can combine and recombine in ways that are self-expanding, either in a revolutionary or evolutionary manner (Garud & Nayyar, 1994; Kogut & Zander, 1992). In other words, the very deployment of knowledge stocks initiates knowledge flows in "continuous wellsprings" (Leonard, 1998).

However, processes required to harness these knowledge-infused resources are different from those used to harness inert resources. Indeed, it would be a mistake to harness knowledge-infused resources with practices that encouraged workers "to do and not to think," a signature of mass production times (Kanigel, 1997). To the extent that cultural mechanisms and the incentives exist for knowledge workers to be responsive – not just responsible – there is every possibility for the post-modern corporation to realize increasing (Arthur, 1991) rather than diminishing returns.

It is useful to pause here to understand the differences between increasing and diminishing returns. Diminishing returns apply when productivity increases with experience but at a diminishing rate (Argote, 1999; Arrow, 1962; Dutton & Thomas, 1985). Such an experience curve effect is typical of mass production environments wherein deskilled workers learn to perform repetitive tasks. The situation is different with knowledge workers. Clearly, knowledge workers also learn by doing. However, the real value lies in their ability meaningfully to frame the ever-increasing volume of information they encounter. In other words, they also learn by reflection (Schon, 1983) to create new knowledge that can yield increasing returns.

To understand this point, it is useful to consider structuration theory as it applies to knowledge (Giddens, 1986). The value of any knowledge is only apparent when it is applied in practice by a knowledge worker who is mindful of local circumstances. In the very act of applying knowledge to a situation at hand, a knowledge worker produces new knowledge. This knowledge is both outcome and medium of action. It is outcome in that the practice-centered application of knowledge results in unique solutions to emergent problems. It is medium in that it adds to the knowledge worker's framework upon which s/he can draw in the future. As Giddens (1986: 144) concluded, "actors are always knowledgeable about the structural framework within which their conduct is carried on, because *they draw upon that framework in producing their action at the same time as they reconstitute it through their action*" (emphasis added).

Such structurational processes may suggest that scaling up is automatic when we are dealing with knowledge-infused resources. To some extent, this is the case because knowledge-infused resources – unlike inert resources – have the potential to be replenished in use. However, structuration at the individual level does not guarantee scalability at the organizational level.

Before scalable structuration can be realized, several challenges have to be met. One challenge stems from the fact that knowledge has a tacit component to it (Nonaka & Takeuchi, 1995; Polanyi, 1967; Spender, 1996; Tsoukas, 1996). Reuse of knowledge even at the individual level can be compromised if the knowledge that is generated remains tacit. Although a knowledge worker may be able to draw upon such tacit knowledge in the future, attrition over time can compromise reuse. Explicating such knowledge can help not only in the preservation of knowledge over time, but also in increasing the range of settings within which it can be deployed.

Although explication can result in increasing knowledge reuse at the individual level, such knowledge may still not be fully scalable to the organizational level. First, all knowledge continues to have a tacit component however much it is explicated (Tsoukas, 1996). If its knowledge workers know more than they can articulate (Polanyi, 1967), how might a firm create collective knowledge? For this to occur, it is important for the firm to foster a community of practice (Brown & Duguid, 1991; Lave & Wenger, 1994; Orr, 1990). Creating and maintaining such a community, however, is not an easy task.

A second, but related, reason for difficulties in scaling up individual knowledge to the organizational level has to do with paradoxes associated with the conversion of private to collective goods (Spender,

1996). Issues of ownership and appropriability come into play. Indeed, firms have to ensure that appropriate cultural mechanisms and incentives are present to encourage their knowledge workers to codify and share knowledge with their colleagues. How these issues are addressed becomes central in determining the extent to which scaleable structuration unfolds.

The need for an overall organizational framework for knowledge accumulation presents yet another challenge for scaling up knowledge from the individual to the organizational level. As Loasby (1999: 91) pointed out, "All knowledge requires a framework. A viable firm provides a particular set of compatible frameworks within which people can pursue their specialism without the need for continual clarification and negotiation, thus reducing the costs of individual transactions." Such an overall framework, or the collective mind (Weick & Roberts, 1993), provides the "knowledge buckets" (Walsh & Ungson, 1991) within which new knowledge can be accumulated.

However, in addressing this challenge, a firm might inadvertently create another one that arises from the potentially recursive nature of knowledge accumulation (Garud & Rappa, 1994). The recognition of new knowledge requires that one has related prior knowledge (Cohen & Levinthal, 1990; Dougherty, 1992). Consequently, new knowledge may accumulate in a progressive, instead of transformative, manner. Worse, accumulated knowledge produced in action may enable synchronically but constrain diachronically (Giddens, 1986). In other words, the accumulation of knowledge within a framework may become path-dependent (David, 1985), thereby rendering a system vulnerable to competency traps (Levitt & March, 1988) and core rigidities (Leonard-Barton, 1992). For scalable structuration to occur, it is important for a firm to avoid such a contingency.

In sum, structurational processes pertaining to the creation and deployment of knowledge resources are not automatically scalable. They have to be induced by the firm. In inducing scalable structuration, however, a firm faces several challenges. First, it needs to deal with resources that are no longer inert, but knowledge-infused. This suggests that organizational processes must be able to harness the knowledge that is produced in use, not only for the individuals involved, but for the organization as a whole. These knowledge-infused resources are socially embedded and the firm has to provide a forum for learning and knowledge creation to occur through interaction. Moreover, a firm's knowledge base has to accumulate in a manner that is not merely

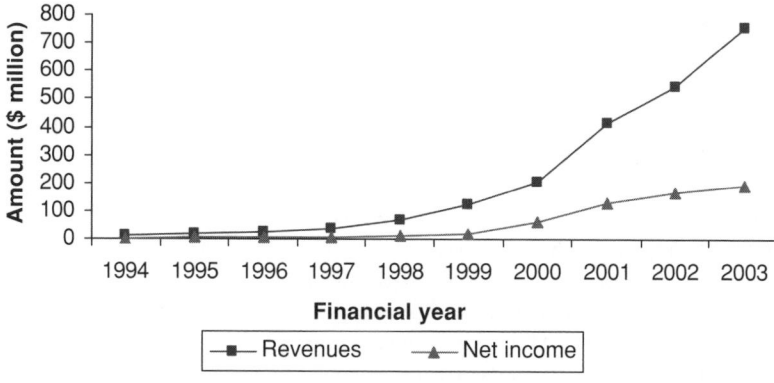

Figure 12.1. Infosys Technologies: growth in revenues and after-tax net income, 1994–2003. (*Source:* Infosys Annual Reports.)

progressive, but also transformative. In the remainder of the chapter, we explore how firms may address these challenges by examining how an exemplary firm has induced scalable structuration.

How Infosys harnesses intellectual capital[1]

Infosys was founded in 1981 when seven professionals collectively invested $250. By fiscal year 2003, Infosys had grown to employ over 15,000 people and had annual revenues of $750 million and net income after taxes of $195 million (Figure 12.1). Growing by over 30% annually, Infosys became a darling of the Indian stock market and was the first Indian company to be listed on the NASDAQ in 1999. Infosys is consistently ranked as the most admired company in India and featured by *Business Week* in its annual Info Tech 100 list. It is also among a select group of companies to have won both the Asian and global Most Admired Knowledge Enterprise (MAKE) awards (see Table 12.1 for chronology).

A key aspect of growth at Infosys is that the company has had to navigate major shifts in the global IT services market without faltering. For instance, at the beginning of the new millennium, the demand for Y2K-related IT services declined considerably. This decline was followed immediately by the boom and bust years in the dotcom and

---

[1] For a detailed thirty-three-page version of the case on Infosys, see Garud, Kumaraswamy, and Malhotra (2003).

Table 12.1. *Infosys Technologies: chronology of events*

1981   • Year of incorporation in India
1987   • Opened first international office in the United States
1992   • IPO in India
       • Launched Bodies of Knowledge (BOK) initiative to codify employees' knowledge
1993   • Listed successfully in India
       • Obtained ISO 9001/TickIT certification
1995   • Set up development centers in several cities across India
1996   • Established e-business practice
       • Set up first European office in Milton Keynes, UK
       • Launched corporate intranet (Sparsh)
1997   • Attained SEI-CMM Level 4 certification
       • Set up office in Toronto, Canada
1998   • Rated first in *Economic Times India*'s "Award for Corporate Excellence"
       • Implemented People Knowledge Map (PKM) on Sparsh
1999   • Crossed $100 million in annual revenues
       • Listed on NASDAQ
       • Attained SEI-CMM Level 5 certification
       • Rated "India's Most Admired Company" by the *Economic Times* survey
       • Opened offices in Germany, Sweden, Belgium, and Australia
       • Established two development centers in the United States
       • Established Domain Competency Group (DCG) and Software Engineering and Technology Labs (SETLabs) for competence building
       • Chartered central KM group and launched company-wide KM program
2000   • Crossed $200 million in annual revenues
       • Became first company to be awarded the "National Award for Excellence in Corporate Governance," conferred by the Government of India
       • Opened offices in France and Hong Kong
       • Set up global development centers in Canada and UK, and third development center in the United States
       • Central knowledge portal (KShop) launched
2001   • Crossed $400 million in annual revenues
       • Ranked "Best Employer of India" by *Business Today*-Hewitt Associates
       • Opened offices in UAE and Argentina
       • Set up new development center in Japan
2002   • Crossed $500 million in annual revenues
       • Opened offices in Netherlands, Singapore, and Switzerland
       • Attained SEI's enhanced CMM Level 5 certification for its onsite and offshore operation
       • Ranked "India's Most Respected Company" in *Business World* survey
2003   • Crossed $750 million in annual revenues
       • Acquired Expert Information Services Pty Limited of Australia
       • Won the global Most Admired Knowledge Enterprise award

telecommunications industry sectors, both major consumers of IT services in the world. A second interesting aspect is the company's reliance on organic growth. Only in 2003 did Infosys make its first and only acquisition, of a small Australian IT services company to consolidate its presence in the region's growing market. This is all the more unique in an era where mergers and acquisitions have driven growth. We explore how Infosys has relied primarily on organic growth to become a global player in the IT services industry, even while navigating such major environmental shifts.

Building human resources

Most firms boast beautiful buildings. This is certainly true of the buildings within the campus-like facilities at Infosys's headquarters near Bangalore, India. But, it would be a mistake to look just at Infosys's well-designed buildings. As one enters the company's campus, it is obvious that Infosys is also continually and systematically building its intellectual capital.

This capacity to build is inherent in its employees who are specifically recruited for what Infosys labels as "learnability." An Infosys word that is both noun and verb, learnability represents the ability of an individual to derive generic conclusions from specific situations and then to apply them to new unstructured situations. Thus, while employees at most firms may be proud of their learning ability, Infoscions are proud of their learnability.

Learnability is much more than routine learning by doing. It includes an ability to reflect in action (Schon, 1983). Infosys's director of HR offered a concrete example of learnability and why it is so important:

The only thing that is constant in our industry is change. If we want our people to cope with change, it does not matter whether they know C++ or Java. More important is whether they are able to figure out how Java is similar to or different from C++ and make appropriate adjustments in applying it. Or, having solved a problem for one customer, can they apply that knowledge in a generic way to some other problem that they face later? This is why we recruit people who possess this generic learning capability that we call learnability.

Besides helping Infoscions cope with ever-changing technologies, learnability also enables them to cope with the rapid career progression that occurs within Infosys. A new recruit within Infosys is expected to ramp up rapidly from mastering technical skills at age 22 to becoming a manager at age 24 and a "manager of managers" by age 26. By 28, this Infoscion may well expect to become a general manager and by age 32, a director of the company. As the associate vice-president of Learning and Development pointed out: "Only those who are able to jump quickly from one paradigm to the next are rewarded. Learnability is key in being able to change and adapt."

Learnability being the key recruitment criterion, new recruits may not possess the technical or domain knowledge required to complete software development projects. Therefore, after recruitment, Infosys invests considerable effort and time in imparting appropriate content knowledge to its new recruits. This training and education is conducted at Infosys's Education and Research (E&R) Center. Initially called the "Training Center," the name of this center was changed to E&R because the term "training" seemed to connote an overly narrow focus on learning by doing instead of encompassing learning by reflection also.

At the E&R Center, new recruits undergo a fourteen-week educational program which not only provides them with relevant technical and managerial skills but also socializes them into the Infosys culture and value system. Formal education for Infoscions, however, does not stop after this intensive training. Every Infoscion is required to undergo at least fifteen days of formal training every year. Such training includes sessions to upgrade technical and managerial skills and to improve appreciation of quality.

A methodology for exercising learnability

Ensuring that employees have the knowledge and capability to reflect and learn is just one aspect of inducing scalable structuration. A firm also needs a methodology that its employees can use to reflect, learn, and create new knowledge. At Infosys, such methods are apparent in an overall framework called the Capability Maturity Model (CMM). Developed by the Software Engineering Institute (SEI) at the Carnegie Mellon University, CMM assesses the maturity level of a software development firm's processes and methodologies on a scale of 1 to 5. Whereas Level 1 represents just an ability to complete a software development project, Level 5 represents an ability to define consistent processes, measure the efficacy of currently defined processes quanti-tatively, question these very processes, and improve them continually (Jalote, 1999: 6–8). It is telling that Infosys is among the few IT firms in the world to be rated by the SEI at CMM Level 5.

Another way to interpret the maturity level of Infosys's processes is to consider them as vesting the firm with dynamic capabilities. Specif-ically, Infosys has used CMM as a framework not just to fine-tune, but also question and change its software development methodologies over time. The head of the Quality Department explained how Infosys's software development methodology has changed since the adoption of CMM:

Way back we implemented long-term software development projects using what is called a "waterfall model" of development. You got all the require-ments and conceived the whole solution upfront and only then did you begin executing the project. We have modified this approach to become more itera-tive. Especially, with the emergence of e-business, both we and the customer are under intense pressure and everyone wants faster time to market. So, after piloting and evaluating this iterative model in several projects, we for-malized it as a completely defined process. But already, we are questioning and modifying this process as we go along.

This philosophy of iterative and incremental action – one that in our literature would be closest to the notion of logical incrementalism (Quinn, 1978) – is not restricted just to software development, but pervades the entire firm. For instance, this methodology is implicit in the measured implementation process prevalent at Infosys. As Infosys's COO noted: "We tend to take small steps in different directions to see what the results will be, before taking big leaps. The philosophy is to take small steps and get feedback for two or three cycles before we scale up."

Remaining connected with the external world

Learnability and CMM are processes at the individual and the orga-nizational levels respectively to ensure that new knowledge is devel-oped even as Infoscions deploy existing knowledge. To ensure that this emerging knowledge base is perpetually connected with the needs of its customers, Infosys insists on establishing close, long-term relationships with its customers. Such close customer relations generate insights on future trends and also enable Infosys to understand customer needs and preferences even as they emerge.

But Infosys does not rely on this mechanism alone to stay abreast of its dynamic environment. For instance, the E&R Center also emphasizes research and piloting of new technologies. Infosys has also created two entities called the Domain Competency Group (DCG) and the Software Engineering and Technologies Labs (SETLabs). The DCG, an internal consulting group, keeps track of customers' industries and also brings together contextual knowledge accumulated by various Infosys units on these industry domains. SETLabs performs applied research in emerging software technologies and development methodologies that Infosys will need to service its clients in the future.

Together, the E&R Center, the DCG, and SETLabs play critical roles not just in sensitizing Infosys to external knowledge, but as crucibles within which external knowledge interacts with internally generated knowledge gleaned from various business units. Thereby, they serve as mechanisms to synthesize or recombine such knowledge that, over time, becomes transformative. The efforts of these units were instrumental in Infosys's smooth transition from Y2K projects to e-business and Internet-related projects at the turn of the century. Indeed, within just one year, Infosys increased its share of revenues from e-business and Internet-related projects from 1.7% in 1Q1999 to nearly 18.1% in 1Q2000.

Infosys has also set up "proximity centers" and development centers in different geographic locations around the world to mine local knowledge and resources. Besides, Infosys periodically undertakes joint projects with start-up firms and makes minority investments in small firms to track or gain access to cutting-edge technologies.

Harnessing distributed knowledge

To be scalable, a firm needs to leverage knowledge that lies distributed among its employees. To accomplish this objective, Infosys has instituted an integrated approach to knowledge management (KM). According to a member of Infosys's KM group: "Our vision is to make every instance of learning within Infosys available to every employee. We want the collective learning of Infosys to back every person wherever they might be located within the company. Our motto is '*Learn once, Use anywhere*'" (emphasis added).

Initially, Infosys created a central KM group to develop an architecture for consistent and integrated deployment throughout the firm. Over time, as various business units take ownership of different content areas, the KM group's role has evolved into that of a cheerleader and facilitator. In other words, the KM initiative is centrally facilitated, yet organizationally distributed (Kochikar, Mahesh, & Mahind, 2002).

Explicating knowledge

The origins of Infosys's KM initiative can be traced to efforts by the E&R Center to create Bodies of Knowledge (BOK). Initiated in 1985, this was an attempt to explicate and capture experiential knowledge in the form of narratives and formal expositions on topics ranging from software methodologies to adapting to new cultures. However, fewer than 5% of Infoscions contributed to the BOK and fewer still used this knowledge. To address this discrepancy, the KM group redesigned the process to create a "system-imposed demand" wherein knowledge codification and capture would become an integral part of everyday activities. A member of the KM group offered the following example:

Suppose someone wanted to know how to execute projects for a large utility company using a specific technology. It used to be difficult to get this information. To solve this problem, corporate marketing used to go around meeting people and writing many case studies manually. That was not sustainable. Instead, we figured that we could have a new template wherein the project plan and other documents have brief write-ups on the client and related issues. Then, we can use an automated tool to extract information from these write-ups. This is likely to be much more successful. Now, we are looking at all the processes and documentation to see what we need to change.

Besides recording internal experiential knowledge in BOK, white papers, and repositories of reusable code, the KM initiative also provides Infoscions with access to publicly available knowledge resources such as websites, glossaries of business and technology terms, technology summaries, online journals and books, external reports, and technology and business news.

Sharing knowledge

Facilitating the sharing of all this knowledge throughout Infosys is the technology architecture that enables Infoscions to access all content and expertise from their very desktops through an intranet portal called the KShop. This infrastructure enables a culture which encourages sharing. As a vice-president in the Delivery Unit pointed out:

We are a very young organization – the average age of employees is 25–26. Most of our young people are very comfortable with sharing. I can pick up the phone and ask anybody who is not in my business unit to help and he/she will. Within 24 hours, we can get information from anywhere in the world on past projects.

Indeed, if a question is posted on the electronic bulletin board that is part of KShop, it is typical for several Infoscions from around the globe to respond within minutes.

The KM group also has created an application called the People Knowledge Map (PKM). The PKM allows Infoscions to "go public" on their specific expertise so that colleagues may consult them. Thereby, this application allows Infoscions to tap the tacit knowledge possessed by colleagues. Also, it caters to those Infoscions who prefer to listen and learn.

Besides such informal mechanisms, Infosys uses other, formal mechanisms to promote knowledge-sharing and synthesis. The rotation of employees among project teams and knowledge domains is one such mechanism. Cross-functional organization of project or business teams is another. Furthermore, periodic meetings between project leaders or business managers serve as communities of practice for discussing topical issues and best practices with one another.

Reusing knowledge

Apart from enabling employees to codify and share knowledge, an important function of any KM initiative is to encourage reuse of existing knowledge. During the initial stages, Infosys's KM group realized that the very time pressures that reuse is intended to alleviate also reduced the propensity of Infoscions to reuse knowledge and software code from various KShop repositories. The head of the E&R Center explained this problem:

If we create a repository and make it too bulky, the chances of getting useful information actually decrease with time. So, there is this trade-off . . . Also, we are implementing many shorter life-cycle projects nowadays – 6 weeks to 3 months duration. Suppose someone searches the repository, gets three documents, takes 2 to 3 days to read them and then finds that they are not useful. This is a considerable waste of time. If this happens, this person might question the very utility of the repository and decide not to use it in the future.

To enable easy retrieval of relevant information, the KM group has adopted a "content architecture." Each "knowledge asset" in a repository is organized within a "knowledge hierarchy" and tagged by multiple paths through the hierarchy. The KM group has also shifted from an automatic repository-based approach to an integrated approach to maintaining content quality and relevance. Under the new approach, whenever new content is submitted for inclusion, a number of volunteer reviewers offer comments to improve its quality and utility. Then, a centralized group of reviewers streamlines and checks the new content for intellectual property (IP) related issues. Only then is it published in a repository.

Addressing the people aspect of KM

Even in a culture such as that of Infosys where sharing is encouraged and embraced, it does not occur automatically. This is because everyday pressures drive employees to complete one project and immediately start another. Also, the rapid pace of change places a premium on learning new technologies instead of pausing to recount or record past experiences. Therefore, even Infosys has to strive to induce knowledge-sharing at all levels.

Apparently, it is the people aspect – not the technology, process, or content – that is an impediment. To address this challenge, the KM group has succeeded in making an employee's ability to codify and reuse knowledge (as part of project execution and closure) an integral component of his/her performance evaluation. Furthermore, the KM group surveys Infoscions periodically on the extent to which they reuse knowledge and confirms that reported reuse actually occurred. According to an Infoscion:

As part of CMM and ISO 9000 processes, we have regular audits. During these audits, every person who reports having reused knowledge is asked specific questions on what was reused and how it was reused. No one can get away with just claiming to have reused knowledge a lot.

In addition to these system-imposed demands, Infosys's KM group has also created a stronger link between knowledge-sharing/reuse and personal benefit. For instance, the KM group has instituted various rewards, recognition, and incentive programs. One innovative incentive is the Knowledge Currency Unit (KCU). Infoscions can earn KCUs for contributing to, reviewing, or using knowledge assets in various repositories such as the BOK. They can also earn KCUs every time their contributions are reused. Periodically, they can exchange these KCUs for a variety of rewards such as time off or bonuses. In addition to being an incentive to promote sharing, KCUs also serve as a metric to regulate content quality and measure the effectiveness of the KM initiative. Realizing, however, that incentivizing knowledge-sharing has the potential to make employees "say more than they know" and also compromise the sharing culture at the company, Infosys's KM group has progressively modified the incentive scheme to emphasize recognition more than monetary rewards.

Governing intellectual capital

In firms such as Infosys, intellectual capital lies distributed among employees who can determine the extent and quality of their intellectual contributions. As Infosys's chairman pointed out, the firm's intellectual assets "walk out of the door every evening" and it is the management's responsibility to ensure that they return the next morning.

Distribution of decision rights

In such a context, traditional distinctions between principals and agents begin to blur. Knowledge workers are not merely deskilled agents who are "paid to do and not to think." Governance processes designed to harness mindlessness in mass-production firms can stifle active intellectual engagement of knowledge workers. Infosys's CFO listed the problems that a traditional bureaucracy generates: "Size inhibits freedom. Bright, young people want to work in smaller companies. So, Infosys needs to retain the flexibility, speed, collegiality and openness of a small company."

Infosys attempts to preserve the attributes of a small company by ensuring that decision rights remain with those who possess relevant knowledge – its front-line employees. Such an emphasis has resulted in inverting the traditional hierarchy. People who are at the bottom take decisions based on their knowledge. Underlying such autonomy is the responsibility of using information mindfully to arrive at superior decisions. A founder director of the company offered the following maxim as a guiding principle for decision-making: "In only God we trust. The rest of you bring facts."

Infoscions are encouraged to challenge one another based on the facts that they can marshal. As a result, Infosys's culture itself is built around a dialectic tension where employees agree to disagree, thereby generating informed consensus. However, as Infosys's CFO explained: "Here, consensus does not mean everyone agrees on everything. It implies finding 'binding aspects.' The range of interpretive differences diminishes as one finds these binding aspects . . . "

Mentoring

What role can top management play if front-line knowledge workers make most decisions? Surely, managers cannot continue to be the keepers of content as was the case in mass-production environments. At Infosys, it appears that managers are part of a larger process of mutual mentorship, a process that the founders hope will create an institution that survives them. Indeed, the philosophy of Infosys's top management is to recruit people who are brighter than themselves and then mentor them.

How can someone mentor a brighter person? At Infosys, this paradox speaks to a deep sense of security that managers possess. These managers ensure that such security does not turn into complacency by becoming a part of the overall knowledge generation and deployment process. On the one hand, they deploy their considerable experience to guide those under them. On the other hand, they learn from the very employees that they teach. Such a co-mentoring approach, coupled with formal training at Infosys's Leadership Institute, has served to increase management depth at Infosys. The importance of such mentoring was highlighted recently by Infosys's chairman, when he assumed the additional role of Chief Mentor.

Fostering transformative change

Without doubt, the capability to create, harness, and govern intellectual capital fully is important. Equally important for a company dealing with continual change is continuity or coherence amidst this change. There are several facets of Infosys that offer such continuity and coherence even as the company confronts continual change.

For instance, it is second nature for Infoscions to offer a model in response to queries pertaining to Infosys's strategy. Whether it is their overall PSPD Model, the Global Delivery Model, or the Customer Relationship Model, these models codify bounds for everyday decisions and actions. For instance, the PSPD Model codifies Infosys's strategic goals. Infosys's CEO and managing director explained:

When we talk about PSPD, we mean that we must build revenue and business models where there is some *predictability*. We must be able to predict that in the next four, eight, or twelve quarters, certain revenue is assured in order to ensure that we manage the growth that is expected from us. Our revenue model has to contain *sustainable* revenue streams, not revenue streams that die out in a few months and need to be replaced by some other revenue stream. Obviously, everything we do has to generate *profits* and deliver earnings to the bottom line. We also should *de-risk*, which means we should not become overly dependent on one technology, one business, or one kind of service offering.

It would be a mistake, however, to think of models such as PSPD as sterile tools applied without reflection to address challenges offered by the continually changing environment. After all, any model is but an aid to decision-making and cannot replace human judgment. Indeed, managers at Infosys who use these models are continually reminded of the need to use their judgment.

A second facet that offers Infosys continuity with change is its culture. For Infosys, such cultural mechanisms are embodied in a set of core values which stress meritocracy. As an Infosys middle manager commented: "The Infosys culture is not an authoritarian or autocratic culture. We all keep each other on our toes. Nobody can rest because this department or that is more powerful than the others."

The meritocratic culture, together with the emphasis on leadership, excellence, and integrity, promotes open communication and sharing among employees. Indeed, a strongly held value within Infosys is that the firm's knowledge is an asset that belongs to every Infoscion. Also, the unwritten rule within the firm is that if someone can help a colleague, he/she should.

Such sharing and openness also is reflected in Infosys's commitment to complete transparency in financial and operational aspects. For instance, Infosys reports its financial results to conform to the GAAP of seven different countries around the world. Infosys's director of Customer Delivery revealed another aspect of transparency: "We are open about our processes and knowledge. For instance, we have published a book on CMM which explains most of our practices. We are also happy to share our knowledge with customers and anyone else who asks."

Indeed, such transparency transforms Infosys into a "naked organization," making continual improvement and transformation critical for staying ahead.

Besides embracing transparency, Infosys has created a forum called the "Voice of the Youth." As part of this forum, a group of junior Infoscions are invited to attend board meetings to voice their opinions freely on any aspects of the business, including Infosys's culture and value system. This forum ensures that the strategy models and core values provide continuity and a common language, but do not become so taken for granted that they stifle change itself.

Beginnings from endings

The two faces of the Greek god Janus symbolize an end as well as a beginning. If one were to apply this image to Infosys, we see that the promise of scalability lies in Infosys's ability continually to evolve from the very platforms it has created. When asked to comment on Infosys's journey and its ability to respond to future challenges, a founder-director had this to say: "Each time we encountered a fundamental challenge, we viewed it as an opportunity to transform the company. We know that the future will pose new challenges. We don't know which capabilities we might need. But, we are confident that we will be able to develop these capabilities and meet these challenges."

This confidence stems from a unique capability to co-evolve with the fluid IT environment within which Infosys operates. Continuity and change are inherent in Infosys's operations as it uses the very resources and capabilities it has built in the past as platforms to explore and exploit emerging opportunities. Scalability lies in Infosys's ability to encapsulate its past experiences such that the accumulated stock and associated flows result not in core rigidities – the perpetuation of Infosys as it once was – but in dynamic capabilities that fuel its continual transformation. That is, Infosys represents a continually upgradable platform, a firm that is always in the making.

Discussion

We began this chapter by noting that knowledge has become a key resource and that processes to harness knowledge to yield productive services are different from the processes used to harness inert resources. Penrose (1995) had pointed out that it is not a firm's inert resources but its managerial capacity to identify and exploit opportunities using these resources that determines its growth potential. For a firm dealing primarily with knowledge-infused resources, however, the responsibility to identify and exploit growth opportunities cannot be confined to top management alone. Instead, it has to be distributed among its many knowledge workers. As opportunities arise in use, it is the knowledge worker who chooses to exploit or ignore them.

Besides the discovery of emergent opportunities, knowledge workers also create new knowledge as they use existing knowledge. As Loasby (1999: 92) pointed out, local engagements can "develop capabilities which can be most effectively used *within the context of discovery*" (emphasis added). Learning occurs as knowledge workers steer a co-evolutionary process that unfolds as they use knowledge in practice under specific circumstances.

In short, in the very act of exploiting existing knowledge, knowledge workers also explore, a capacity that represents "knowledgeability" (Giddens, 1986: 144). Yet, for such knowledge to result in scalable structuration, a firm must address three challenges. First, it must explicate this knowledge for future use. Secondly, it has to develop mechanisms that make this knowledge a collective asset accessible by all of its knowledge workers. Thirdly, it has to free itself from path-dependencies in knowledge accumulation that give rise to competency traps and core rigidities.

An exploration of Infosys's practices offers several insights into how a firm might address these challenges. Consider, first, the challenge of managing the tacit–explicit dimensions of knowledge. Infosys not only recruits its employees for learnability, but it also trains them to exercise "critical judgment." Additionally, Infosys encourages its employees to learn even as they deploy their knowledge by providing them with a systematic framework – its CMM Level 5 methodology. Indeed, given its willingness to share its best practices with customers and competitors alike, such learning and the continual improvements that it generates become critical sources of Infosys's performance advantage.

Such learning involves much more than learning by doing, which remains tacit and, hence, may degenerate or be forgotten over time. It requires cultivating a readiness to continually ask "why" or "why not," draw rough inferences, and construct tentative hypotheses (Garud, 1997; Schon, 1983; Zuboff, 1984). As these tentative hypotheses are applied and modified from one context and time to another, new knowledge is created through analytical induction (Boland & Collopy, 2004; Georges and Romme, 2003; Glaser & Strauss, 1967). Thereby, learning by reflection allows knowledge workers to say more about what they know and also to do more with it.

Mechanisms to manage the tacit–explicit dimensions are also evident in Infosys's knowledge management (KM) initiative. For instance, the People Knowledge Map enables any Infoscion to interact directly with experts and tap their tacit knowledge. Its BOK repositories contain not only the knowledge that arises from reflective thinking on experiences, but also narratives of experiences in specific contexts (Czarniawska, 1997; Weick, 1995: 127). These narratives, when coupled with the learnability inherent in each Infoscion, provide the basis for utilizing past experiences in new ways in the future.

In sum, these mechanisms not only enable Infoscions to address emerging issues pertaining to their current knowledge and contexts, but they also result in the creation of new knowledge for the future. But, the utility of such knowledge would be limited if it remained resident in individual employees. Therefore, this private knowledge generated by individuals needs to be converted into a collective good that is also available for use by others within the firm. We have already discussed many of the pressures that prevent private knowledge from becoming organizational. These include ownership and appropriability issues as well as the lack of a forum to harness such private knowledge. Infosys suggests other reasons. For instance, time pressure can prevent people from "closing" projects in such a way that they are easily accessible for reuse in the future. When closure and search costs are high, private knowledge remains so and does not benefit the firm.

Overcoming this challenge requires the firm to pay attention to cultural mechanisms that promote explication of private knowledge for others to use in the future. Such cultural mechanisms are evident within Infosys in statements such as "Every instance of learning within Infosys should be available to every employee," "Learn once, Use anywhere," and "If you can help a colleague, you should." They are also evident in the nested co-mentorship processes wherein leaders are willing to "listen and learn" (Leonard, 1998: 265) even as they teach those under them.

But Infosys does not rely on cultural mechanisms alone to induce scalable structuration at the organizational level. It has incentivized the system – for instance, by awarding Knowledge Currency Units (KCUs) – to entice Infoscions to explicate their knowledge for use by others. Recognizing that such explicated knowledge does not become a collective good unless it is used, Infosys awards KCUs even to those who reuse explicated knowledge resident in its repositories.

Indeed, the very ways in which knowledge is organized within Infosys's KShop portal and the ways in which this knowledge is used in real time co-evolve in an adaptive manner (Bowker & Star, 2000). These dynamics are consistent with the process that DeSanctis and Poole (1994: 122) describe: "There is a duality of structure whereby there is an interplay between the type of structures that are inherent to advanced technologies (and hence anticipated by designers and sponsors) and the structures that emerge in human action as people interact with these technologies." Such co-evolution in an adaptive manner provides Infosys with an automatic and mindful selection mechanism, the key to evolution in high-velocity environments (Eisenhardt & Martin, 2000).

These cultural mechanisms and incentives lay the foundation for an integrated KM initiative within Infosys. Realizing that knowledge is dispersed, Infosys's KM initiative is not centrally controlled, but centrally facilitated. Such central facilitation ensures consistency of implementation throughout the firm, but provides considerable flexibility to different units or content areas to organize and manage their own "knowledge nodes." Furthermore, through mechanisms such as E&R Center, DCG, and the SETLabs, the KM initiative synthesizes codified knowledge about the different domains or technologies, thereby transforming partial and context-specific private knowledge into useful collective knowledge at a higher level of abstraction. Above all, the KShop portal serves as a common forum for Infoscions, irrespective of their geographic location, to interact with one another, tap each other's private knowledge, and create collective knowledge that benefits the entire firm. In this sense, the KM initiative has set the stage for the creation of "digital options" (Sambamurthy, Bharadwaj, & Grover, 2003) that Infosys can strike when the time is right.

The third challenge that a firm faces in inducing scalable structuration is to ensure that it does not become enmeshed in core rigidities. The potential to fall into these traps is ever present because knowledge development can be a recursive process. What is learned and what is useful knowledge is determined by the absorptive capacity of the individual and the organization (Cohen & Levinthal, 1990). If this cycle is not broken, there is a likelihood that the firm progresses in a path-dependent manner till it eventually hits an evolutionary wall (Garud & Karnoe, 2001).

There are several mechanisms at Infosys to prevent this eventuality. First, Infosys ensures that decision rights are distributed among its knowledge workers. Such distribution of decision rights empowers Infoscions not just to exercise learnability, but also to act in a timely manner on the basis of their learning.

Moreover, Infosys continually keeps abreast of its exceedingly dynamic environment, thereby matching its internal knowledge initiatives with its ever-changing environment. For instance, close, long-term relationships with its customers enable Infosys to anticipate their emerging needs and preferences. Such close relationships also enable Infosys to tap into its customers' innovative potential. Finally, together with the iterative development process, they allow Infosys to skirt around the challenge posed by "sticky information" (von Hippel, 1994) in addressing customer needs.

In addition, Infosys employs other mechanisms to make sense of its changing environment. Its dispersed development and proximity centers sensitize Infosys to emerging trends over and above those revealed by its existing customers. Likewise, joint projects and invest-ments in start-up companies enable Infosys to bridge emerging tech-nologies and competencies.

The recombination of knowledge is another mechanism for induc-ing variation (Kogut & Zander, 1992). Rotation of personnel and the cross-functional sharing of knowledge (Nonaka & Takeuchi, 1995) are common occurrences at Infosys as at other firms. But equally important, Infosys has institutionalized this process through structural means. Specifically, Infosys's E&R Center, DCG, and SETLabs combine externally acquired knowledge with the knowledge that Infosys's busi-ness units have accumulated by working on various projects for their respective customers. Thereby, knowledge generated through practice and that generated about possibilities complement one another (cf. Hargadon, 2003), yielding new and unique solutions.

Any other firm would have been content with these mechanisms to ensure that transformation rather then progression results. How-ever, transformation has to be accomplished mindfully. To ensure this, Infosys has created a shared context (Fahey & Prusak, 1998) and a shared identity (Orlikowski, 2002) to inform its decisions and actions. Its strategy models codify key priorities for making decisions, whereas its core values such as sharing and transparency prescribe norms for action. Even as these models and values serve as selection mecha-nisms to harness variation beneficially, they also provide continuity and coherence amidst continual change.

Over time, however, even these models and values may become taken for granted and stifle change. Therefore, it is necessary for the firm to encourage critical inquiry of these very models and core values. Within Infosys, the "Voice of the Youth" serves such a purpose. By ensuring that even junior employees have the power to question the values and models driving the firm, Infosys has instituted a mechanism for innocent questions to challenge taken-for-granted approaches of the past. In addition, Infosys's insistence on transparency ensures that investors and other stakeholders know enough to question its direction and actions.

In sum, Infosys's initiatives at different levels within the firm serve to induce scalable structuration. As employees socialized into the shared context and endowed with learnability use CMM methodology to learn, they refine existing knowledge and create new knowledge. The KM initiative induces the articulation, codification, and prioritization of this private knowledge, thereby converting dispersed and fragmented knowledge into useful collective knowledge. As environmental scanning matches this collective knowledge with emerging trends, experiments in redeploying knowledge are initiated resulting in the recombination of new knowledge with old. Such recombination, in turn, initiates a reappraisal of the organization's learning routines and shared context, thereby resulting in organizational transformation that is consistent with the direction of environmental change. Not only do these interactions allow Infosys to co-evolve with its environment, but they also are enabling it to grow and move up the value chain in IT services.

Conclusion

In this chapter, we have attempted to identify processes through which a firm can induce scalable structuration. We suggested that such processes need to address several challenges. They need to address the tacit–explicit dimensions of knowledge, effect a conversion of private knowledge resident in individual employees into collective organizational knowledge available to others, and prevent path-dependent accumulation of knowledge. In this regard, our inquiry into Infosys revealed a nested set of co-evolutionary processes unfolding at different levels within the firm. "Knowledgeability" at the individual level involves reflective learning from deployment. New knowledge created in this process co-evolves with the firm's collective knowledge which, in turn, determines and is determined by the unfolding governance processes that we described.

Such nesting implies that there are connections between levels – "an interlocking set of experiments" (Loasby 1999: 92) – that foster knowledge accumulation. At the same time, autonomy and dispersion of decision rights ensure that there is sufficient variation to effect transformation. In sum, the nested co-evolutionary processes ensure that there is continuity and change built in.

Our perspective on scalable structuration yields several insights. First, it is no longer appropriate to think in terms of knowledge stocks and knowledge flows. Structuration implies that structure is both medium and outcome of action. Consequently, a knowledge-infused resource is simultaneously stock and flow. In its very deployment, it generates new knowledge. In other words, in the context of a firm, "knowledge" is akin to words such as "building," "construction," and "work," designating both a process and its finished product (Dewey, 1934: 51).

A second implication pertains to the dichotomy between exploration and exploitation (March, 1991). Emerging landscapes may have a disruptive impact on a firm to the extent that organizing for exploration is distinct from organizing for exploitation. If a firm were to (re)organize for exploration, its exploitation activities would be disrupted. Alternatively, if a firm were to focus its energies on exploitation, it is likely to hit limits in the future as radical or architectural innovations emerge (Henderson & Clark, 1990). Under scalable structuration, however, this problem does not arise because exploration is a byproduct of exploitation. Also, as the firm co-evolves with its environment, it endogenizes discontinuities into a series of small, iterative changes (Gavetti & Levinthal, 2000; Quinn, 1978), thereby mitigating their negative impact.

Finally, scalable structuration compels us to think of knowledge as being both tacit and explicit, instead of being either tacit or explicit. As Tsoukas (1996) argued, any articulable knowledge only makes sense given a tacit background. Therefore, transporting knowledge across time and space involves much more than transferring formulae. It includes the context – people, culture, and the social relationships – that also has to be transported across time and space. Viewed thus, knowledge transfer becomes an active process of translation (Callon, 1986; Latour, 1991; Law, 1992) and not one of diffusion.

In conclusion, the promise of the post-modern corporation lies in its ability to harness knowledge-infused resources. Mechanisms and processes to harness such knowledge-infused resources are very different from those required to harness inert resources. Implemented properly, these mechanisms and processes can induce scalable structuration, wherein a nested set of co-evolutionary dynamics results in new, transformative knowledge being generated as a byproduct of the application of existing knowledge. Our chapter is an attempt to outline how a firm might induce scalable structuration and benefit from the increasing returns that accrue.

References

Alavi, M. & Leidner, D. 2001. Review: Knowledge management and knowledge management foundations and research issues. *MIS Quarterly*, 1: 107–136.

Argote, L. 1999. *Organizational Learning: Creating, Retaining, and Transferring Knowledge*. Boston: Kluwer Academic.

Arrow, K. 1962. The economic implications of learning by doing. *Review of Economic Studies*, 29 (June): 155–173.

Arthur, W. B. 1991. Now capital means brains not bucks. *Fortune*, 14 (January): 31–32.

Barley, S. R. 1986. Technology as an occasion for structuring: evidence from observations of CT scanners and the social order of radiology departments. *Administrative Science Quarterly*, 31: 78–108.

Barney, J. 1991. Firm resources and sustained competitive advantage. *Journal of Management*, 17: 99–120.

Boland, R. J., Jr., & Collopy, F. (eds.) 2004. *Managing as Designing*. Stanford: Stanford University Press.

Bowker, G. S. & Star, S. L. 2000. *Sorting Things Out: Classification and Its Consequences*. Cambridge, MA: MIT Press.

Brown, J. S. & Duguid, P. 1991. Organizational learning and communities of practice: toward a unified view of working, learning, and innovation. *Organization Science*, 2: 40–57.

Brown, S. L. & Eisenhardt, K. M. 1998. *Competing on the Edge: Strategy as Structured Chaos*. Boston: Harvard Business School Press.

Business Week. 1992. Industrial policy: call it what you will, the nation needs a plan to nurture growth. *Business Week*, 6 (April): 70–104.

Callon, M. 1986. The sociology of an actor-network: the case of the electric vehicle. In M. Callon, J. Law & A. Rip (eds.), *Mapping the Dynamics of Science and Technology*. London: Macmillan.

Christensen, C. & Raynor, M. 2003. *The Innovator's Solution*. Boston: Harvard Business School Press.

Cohen, M. D. & Bacdayan, P. 1994. Organizational routines are stored as procedural memory: evidence from a laboratory study. *Organizational Science*, 5: 554–568.

Cohen, W. & Levinthal, D. A. 1990. Absorptive capacity: a new perspective on learning and innovation. *Administrative Science Quarterly*, 35: 128–152.

Collis, D. J. & Montgomery, C. A. 1997. *Corporate Strategy: A Resource-Based View*. New York: Irwin/McGraw-Hill.

Czarniawska, B. 1997. *Narrating the Organization: Dramas of Institutional Identity*. Chicago: University of Chicago Press.

David, P. A. 1985. Clio and the economics of QWERTY. *American Economic Review*, 75: 332–337.

DeSanctis, G. & Poole, M. S. 1994. Capturing the complexity in advanced technology use: adaptive structuration theory. *Organization Science*, 5: 121–147.

Dewey, J. 1934. *Art as Experience*. New York: Minton, Balch & Company.

Dierickx, I. & Cool, K. 1989. Asset stock accumulation and sustainability of competitive advantage. *Management Science*, 35: 1504–1511.

Dosi, G. & Marengo, L. 1994. Some element of an evolutionary theory of organizational competencies. In R. W. England (ed.), *Evolutionary Concepts in Contemporary Economies*. Ann Arbor: University of Michigan Press.

Dougherty, D. 1992. A practice-centered model of organizational renewal through product innovation. *Strategic Management Journal*, 13: 77–92.

Drazin, R. & Sandelands, L. 1992. Autogenesis: a perspective on the process of organizing. *Organization Science*, 2: 230–249.

Dutton, J. M. & Thomas, A. 1985. Relating technological change and learning by doing. In R. D. Rosenbloom (ed.), *Research on Technological Innovation, Management, and Policy*. Greenwich, CT: JAI Press.

Eisenhardt, K. M. & Martin, J. M. 2000. Dynamic capabilities: what are they? *Strategic Management Journal*, 21: 1105–1121.

Fahey, L. & Prusak, L. 1998. The seven deadliest sins of knowledge management. *California Management Review*, 40(3): 265–276.

Feldman, M. S. & Pentland, B. T. 2003. Reconceptualizing organizational routines as a source of flexibility and change. *Administrative Science Quarterly*, 48: 94–118.

Fortune 1991. The most fascinating ideas for 1991: managing. *Fortune*, 123(1): 30–33.

Foss, N. J. & Robertson, P. L. 2000. *Resources, Technology and Strategy: Explorations in the Resource-Based Perspective*. New York: Routledge.

Galbraith, J. R. & Kazanjian, R. K. 1986. *Strategy Implementation: Structure, Systems and Process*. St. Paul: West Publishing Company.

Garud, R. 1997. On the distinction between know-how, know-why and know-what in technological systems. In J. Walsh & A. Huff (eds.), *Advances in Strategic Management*. Greenwich, CT: JAI Press.

Garud, R. & Karnoe, P. 2001. Path creation as a process of mindful deviation. In R. Garud & P. Karnoe (eds.), *Path Dependence and Creation*. Mahwah, NJ: Lawrence Erlbaum Associates.

Garud, R., Kumaraswamy, A., & Malhotra, M. 2003. Infosys: architecture of a scalable corporation. Stern School of Business Case, New York University.

Garud, R. & Nayyar, P. 1994. Transformative capacity: continual structuring by inter-temporal technology transfer. *Strategic Management Journal*, 15: 265–385.

Garud, R. & Rappa, M. 1994. A socio-cognitive model of technology evolution. *Organization Science*, 5: 344–362.

Gavetti, G. & Levinthal, D. 2000. Looking forward and looking backward: cognitive and experiential search. *Administrative Science Quarterly*, 45: 113–137.

Georges, A. & Romme, L. 2003. Making a difference: organization as design. *Organization Science*, 14(5): 558–573.

Giddens, A. 1986. *Central Problems in Social Theory*. Berkeley: University of California Press.

Glaser, B. & Strauss, A. 1967. *The Discovery of Grounded Theory: Strategies of Qualitative Research*. London: Weidenfeld and Nicolson.

Grant, R. M. 1996. Toward a knowledge-based theory of the firm. *Strategic Management Journal*, 17 (Special Issue): 109–122.

Hargadon, A. 2003. *How Breakthroughs Happen: The Surprising Truth About How Companies Innovate*. Boston: Harvard Business School Press.

Hayek, F. A. 1945. The use of knowledge in society. *American Economic Review*, 35(4): 519–532.

Henderson, R. M. & Clark, K. B. 1990. Architectural innovation: the reconfiguration of existing product technologies and the failure of established firms. *Administrative Science Quarterly*, 35: 9–30.

Jalote, P. 1999. *CMM in Practice: Processes for Executing Software Projects at Infosys*. Reading, MA: Addison-Wesley.

Kanigel, R. 1997. *The One Best Way: Fredrick Winslow Taylor and the Enigma of Efficiency*. New York: Viking.

Kochikar, V. P., Mahesh, K., & Mahind, C. S. 2002. Knowledge management in action: the experience of Infosys technologies. In V. Hlupic (ed.), *Knowledge and Business Process Management*. Hershey: PA Idea Group.

Kogut, B. & Zander, U. 1992. Knowledge of the firm: combinative capabilities and the replication of technology. *Organization Science*, 3: 383–397.

Latour, B. 1991. Technology is society made durable. In J. Law (ed.), *A Sociology of Monsters – Essays on Power, Technology and Domination*. London: Routledge.

Lave, J. & Wenger, E. 1994. *Situated Learning: Legitimate Peripheral Participation*. Cambridge: Cambridge University Press.

Law, J. 1992. Notes on the theory of the actor-network: ordering, strategy and heterogeneity. *Systems Practice*, 5: 379–393.

Lei, D., Hitt, M. A., & Bettis, R. 1996. Dynamic core competences through meta-learning and strategic context. *Journal of Management*, 22(4): 549–569.

Leonard, D. 1998. *Wellsprings of Knowledge*. Boston, MA: Harvard Business School Press.

Leonard-Barton, D. 1992. Core capabilities and core rigidities: a paradox in managing new product development. *Strategic Management Journal*, 13: 111–125.

Levinthal, D. 1997. Adaptation on rugged landscapes. *Management Science*, 43: 934–950.

Levitt, B. & March, J. G. 1988. Organizational learning. *Annual Review of Sociology*, 14: 319–340.

Loasby, B. J. 1999. *Knowledge, Institutions and Evolution in Economics*. New York: Routledge.

Mahoney, J. & Pandian, J. 1992. The resource-based view within the conversation of strategic management. *Strategic Management Journal*, 13: 363–380.

March, J. G. 1991. Exploration and exploitation in organizational learning. *Organization Science*, 2: 71–87.

March, J. G. & Simon, H. A. 1958. *Organizations*. New York: Wiley.

Metcalfe, J. S. & James, A. 2000. Knowledge and capabilities: a new view of the firm. In N. J. Foss & P. L. Robertson (eds.), *Resources, Technology and Strategy: Explorations in the Resource-Based Perspective*. New York: Routledge.

Miller, D. & Friesen, P. 1980. Momentum and revolution in organization adaptation. *Academy of Management Journal*, 23: 591–614.

Nelson, R. & Winter, S. 1982. *An Evolutionary Theory of Economic Change*. Cambridge, MA: Harvard University Press.

Nonaka, I. & Takeuchi, H. 1995. *The Knowledge Creating Company*. New York: Oxford University Press.

Orlikowski, W. J. 1992. The duality of technology: rethinking the concept of technology in organizations. *Organization Science*, 3: 398–427.

2002. Knowing in practice: enacting a collective capability in distributed organizing. *Organization Science*, 13: 249–273.

Orr, J. E. 1990. Sharing knowledge, celebrating identity: community memory in a service culture. In D. Middleton & D. Edwards (eds.), *Collective Remembering*. London: Sage.

Penrose, E. 1995. *The Theory of the Growth of the Firm*. Oxford: Oxford University Press.

Petaraf, M. A. 1993. The cornerstones of competitive advantage: a resource-based view. *Strategic Management Journal*, 14: 179–191.

Polanyi, M. 1967. *The Tacit Dimension*. Garden City, NY: Anchor.

Quinn, J. B. 1978. Strategic change: logical incrementalism. *Sloan Management Review*, 20(1): 7–21.

Sambamurthy, V., Bharadwaj, A., & Grover, V. 2003. Shaping agility through digital options: reconceptualizing the role of information technology in contemporary firms. *MIS Quarterly*, 27: 237–263.

Schon, D. A. 1983. *The Reflective Practitioner*. New York: Basic Books.

Spender, J. C. 1996. Making knowledge the basis of a dynamic theory of the firm. *Strategic Management Journal*, 17 (Special Issue): 45–62.

Teece, D., Pisano, G., & Shuen, A. 1997. Dynamic capabilities and strategic management. *Strategic Management Journal*, 18: 509–534.

Thompson, J. 1967. *Organizations in Action*. New York: McGraw-Hill.

Tsoukas, H. 1996. The firm as a distributed knowledge system: a constructionist approach. *Strategic Management Journal*, 17 (Special Issue): 11–25.

Tushman, M., Smith, W., Wood, R., Westerman, R., & O'Reilly, C. 2004. Innovation streams and ambidextrous organizational designs: on building dynamic capabilities. Paper presented at conference on Innovation. University of Maryland.

von Hippel, E. W. 1994. "Sticky information" and the locus of problem solving: implications for innovation. *Management Science*, 40(4): 429–439.

Walsh, J. P. & Ungson, G. R. 1991. Organizational memory: information acquisition, retention, and retrieval. *Academy of Management Review*, 16: 57–91.

Weick, K. E. 1995. *Sensemaking in Organizations*. Thousand Oaks, CA: Sage.

Weick, K. E. & Roberts, K. 1993. Collective mind in organizations: heedful interrelating on flight decks. *Administrative Science Quarterly*, 38: 357–381.

Wernerfelt, B. 1984. A resource-based view of the firm. *Strategic Management Journal*, 5: 171–180.

Winter, S. G. 1987. Knowledge and competence as strategic assets. In D. J. Teece (ed.), *The Competitive Challenge: Strategies for Industrial Innovation and Renewal*. Cambridge, MA: Ballinger.

Zollo, M. & Winter, S. G. 2002. Deliberate learning and the evolution of dynamic capabilities. *Organization Science*, 13: 339–351.

Zuboff, S. 1984. *In the Age of the Smart Machine*. New York: Basic Books.

13 | *Stay tuned: knowledge brokering via inter-firm collaboration in satellite radio*

CHAD NAVIS, MARYANN GLYNN, AND
ANDREW HARGADON

I N dynamic business environments, opportunities often arise faster than entrenched players can form a response. Many organizations have been taken by surprise, unable to see or anticipate new opportunities. For instance, in 1876 William Orton of the Western Union Telegraph Company rejected an offer by Alexander Graham Bell to sell his telephone patents because Western Union could not envision how the telephone would be successful. From 1974 to 1984 the Swiss watch industry lost 30% of the world export market because it was unable to recognize the merits of quartz and electronic technology (Glasmeier, 1991). By 1979, Xerox Corporation's Palo Alto Research Center (PARC) had developed graphical user interfaces, mice, windows and pull down menus, laser printing, distributed computing, and Ethernet, but Xerox failed to exploit these innovations because of management's preoccupation with Japan's encroachment on its core copier business (Port, 1997). UPS, Emery Air Freight, and USPS each considered the idea of an overnight delivery service like that of FedEx, but rejected the concept because they could not foresee a market need (Collins & Lazier, 1992).

In hindsight, it is easy to dismiss these unfortunate business decisions as irrational or even incompetent. Such arguments recognize the competency traps faced by established firms: that despite longer-term returns, most firms are unable to overcome (or see beyond) the short-term costs of adopting new technologies and pursuing new strategies (Christensen, 1997; Leonard-Barton, 1992; March, 1991). The Swiss watchmakers had been building watches the same way for centuries. So why turn away from a time-tested business model? Western Union only understood the telephone as "an electric toy" (Evenson, 2000). So why invest in a trivial fad? Xerox was entrenched in a fierce battle for the company's core market. So why invest resources in an unproven endeavor? UPS, Emery Air Freight, and USPS had established a parcel delivery network that was adequately meeting the delivery requests of their customers. So why fix something that is not broken? Viewed from an economic perspective, the competency trap reflects the inability to balance short- and long-term needs and suggests that overcoming such barriers to change lies in changing the time horizons of the decision-makers.

However, when viewed from an institutional perspective, these same unfortunate business decisions suggest a different set of causes and highlight a different set of strategic opportunities for enabling innovation-driven organic growth. The lens of institutional theory reveals how, within established social systems, entrenched norms or taken-for-granted routines can constrain the very *perceptions* of opportunity and limit creative responses. As importantly, those same entrenched norms and routines that constrain innovation can also, when understood, provide the raw materials and strategic advantage in constructing new innovations.

Institutional theory has much to offer those who pursue and study innovation-driven organic growth. Institutionalized norms and routines are powerful forces that shape and often constrain action and beliefs within organizational fields. These forces shape both perception and action by defining the normative, cognitive, and regulatory environments in which we act and – equally – in which others respond to our actions (Hargadon & Fanelli, 2002; Scott, 1995). In short, institutional conditions shape what we think we "ought to do," what we think is possible, and what others allow us to do, filtering organizational perceptions of what options are appropriate, possible, and allowed (Zucker, 1983). As seen in the earlier examples, the taken-for-granted ways of doing business limited the incumbent firms' perceptions of, and responses to, emerging opportunities. Overcoming such institutional constraints is an important condition for enabling organic growth (Benner & Tushman, 2003; March, 1991). Yet, because the institutional environment permeates established social systems, organizations must find ways of overcoming the embedded constraints. The strategy of inter-firm collaboration can be a mechanism of knowledge brokering that overcomes institutional forces within the field of the focal organization, thereby enabling organic growth.

Inter-firm collaboration, by linking knowledge domains across organizations and across institutional environments, enables firms to enhance their creativity and to grow organically. Resource-based view and knowledge-based view perspectives cite inter-firm collaboration as a mechanism for gaining access to firm-specific resources that are rare, valuable, and difficult to imitate (Ahuja, 2000; Dyer & Singh, 1998; Goes & Park, 1997; Grant, 1996; Gulati, Nohria, & Zaheer, 2000; Stuart, Hoang, & Hybels, 1999). The creativity research often bridges inter-firm collaboration concepts by using a neo-institutional framework that cites collaborative relationships as necessary for "technology brokering" (Hargadon, 2003; Hargadon & Sutton, 1997); that is, the process of bridging institutional frames to enable recombinant innovation. In other words, technology brokering involves connecting neighboring environments as an integrative mechanism that enables recombinant innovation, or the creation of "new products that are original combinations of existing knowledge from disparate industries" (Hargadon & Sutton, 1997). Thus, in addition to bringing stocks of knowledge to firms in collaboration, inter-firm linkages also can provide fresh perspectives that can over-ride entrenched, traditional, and institutionalized ways of thinking and capitalizing on new opportunities.

Our chapter contributes to the research on how firms assemble knowledge to enable innovation by examining the mechanism of inter-firm collaboration, which we view as a mechanism for enabling organizational innovation and organic growth. We organize our chapter as follows. First, we review the extant literatures on institutional theory and innovation to develop a framework of how institutional forces can limit an organization's propensity for creativity. Next, we build on this foundation by introducing the literature on inter-firm collaborations, demonstrating how these partnerships can overcome local institutional constraints to serve as a mechanism for organic growth; in this, we focus on internal growth and not through an exchange of equity, as with mergers or acquisitions. We illustrate our theoretical perspective using examples from the satellite radio industry,[1] which offers a window on the phenomena we sought to explain. Changes in FCC regulations presented firms with new opportunities and new

---

[1] The vast majority, approximately 97%, of the over 200 partnerships in satellite radio did *not* involve an equity investment. The few exceptions include strategic partners that involved stock deals: GM, Honda, DIRECTV, Clear Channel Communications, Hughes Electronics, Ford, and DaimlerChrysler. As well, we note that the FCC license guidelines had no provisions against selling the license to a third party. Thus, the firms chose the strategy of organic growth.

needs, which required creativity. Our chapter concludes with practical implications for managing organic growth.

Organic growth and institutional environments

Institutional environments place pressures on organizations that can enable or constrain opportunities for organic growth. Hence, understanding the institutional environments in which organizations operate is important to understanding how organic growth can occur.

The seminal work upon which organizational theories of institutionalism rests is that of Selznick (1948, 1949, 1957). Early institutional pioneers characterized organizations as rational actors that adapt to the demands of the broader institutional environment. Hence, organizational structures are seen as being carefully designed, calculated, and considerate of local environmental circumstances (Selznick, 1949). Organizations were viewed by early institutional theorists as having sizable agency; that is, they could readily respond when new values, interests, and emerging coalitions penetrated the established institutional environment. Exemplifying this agency is the story of the evolution of the Young Men's Christian Association (YMCA). Originally founded in London in 1844 as an association for young Christian men, the YMCA continually morphed throughout its turbulent history, shedding its emphasis on young Christian males as the target audience for its services over time (Zald & Denton, 1963) to embrace a broader audience, with broader needs. Its changes came in response to shifting institutional pressures, arising from client interests and needs. In this case, institutional pressures enabled organizational growth, change, and expansion, but this is not always so; in fact, the reverse is more often the case.

Neo-institutionalists shifted the model of organizations from one of adaptable, agentic actors to that of embedded actors, largely shaped by the institutional niche or field they occupied. DiMaggio and Powell (1983) broadened the organizational landscape, from that of the local environment to that of the wider "field" or industry level. At this level, multiple institutional environments interact, including the state, professional associations, competitors, and other organizations (DiMaggio & Powell, 1991), thus compounding and complicating the set of pressures to which organizations respond. Thus, rather than being nimble change agents, as Selznick posited, organizations became captives of their institutional environment, adapting to environmental pressures in order to secure legitimacy. Institutionalism bred isomorphism, or conformity to the status quo.

Under conditions of strong institutionalization, then, organizations tended towards isomorphism, or similarity in structure (DiMaggio & Powell, 1983), strategy (Deephouse, 1996), and symbol (Glynn & Abzug, 2002), with fewer displays of differentiation or creative deviance. Scholars of the "new" or "neo" institutionalism movement explain the ubiquitous tendency towards isomorphism as a natural outcome of an organization's obligatory pursuit of institutional legitimacy. The result is that organizations conform to the routines, values, norms, beliefs, and taken-for-granted assumptions (Barley & Tolbert, 1997) of their institutional environments.

DiMaggio and Powell (1983) explain that institutional isomorphism occurs through coercive, mimetic, and normative mechanisms. Coercive isomorphism arises when organizations are influenced by dominant institutions, such as political, regulatory, or governmental bodies, or from organizations on which organizations have a dependency (DiMaggio & Powell, 1983). These pressures may be forceful, persuasive, or inviting of collusion. Mimetic isomorphism arises when organizations are immersed in environments of uncertainty or ambiguity (DiMaggio & Powell, 1983), in which legitimacy is purchased by imitating similar organizations or modeling those perceived as successful. Normative isomorphism arises when forces of "professionalization" push organizations towards conformity, as norms are developed and diffused through formal education, professional socialization, or professional networks that span organizations (DiMaggio & Powell, 1983). Ultimately, the tendency towards isomorphism reinforces cycles of persistence and stability in institutional environments. These pressures have the effect of constricting learning, creativity, and change in organizations (DiMaggio & Powell, 1983, 1991). So potent are these forces that neo-institutional scholars have asserted that institutional pressures limit what individuals are even capable of imagining as possible (Zucker, 1983).

Institutional forces clearly impose powerful pressures towards organizational conformity. Nevertheless, many creative inventions have found a way to emerge from deeply entrenched institutional environments, thus enabling organizations to achieve remarkable organic growth. An explanation for this phenomenon can be seen in the organizational capabilities developed through the acute management of knowledge resources. Borrowing from the knowledge-based view of organizations, research has shown that exploring new opportunities and exploiting old certainties (Benner & Tushman, 2003; March, 1991) is fundamentally dependent on how an organization's knowledge bases are developed, managed, and applied (Cohen & Levinthal, 1990; Kazanjian & Drazin, 1987; Kogut & Zander, 1992). March (1991) advocates a balance between exploration and exploitation as a key driver of competitive advantage, where relative primacy is awarded to organizations that best achieve this balance. According to March, organizations tend to favor exploitation, with its more predictable and near-term positive benefits, over exploration, which has less certain, distant, and often negative outcomes. Consequently, the locus and certainty of knowledge necessary to explore new opportunities and realize explorative returns is often far more distant than necessary for exploitative returns. Organizations thus frequently trade exploration for exploitation, leading to "suboptimal stable equilibria" (p. 71). In return, creativity-enabling activities including search, variation, discovery, and experimentation (March, 1991) are often sacrificed.

While March aptly positioned the exploitation/exploration problem as a key strategic consideration, little research has since emerged to uncover the mechanisms of how firms surmount existing constraints and broker new knowledge in the service of exploration and exploitation. We propose that inter-firm collaborations serve as a viable mechanism for doing so, by providing complementary resources that can enable opportunistic innovations, as well as different perspectives that delimit (or debunk) existing institutional constraints that can rein in learning, creativity, and change. Collaborative relationships can help develop absorptive capacity (Powell & Koput, 1996), thus broadening a firm's appreciation of new project opportunities and the repertoire of potential responses.

Linking to, and collaborating with, other firms, which occupy different institutional niches, can help organizations overcome specific competency limitations (Mitchell & Singh, 1996). Embedded within institutions are a series of social networks, where sets of actors "know one another, are aware of the same kinds of opportunities, have access to the same kinds of resources, and share the same kinds of perceptions" (Burt, 1983). Viewed in isolation, one would naturally expect suboptimal creativity, average returns, and limited organic growth to arise from arrangements of this sort. Yet the same institutions that bind what is thinkable in isolation, proliferate opportunity once interconnected.

One of the primary incentives for inter-firm collaboration is organizational learning. Powell & Koput (1996) succinctly indicate the motive for these linkages: "Research breakthroughs demand a range of intellectual and scientific skills that far exceed the capabilities of any one organization." As knowledge is brokered across institutional frames, opportunities for creativity and recombinant innovation are dramatically enabled:

Knowledge is imperfectly shared over time and across people, organizations, and industries. Ideas from one group might solve the problems of another, but only if connections between existing solutions and problems can be made across the boundaries between them. When such connections are made, existing ideas often appear new and creative as they change form, combining with other ideas to meet the needs of different users. (Hargadon & Sutton, 1997)

We propose that an important mechanism by which the boundaries of institutional fields can be spanned is that of inter-firm collaboration. Specifically, we see inter-firm collaboration best used as a middle-range strategy between exploration and exploitation. In contrast to true "green field" exploration, where the creative discovery process has little guidance, we see inter-firm collaboration as a fruitful strategy in situations when opportunities have already presented themselves. Figure 13.1 depicts this concept, demonstrating how the mechanism of inter-firm collaboration relates across multiple strategic contexts and knowledge domains.

We seek to contribute to the existing literature in a number of ways. First, we demonstrate how inter-firm collaboration can enable growth at an intermediary level between exploration and exploitation. Second, we show how institutional environments can act as a constraint when organizations are confined to a particular niche, but as an opportunity when interconnected. As our earlier examples of the Swiss watchmakers, Western Union, Xerox executives, and FedEx competitors illustrated, institutional forces are often powerful forces for inaction and non-responsiveness to new opportunities. However, by enlarging the organizational field through inter-firm collaborations, organizations can thrive in richer institutional fields, which can serve as wellsprings for creativity and sources of knowledge resources. Third, we look at

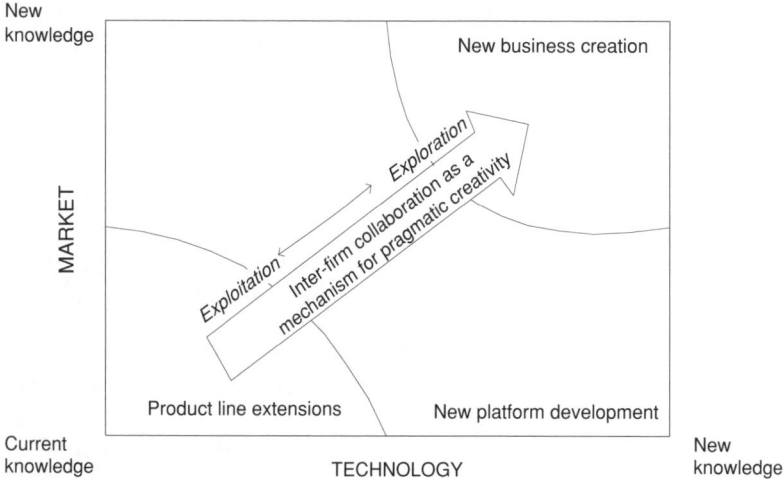

Figure 13.1. Inter-firm collaboration as a mechanism of organizational growth.

change mechanisms that extend beyond the firm level and can ripple through and transform an institutional field.

Inter-firm collaboration in satellite radio

When Guglielmo Marconi began experimenting with "Hertzian Waves" in 1894, the world was on the brink of becoming a much smaller place. Marconi laid the foundation for what would later become radio. It was only after a series of voice transmitters, amplifiers, frequency alternators, and receivers were developed in other environments though, that the industry evolved into a legitimate offering. Marconi did not, and could not, have achieved this outcome by himself, despite his advanced scientific knowledge. Rather, the development of the radio industry required an extensive network of complementary resources, with each leveraging knowledge gains in one area to propagate industry advances in others. By 1935, the radio industry had rapidly evolved to the point where two out of three American households had radio sets. Leblebici and colleagues chronicled this rich evolution over three periods from 1920 through 1965, highlighting how many of the changes to the industry emerged only after disparate organizational actors began interacting:

In each historical period most new practices were introduced by the less central parties of the period. They were initiated by shady traders, small independent stations, renegade record producers, weaker networks, or enterprising advertising agencies. (Leblebici, Salancik, Copay, & King, 1991)

Although the radio industry experienced substantial transformation in its early years, by the 1960s it had reached a stage of maturity where dominant institutional pressures emerged and, in general, motivation for change was squelched (Leblebici, Salancik, Copay, & King, 1991). Amidst these forceful institutional pressures, knowledge, creativity, and growth were largely stifled:

The powerful parties who had vested interests in the institutionalized conventions used their resources to maintain the status quo or introduced practices that confirmed established conventions. Industry routines have been reinforced, norms solidified, and broadcast content generalized. (Leblebici, Salancik, Copay, & King, 1991).

With FM broadcasting as the last discernible innovation in the radio industry prior to the nearly forty-year period of maturity begun in the 1960s, the industry had become relatively stable, secure, and complacent. In April 1997, however, the Federal Communications Commission (FCC) disrupted the institutional order. Through an auction-style proceeding, the FCC licensed a portion of its broadcast frequency spectrum to two emerging competitors with the intent of cultivating a new and unique satellite radio service offering. The FCC believed that the new offering would foster a new form of competition with traditional local station providers, which, in turn, would create enhanced listening services for the public.

The winners of the FCC auction were two competitors that had received little public attention prior to being awarded the license: American Mobile Radio (now XM Satellite Radio, but originally a wholly owned subsidiary of Motient Corporation) and Satellite CD Radio (now SIRIUS). Interestingly, these firms were not particularly powerful market players at the time, and in order simply to gain access to this lucrative new market, each had to raise funds in excess of $80 million to win their bids. Further, this figure did not even begin to consider the costs associated with building infrastructures, establishing service offerings, creating distribution channels, or accumulating market awareness. Nevertheless, finances were just the first of the many challenges that these firms would face.

Subset of institutional force field

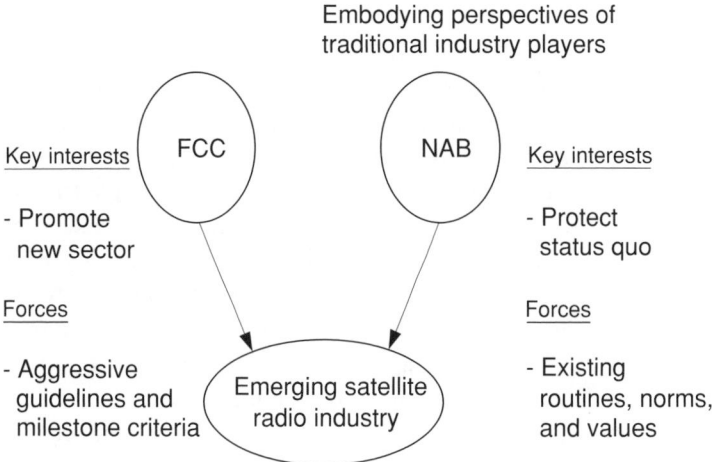

Figure 13.2. Institutional forces in satellite radio.

Institutional pressures for and against change

Although they operated within the radio industry, the two new radio satellite firms, XM and SIRIUS, found themselves facing new sets of institutional pressures that offered both opportunities and constraints. Foremost among these were the FCC, fostering institutional change to established radio firms, and the National Association of Broadcasters (NAB), which resisted institutional change vehemently and sought a prolonged continuation of existing values, routines, norms, and technologies. Although many other actors, such as the record labels and existing infrastructure support providers, constituted the new satellite radio field, we limit our focus to the FCC and NAB. We have chosen these two because of their prominent influence on satellite radio. A depiction of the institutional force field imposed by the FCC and NAB is shown in Figure 13.2.

The FCC exerted pressures for change by establishing a set of aggressive milestones that each new satellite radio provider was required to meet in order to maintain its eight-year dedicated license, although, interestingly, the milestones did not preclude these firms from selling their new licenses to other firms. In the first year, XM and SIRIUS were required to contract for their first satellite space station or begin this effort internally. In the second year, each was to have met the same requirements as in year one, but for a second satellite. In the fourth year, each was to have had at least one satellite in orbit and/or, in the sixth year, each was to have full operation of its satellite system. With little prior experience in this realm and no time to waste, XM and SIRIUS were expressly challenged on how to meet these deadlines. Both chose to grow organically instead of through acquisition or selling their licenses. Furthermore, the strategic choices available to XM and SIRIUS were limited by the regulatory scrutiny of the FCC; that is, strategic considerations such as intellectual property management and competitive positioning were all bounded by the purview of the FCC's regulatory eye. For the FCC, it was crucial that a consumer-focused, competitive satellite radio industry develop with clear and timely progress demonstrated towards this end. Thus, innovation was essential to success, but given the regulatory requirements imposed by the FCC, it had to be pragmatic and directed towards meeting the FCC's targeted objectives.

In contrast to the FCC pressure for institutional change, the NAB was a formidable force of resistance, arguing vehemently that the establishment of the satellite radio industry would contravene the public interest.[2] The NAB rationalized the existing institutional order, prior to the FCC changes. From the NAB's perspective, local radio stations "serve[d] to promote and reinforce traditional American values of community cohesion and local identity."[3] The NAB and its members contended that the public interest was best served in the "form of local programming, local announcements, local identity, local diversity and local connectedness."[4] In a similar argument, the NAB urged the FCC to "preserve the fruits of fifty years of public policy promoting . . . local radio service."[5]

The resistance of the NAB to satellite radio was understandable; it was geared towards preserving the boundaries around the established local environment rather than the newly created and broader field that

---

[2] See Federal Communications Commission, Comments of the National Association of Broadcasters to Frequency Establishment NPRM, GEN Docket No. 90–357, RM No. 8610 (1995).
[3] Ibid.   [4] Ibid.
[5] http://www.lawtechjournal.com/archives/blt/i1-jm.html#n9.

the FCC envisioned with the regulatory changes. Over 12,000 radio stations in the United States employed over 125,000 people[6] from deejays, to station managers, to newscasters. Beyond questions of job security, many of these individuals were veteran employees who, over many years, had internalized the entrenched norms, values, and routines of the local radio institution. Thus, fierce resistance to satellite radio was a natural response. And, as such, the emerging satellite radio environment was one of institutional contest, with forces for innovation and growth propelled by, and predicated upon, changes in the regulatory environment, and forces against innovation and growth propelled by, and predicated upon, mobilized units designed to protect existing institutional boundaries.

Response to institutional pressures: inter-firm collaboration

Considering the intense time and technology challenges precipitated by the FCC rulings, as well as the institutional resistance of the NAB, XM and SIRIUS were faced with a vexing, but not uncommon dilemma that confronts firms in changing and fast-paced business environments. The taken-for-granted assumptions embedded within the existing environment were such that the present institutional order was not likely to present feasible innovations to address the opportunities of a brandnew medium. As well, the FCC's time and technology pressures, in conjunction with the firms' pursuit of first-to-market advantage, required a specialized set of knowledge that could neither be developed internally nor acquired and assembled through hiring practices in a reasonable time-frame. Consequently, XM and SIRIUS had to look outside their institutional frame of reference for creative solutions. As a result, the firms deliberately pursued strategies that enabled them to gain knowledge from different institutional environments that could, in turn, be recombined for innovation. They achieved this end by engaging in purposeful, goal-oriented inter-firm collaborations.

Triggering the process of collaboration was a knowledge gap assessment that identified the specialized skills and technologies required to develop the satellite radio market and service offering. Both XM and SIRIUS could not have predicted with reasonable accuracy how the

---

[6] http://www.bctv.net/telcom/radio.html.

new satellite radio industry would take shape, but they did have a general idea of where functional areas would need to be cultivated. For the sake of parsimony, we have placed these functional areas into four groupings: (1) infrastructure development and maintenance; (2) content and programming; (3) hardware (product) development; and (4) marketing and distribution. By first selecting collaborators with particular knowledge and technologies in each of these areas, and then brokering this knowledge across the disparate institutional frames of complementary partners, innovation could be fostered and the challenge of the new frontier of satellite radio met.

Stages of knowledge brokering in inter-firm collaboration

The process by which XM and SIRIUS brokered knowledge had two stages: the first was characterized by a mass-market focus, which emphasized legitimacy-seeking and rapid deployment, while the second, which was still under way at the time of writing, was more specialized. Here, enabled by partner-driven knowledge, recombination and bricolage created "new" outlets for "old" ideas.

Although the two stages are somewhat overlapping and not dichotomous, they serve to illustrate parsimoniously the evolution of the industry. Specifically, the stages demonstrate how the dynamics of knowledge brokering were managed over time to respond to institutional pressures and breed the recombinant innovation necessary for organic growth. We next look more closely at the characteristics of the two stages.

Stage 1: Mass-market legitimacy and rapid deployment

At the time when XM and SIRIUS were awarded FCC approval, few consumers had even heard of satellite radio. Just as the established radio field resisted change, so too did everyday consumers. The institutional order equips participants with conceptual apparatus that tends to downplay the opportunities inherent in the unfamiliar; the familiar, with its taken-for-grantedness, is what is more easily perceived and more cognitively legitimate (Hargadon & Douglas, 2001; Suchman, 1995). For the new service to be accepted, XM and SIRIUS had to position satellite radio within the existing understandings and routines while simultaneously setting it apart from what already existed (Hargadon & Douglas, 2001). As a consequence, achieving legitimacy was a key emphasis in the first stage of XM and SIRIUS's partnership strategy.

The satellite radio firms achieved legitimacy through two important mechanisms. First, they structured their early partnerships in a way that positioned their service towards a familiar mass-market medium. Initially, the entrants sought "to pioneer and commercialize a digital quality, multi-channel radio service broadcast directly from satellites to vehicles."[7] XM and SIRIUS viewed the automobile as an outlet that could reach many radio listeners in a way that was already familiar to consumers. By mirroring existing institutional understandings and targeting listeners in their vehicles, XM and SIRIUS reached the widest, but not necessarily the most profitable, audiences first.

The second mechanism through which XM and SIRIUS achieved legitimacy was by targeting collaborative partners with established reputations and promoting these through the media. For instance, in the early XM press releases and annual reports, president and CEO, Hugh Panero, advocated the reputations of partnering firms in lieu of more tangible operational features whenever remarking on new collaborative arrangements: "I am very proud of XM's partnerships with the world's leading radio and audio system manufacturers and leading car computer chip maker" (collaboration with Alpine, Pioneer, and Sharp: November 18, 1998); "XM is thrilled to announce this dream-team alliance with General Motors, DIRECTV, and Clear Channel, the largest car manufacturer, the largest direct broadcast satellite company, and one of the largest and most profitable radio groups in the United States" (collaboration with GM, DIRECTV, and Clear Channel: June 8, 1999); "It is a great honor to have this prestigious news organization join XM's channel lineup . . . BBC will complement our other brand name programmers" (collaboration with the BBC: July 26, 1999).

In later years, as satellite radio gained legitimacy, the operational justifications dominated the rationalizations voiced for new collaborative partners, eclipsing earlier concerns for legitimacy and reputational promotion.

Beyond a quest for legitimacy, XM and SIRIUS used the first stage of growth to pursue rapid knowledge brokering. Collaboration partners were engaged to cultivate a consumer mass market and vigorously develop the satellite radio industry. To build a satellite network

---

[7] 1997 Annual Report for CD Radio, Inc. (now SIRIUS Satellite Radio).

infrastructure and meet the aggressive deployment schedule mandated by the FCC, XM and SIRIUS called on firms like Hughes Space & Communications and Loral CyberStar Inc., with their well-established space technology expertise. Similarly, to access the automotive industry and its network of suppliers and distribution channels, XM and SIR-IUS engaged major automotive manufacturers as strategic partners. In 1999, General Motors partnered with XM and DaimlerChrysler with SIRIUS. Within a year, the satellite radio providers had partner arrangements with most major automotive manufacturers. Likewise, to establish a technology foundation, XM and SIRIUS entered agreements with STMicroelectronics and Lucent. These two firms manufactured the receiver "chipsets" upon which partners like Alpine, Delco-Delphi, Motorola, Clarion, and Panasonic relied to create innovative new product pipelines. And finally, in order to rapidly build a content line-up for their consumer audiences, XM and SIRIUS engaged mainstream broadcast organizations like USA Today, Bloomberg, BBC World Service, Salem Communications, and Radio One, Inc.

Together, the collaborations that characterized this first stage of growth brought together a broad set of complementary knowledge resources. With the exception of Loral Cyberstar, which entered into a relationship with SIRIUS prior to 1998, the firms included in the above examples constituted just a small subset of the inter-firm collaborations entered over the twenty-four months of 1998 and 1999. In total, over 150 inter-firm collaborations occurred between 1998 and 2002 for the two firms. More remarkably, the magnitude of this number represents nearly half the number of *employees* of either firm.[8] By carefully selecting and brokering these partnerships, XM and SIRIUS were able rapidly to achieve their initial mainstream market objectives of legitimizing satellite radio and developing the nascent industry despite having little initial skill or experience of their own.

Stage 2: Specialized markets and recombinant innovation

By the end of 2002, XM and SIRIUS had saturated the inter-firm relationships needed to adequately span and nurture the mainstream satellite radio market. Hence, in order to maximize growth opportunities,

---

[8] As of March 14, 2003, SIRIUS had 304 employees (*Source:* SIRIUS 2002 Annual Report). As of December 31, 2002, XM had 384 employees (*Source:* XM 2002 Annual Report).

these firms needed to explore and then exploit (March, 1991) new markets for their technologies. The legitimacy gained in the first stage allowed subsequent growth to target, fruitfully, fringe industry markets. We now explain the mechanisms by which this was possible. Briefly, XM and SIRIUS leveraged the already present social networks of their collaborative partners to explore specialized new markets. Creative inventions, largely arising from processes of knowledge brokering across partnerships, enabled these new markets to be exploited.

In this second growth stage, although a number of brand-new, independently identified collaborations were forged by XM and SIRIUS, a substantial portion of their explorative activity was enabled through the social networks of previously forged collaborations. Consider, for instance, the partnership between SIRIUS and Clarion. This electronics manufacturer had a history of experience in developing waterproof marine radios. Consequently, Clarion's preexisting social networks opened up new market opportunities for SIRIUS in the boating industry. In particular, the Clarion partnership helped lead to two major boating partnerships for SIRIUS: one with Genmar Boats, manufacturer of sixteen different brands including Carver and Four Winns, and the other with Thunderbird Products, manufacturer of the Formula brand. A similar example is found with XM in its partnership with LiveTV, the leading supplier of real-time programming from DIRECTV on commercial aircraft. Originally entered as an arrangement to make the XM service available to airline passengers, the LiveTV collaboration set the stage for a later marketing agreement with DIRECTV, as well as a broadcasting agreement with Jet Blue, the parent company of LiveTV. Table 13.1 elaborates upon the many markets and strategic opportunities enabled by the partnerships that XM and SIRIUS entered.

The knowledge brokering enabled through the diverse partnerships into which XM and SIRIUS entered also fostered the rapid innovation required to exploit new opportunities. When the first satellite radio-enabled vehicles were introduced at the Consumer Electronics Show in 2000, they were equipped with basic satellite radio receivers containing few advanced features. Over the next four years, the creativity driving satellite radio's advancement erupted. For example, the year 2002 brought radio units that integrated song and artist displays, provided the ability to preview and search channels by artists and song titles, and enabled touch-screen operation. The year also delivered

Table 13.1. *Strategic markets and capabilities enabled through selective partnering*

Hardware (product) development		Infrastructure & programming and content		Marketing and distribution	
Partners	Strategic value	Partners	Strategic value	Partners	Strategic value
Terk, Antenna Specialists	GPS and PCS antenna technologies	Cisco, Encoda Systems, Dalet, Harris Corporation, Lawson Software, Object Builders, Oracle, Portal Software, Siebel, Sun Microsystems, Telos Systems, Veritas, Vitria, Applied Media Technologies Corporation	Network support for broadcast infrastructure and data management	Clear Channel Communications	Access to 700,000 outdoor advertising displays and 26,000 live entertainment events annually
Audiovox, Panasonic, Sanyo, Jensen	After-market radio production			House of Blues, Radio City (Music Hall) Entertainment	Access to concert series, clubs, special events, and artist programs
Bontec, Hyundai Autonet, Delphi, Mitsubishi Electric	Traditional suppliers of OEM components to major automotive companies				
Clarion	Car multimedia technologies, integrating audio, video, entertainment and navigation, including the boating market	Acoustic Systems Inc., Genelec	Sound improvement technologies	LiveTV	In-flight entertainment programming on AirTran and Jet Blue
		Lucent Technologies, Klotz Digital, STMicroelectronics	Receiver chipset software and integration	NASCAR, ISC Motorsports	America's largest spectator sport, with track and race sponsorships
Sony	Audio, video, information, and communication technologies, and portable electronics specialist	Boeing, Loral Cyberstar Inc.	Satellite technology capabilities	Dell	Trial exposure with computer sale (including Internet listening)
		DIRECTV, Echostar (Dish Network), TiVo	Digital broadcasting and technology expertise and network access	Avis, Hertz	Automotive rental market

Eclipse-Fujitsu Ten, Pioneer	Integrated multimedia technologies, including audio-video	Collegiate athletic conferences (Big 10, ACC, Pac 10), professional sports and NASCAR, WorldSpace / Capability to broadcast local content (athletic events, African and Asian programming) to subscribers regardless of their location in the US	All major automotive manufacturers	Automotive sales market
Visteon	OEM supplier to automotive market. Innovator in multimedia integration with affiliate ties to Microsoft, Intel, Bang Olufsen, Nintendo, Texas Instruments, and Fujitsu		Genmar Boats, Thunderbird Products; Winnebago Industries; Applied Media Technologies Corp.	Boating market; RV market; Alternative electronic marketing technologies, similar to Muzac's "elevator music" offering
Heads Up Technologies	OEM supplier to major aircraft manufacturers including Cessna, Bell Helicopter, Bombardier Aerospace, LearJet, Raytheon, Sikorsky, and Gulfstream Aircraft	Weather Channel, Mobility Technologies / Capability to broadcast live weather and sophisticated live traffic updates in major metro areas		
Motorola	Integrated technologies, including navigation, communication and terrestrial radio reception		Al and Ed's Autosound, Best Buy, Car Toys, Circuit City, Cowboy Maloney's Electric City, Good Guys, Magnolia Hi-Fi, Mobile One Auto Sound, Sears, Sound Advice, Tweeter, Ultimate Electronics, Wal-Mart, Radio Shack	After-market automotive equipment sales (as well as emerging satellite radio applications)
Pana-Pacific	Leading producer of radio equipment for large trucks, including supplier to Caterpillar, Freightliner, International, Kenworth, Mack, Sterling, Volvo, and Western Star		Crutchfield	Mail-order electronic sales channel

Table 13.2. *Representative partnerships and annual partnership totals by firm and functional area*

Year	Infrastructure		Content and programming		Hardware (product) development		Marketing and distribution	
	XM	SIRIUS	XM	SIRIUS	XM	SIRIUS	XM	SIRIUS
Pre-1999	Hughes Space & Comm.	Loral CyberStar	USA Today Bloomberg Salem Com.	Bloomberg C-SPAN Sports Byline	Alpine Pioneer STMicroelec.	Lucent		MediaAmerica
	(1)	(1)	(9)	(5)	(4)	(1)	(0)	(1)
1999	LCC Interntl.	Globecomm Black and Veatch	Clear Channel CNN Weather Chan.	BBC NPR PRI	Motorola Mitsubishi Elec. Delco-Delphi	Delco-Delphi Matsushita Clarion	General Motors	DaimlerChrysler Ford BMW
	(1)	(2)	(5)	(9)	(4)	(4)	(1)	(3)
2000	Alcatel Space Klotz Digital Telestat		NASCAR AP Radio Sesame Wkshp.	CNBC Playbill World Radio	Sony OnStar (GM) Fujitsu Ten	Audiovox Kenwood Visteon	Honda Freightliner Best Buy	Honda Circuit City Crutchfield
	(9)	(0)	(5)	(6)	(10)	(6)	(23)	(8)

Year							
2001	(0)	(0)	Sporting News, CNET, Ntl. Lampoon (12)	Discovery Chan., ABC Radio, EI Entertain. (9)	Fujitsu Ten, Harman Intl. Ind. (2)	GMAC, Porsche NA (2)	Porsche NA (1)
2002	Coding Tech., Neural Audio (2)	Ibiquity Digital (1)	MediaBay, Radio Classics, Playboy (2)	Command Audio Corp. (1)	(0)	Wal-Mart, DIRECTV, Volkswagen (6)	Volkswagen, Hertz (2)
2003	(0)	(0)	MSNBC (1)	NBA, NHL, NFL (5)	USA Today, Bloomberg, Salem Com. (9)	AirTran, Jet Blue, Carat NA (4)	Genmar Boats, Winnebago, Applied Media (5)
Through April 2004	(0)	(0)	(0)	TiVo (1)	Creston, STMicroelec., Tivoli (7)	(0)	Echostar, Penske, Kenworth (8)

satellite-capable receiver adapters that plugged in to any traditional FM radio equipped with auxiliary inputs. Additionally, portable "boom-box" units were unveiled, signaling an adaptation away from the industry's initial automobile focus. In 2003, more sophisticated applications were explored. For instance, XM teamed up with Weather Works (Baron Services) to introduce an advanced weather service delivering real-time, detailed graphical weather data to mobile users in the marine, aviation, and emergency management markets, signaling a foray into Global Positioning System (GPS) applications. In a separate leap, SIRIUS unveiled a Kenwood receiver that doubled as a mobile video system, capable of receiving satellite-beamed video as well as radio broadcasts. Meanwhile, the traditional automobile receiver models continued to evolve. New receivers were reduced in size by 40% and manufacturers began to unveil cheaper, customizable, and more stylized models. In fact, an Audiovox model built for SIRIUS enabled listeners to capture ten favorite songs and have the system continually search the radio frequency for those songs, alerting the user when they are found playing on other channels. And in the home market, advanced home receivers were also unveiled. In 2004, innovation continued to proliferate. Receivers were integrated into traditional trucking information systems and video and GPS applications were being enhanced with satellite radio receivers.

Remarkably, all of the above were spawned from only one of the functional areas of the satellite radio firm's partnerships – hardware (product) development. During this same time, content and programming were also introducing creative enhancements, incorporating such features as location-specific weather and traffic reports. Similarly, in the area of marketing and distribution, specialized new outlets were being exploited in such markets as business radio services (similar to Muzak) and online listening, promoted through a recent collaboration with Dell Computers. Table 13.2 illustrates representative collaborations and annual collaboration totals by firm and functional area.

Implications for organic growth

The staged evolution of the aforementioned partnerships is represented visually by functional area in Figure 13.3, and is represented conceptually in Figure 13.4.[9]

---

[9] A full annotation of these partnerships is available upon request from the authors.

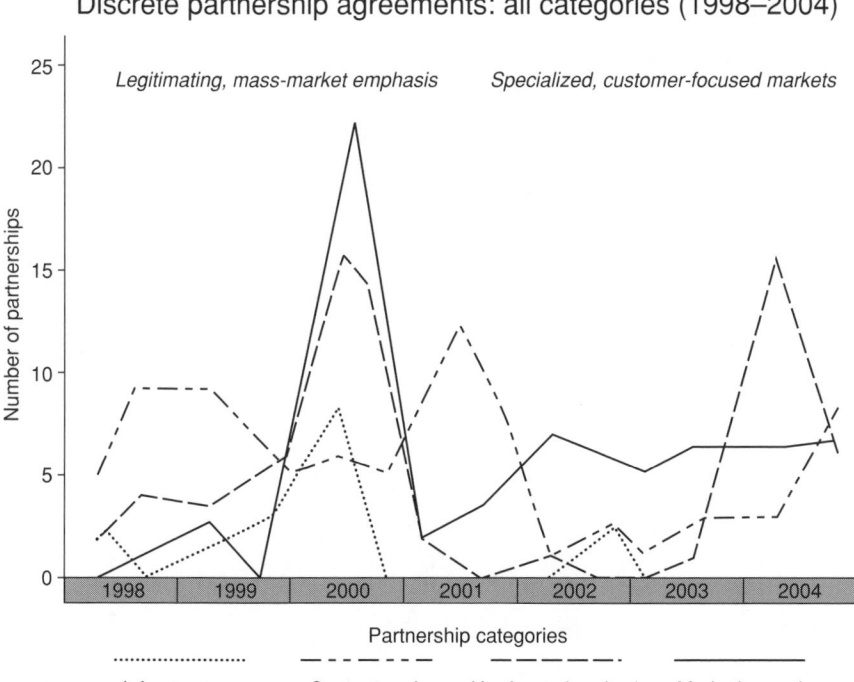

Figure 13.3. Stages of inter-firm collaboration.

Initially, the two satellite radio firms' activity targeted collaborations to access mass-market outlets and attain legitimacy. It also set the stage for future growth. Subsequent collaborations explored and exploited the fringe and specialized markets of the satellite radio industry, targeting unique customer-focused niches.

Innovations emerged at a breakneck pace as knowledge was brokered across partnerships over this brief period of time. This translated to rapid organic growth for XM and SIRIUS. Notably, both firms experienced double-digit subscriber growth in each quarter after their respective service launches. In fact, in 2003, XM surpassed the one million subscriber mark making it the second fastest mass-market technology product (after DVD players) to achieve this milestone.[10]

---

[10] According to Greystone Communications (Yankee Group) and measured by customers or subscribers.

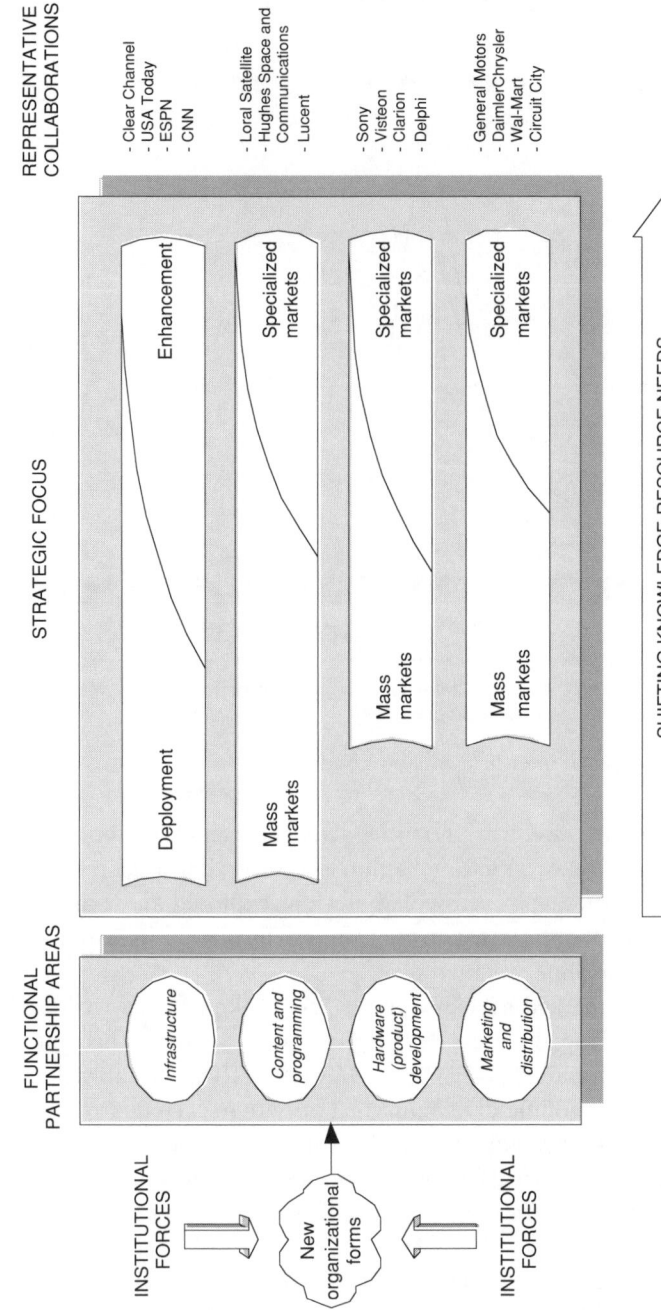

Figure 13.4. Satellite radio knowledge brokering process conceptualization.

Importantly, the growth of these firms did not sacrifice quality for speed, demonstrating how recombinant innovations – in this case pieced together through inter-firm collaborations – can enable firms to side-step many of the traditional trade-offs between the efficiencies of exploiting existing knowledge and the exploration of new options.

XM and SIRIUS have won numerous awards, including "Leading Communications Company," from *Scientific American*, "Product of the Year," from *Fortune Magazine*, "2001 Invention of the Year," from *Time Magazine*, and "Best of What's New," from *Popular Science*. And, in a survey by Crutchfield, an astonishing 98% of XM and SIRIUS users would recommend a purchase to their friends and family. These results have translated to the firms' financials. XM has already reached its cash flow break-even point – much sooner than originally forecast – while SIRIUS appears to be well on the way to achieving this milestone. This growth and financial performance was achieved despite the mammoth investments required to establish the emerging industry's infrastructure.

Conclusion

In this chapter, we explored how traditional institutional fields often impose powerful forces for inaction, thereby disabling the innovation and change required to explore and exploit emerging opportunities. As well, we presented the process of knowledge brokering, enabled by inter-firm collaboration, as a way of overcoming this inertia to expand institutional fields and proliferate creative opportunity. We saw that inter-firm collaborations, when managed in pursuit of new combinations of existing institutional resources, have the means to create organic growth by converting the traditionally constraining nature of such resources into the raw materials that provide the critical awareness, opportunity, and legitimacy that new ventures need.

Our findings have important practical implications. As alternative opportunities for rapid growth – through acquisitions or expanding markets – decline, the ability to enter new markets effectively and create new opportunities in old markets will increasingly depend on inter-firm collaborations. In this way, the case studies of the XM and SIRIUS satellite radio ventures offer valuable lessons for how organizations can manage and pursue innovation-driven growth.

References

Ahuja, G. 2000. The duality of collaboration: inducements and opportunities in the formation of interfirm linkages. *Strategic Management Journal*, 21(3): 317–343.

Barley, S. R. & Tolbert, P. S. 1997. Institutionalization and structuration: studying the links between action and institution. *Organization Studies*, 18(1): 93–117.

Benner, M. J. & Tushman, M. L. 2003. Exploitation, exploration, and process management: the productivity dilemma revisited. *Academy of Management Review*, 28(2): 238–256.

Burt, R. S. 1983. Range. In R. L. Burt & M. J. Minor (eds.), *Applied Network Analysis: A Methodological Introduction*. Beverly Hills, CA: Sage.

Christensen, C. M. 1997. *The Innovator's Dilemma: When New Technologies Cause Great Firms to Fail*. Boston: Harvard Business School Press.

Cohen, W. M. & Levinthal, D. A. 1990. Absorptive capacity: a new perspective on learning and innovation. *Administrative Science Quarterly*, 35(1): 128–153.

Collins, J. C. & Lazier, W. C. 1992. *Beyond Entrepreneurship: Turning Your Business into an Enduring Company*. Englewood Cliffs, NJ: Prentice-Hall.

Deephouse, D. L. 1996. Does isomorphism legitimate? *Academy of Management Journal*, 39: 1024–1039.

DiMaggio, P. J. & Powell, W. W. 1983. The iron cage revisited: institutional isomorphism and collective rationality in institutional fields. *American Sociological Review*, 48: 147–160.

    1991. Introduction. In P. J. DiMaggio & W. W. Powell (eds.), *The New Institutionalism in Organizational Analysis*. Chicago: University of Chicago Press.

Dyer, J. H. & Singh, H. 1998. The relational view: cooperative strategy and sources of interorganizational competitive advantage. *Academy of Management Review*, 23(4): 660–679.

Evenson, A. E. 2000. *Telephone Patent Conspiracy*. Jefferson, NC: McFarland.

Glasmeier, A. 1991. Technological discontinuities and flexible production networks: the case of Switzerland and the world watch industry. *Research Policy*, 20(5): 469–485.

Glynn, M. A. & Abzug, R. 2002. Institutionalizing identity: symbolic isomorphism and organizational names. *Academy of Management Journal*, 43(1): 267–280.

Goes, J. B. & Park, S. H. 1997. Interorganizational links and innovation: the case of hospital services. *Academy of Management Journal*, 40(3): 673–696.

Grant, R. M. 1996. Prospering in dynamically-competitive environments: organizational capability as knowledge integration. *Organization Science*, 7(4): 375–387.

Gulati, R., Nohria, N., & Zaheer, A. 2000. Strategic networks. *Strategic Management Journal*, 21(3): 203–215.

Hargadon, A. 2003. *How Breakthroughs Happen: The Surprising Truth About How Companies Innovate*. Boston: Harvard Business School Press.

Hargadon, A. B. & Douglas, Y. 2001. When innovations meet institutions: Edison and the design of the electric light. *Administrative Science Quarterly*, 46: 476–501.

Hargadon, A. B. & Fanelli, A. 2002. Action and possibility: reconciling dual perspectives of knowledge in organizations. *Organization Science*, 13(3): 290–302.

Hargadon, A. B. & Sutton, R. I. 1997. Technology brokering and innovation in a product development firm. *Administrative Science Quarterly*, 42(4): 716–749.

Kazanjian, R. K. & Drazin, R. 1987. Implementing internal diversification: contingency factors for organization design choices. *Academy of Management Review*, 12(2): 342–354.

Kogut, B. & Zander, U. 1992. Knowledge of the firm, combinative capabilities, and the replication of technology. *Organization Science*, 3: 383–397.

Leblebici, H., Salancik, G. R., Copay, A., & King, T. 1991. Institutional change and transformation of interorganizational fields: an organizational history of the US radio broadcasting industry. *Administrative Science Quarterly*, 36(3): 333–363.

Leonard-Barton, D. 1992. Core capabilities and core rigidities: a paradox in managing new product development. *Strategic Management Journal*, 13: 111–125.

March, J. G. 1991. Exploration and exploitation in organizational learning. *Organization Science*, 2(1): 71–87.

Mitchell, W. & Singh, K. 1996. Survival of businesses using collaborative relationships to commercialize complex goods. *Strategic Management Journal*, 17(3): 169–196.

Port, O. 1997. Xerox won't duplicate past errors, *Business Week*, September: 98–103.

Powell, W. W. & Koput, K. W. 1996. Interorganizational collaboration and the locus of innovation: networks of learning in biotechnology. *Administrative Science Quarterly*, 41(1): 116–145.

Scott, W. R. 1995. *Institutions and Organizations*. Thousand Oaks, CA: Sage.

Selznick, P. 1948. Foundations of the theory of organization. *American Sociological Review*, 13: 25–35.

    1949. *TVA and the Grass Roots*. Berkeley: University of California Press.

    1957. *Leadership in Administration*. New York: Harper & Row.

Stuart, T. E., Hoang, H., & Hybels, R. C. 1999. Interorganizational endorsements and the performance of entrepreneurial ventures. *Administrative Science Quarterly*, 44(2): 315–349.

Suchman, M. C. 1995. Managing legitimacy: strategic and institutional approaches. *Academy of Management Review*, 20(3): 571–610.

Zald, M. N. & Denton, P. 1963. From evangelism to general service: the transformation of the YMCA. *Administrative Science Quarterly*, 8(2): 214–234.

Zucker, L. 1983. Organizations as institutions. *Research in the Sociology of Organizations*, 2: 1–47.

14 New directions for the study of organizational growth

ROBERT DRAZIN, ROBERT K.
KAZANJIAN, AND EDWARD D. HESS

A s we contemplated hosting the "Hitting the Growth Wall" conference at the Goizueta Business School of Emory University, and editing this book, we observed that little had actually been written about organic growth in recent years. Work by Penrose (1995) and Chandler (1962) had set the stage for viewing growth from an evolutionary economics perspective. Much of the work that followed then shifted into research on organizational resources and the linkage between strategy and structure. However, the most dominant growth-related theme that exercised researchers and practitioners alike was the study of innovation processes and outcomes. Our understanding of innovation grew dramatically from the 1980s as the topic took on increasing practical and theoretical significance. This literature covered a broad range of topics and concepts, extending from paradigm shifts (Anderson & Tushman, 1990), to corporate entrepreneurship (Hitt, Ireland, & Tuggle, this volume, ch. 8; Stopford & Baden-Fuller, 1994), intelligent organizations (Quinn, 1992), mastering change (Kanter, 1983), and time-based competition (Eisenhardt, 1989). Most of these were ideas in good currency, enjoying unparalleled popularity among managers and envious citation rates among scholars. Surely such a wealth of information signaled the arrival of a dominant theoretical model for the role of organizations in creating innovation. But what about growth?

Whereas each book or journal article provided its own valuable contribution, we were disappointed to discover that no dominant theoretical perspective had emerged to integrate the multiple streams of innovation into a more comprehensive and substantive view of growth. Unlike other evolving fields of organizational inquiry, such as organizational economics (Williamson, 1975), contingency theory, organizational ecology (Hannan & Freeman, 1977), or institutional theory (Scott, 1992), little in the way of common theoretical underpinnings has been offered to guide the development of growth research in

Table 14.1. *Organic growth issues: defining the business and delivery logics*

Issue	Case examples										
	Siemens	Home Depot	SYSCO	UPS	Joyce	Hitt *et al.*	McGrath	Anderson	Bowman & Narayandas	Garud *et al.*	Navis *et al.*
Organizational transformation	✓	✓									
Elements of business logic											
Developing a platform for growth	✓	✓	✓	✓	✓	✓	✓				✓
Growth via geographic expansion	✓	✓	✓	✓	✓	✓		✓			
Developing innovative products and services	✓	✓	✓	✓	✓	✓	✓	✓	✓	✓	✓
Customer centeredness	✓	✓	✓	✓					✓		
Elements of delivery logic											
Efficiency and the use of technology	✓	✓	✓	✓	✓	✓	✓				
Role of people and leadership	✓	✓	✓	✓						✓	✓
Role of measurements, rewards, and employee ownership	✓	✓	✓	✓	✓						
Organizational structures and processes						✓	✓	✓		✓	✓

organizations. While these other approaches are not free from internal debate, each has, at its core, a set of theoretical principles and a group of advocates that drive its theoretical and empirical development.

Our purpose in conducting the conference and publishing this book was to provide a foundation for the study of organizational growth. We wanted to provide guidance to researchers and managers in their quests to understand and implement growth. In a sense, we are placing a flag in the ground to challenge all involved in managing growth to develop a deeper understanding of the phenomena and to share their knowledge. In this chapter we present an integrated view of organic growth that we believe has emerged from the combined efforts of all our contributors.

In the management literature, the notion of logic has been an important part of theorizing about organizations (Drazin, Glynn, & Kazanjian, 2004). Prahalad and Bettis (1986) articulated perhaps one of the earliest and most forceful arguments for considering the role of logic in explicating organizational performance. They advanced the construct of dominant logic as "the way in which managers conceptualize the business and make critical resource allocation decisions" (Prahalad & Bettis, 1986: 490). As we noted in Chapter 1, several themes emerged from a close review of our colleagues' chapters. We interpret these themes, presented again in Table 14.1, as constituting two distinct logics necessary for organic growth. These twin logics then provide the path to organic growth.

Successful growth results, in part, from a *business logic* that defines a particular mix of products and services that are responsive to the customer needs, suggesting a strong role for customer centeredness. Further, this mix must be easily replicated in new geographic markets, such that the firm can expand from local to national and ultimately global scope. Alternatively, the business logic might emphasize supplementing the original mix with new products and services to current customers in the same geographic market. Consistent with this view, several authors emphasized the importance of developing innovative products and services as well as growth via geographic expansion. Either way, the business logic must be easily and quickly replicable for high levels of organic growth to result.

The second requisite logic is what we call the *delivery logic*. This defines the operational and organizational capabilities that cost-effectively distribute products and services to customers consistent with their needs and preferences. In offering the notion of delivery logic, we note that several chapters discussed the importance of operational efficiency and the aggressive use of appropriate technology to support growth. A number of authors also emphasized the importance of organizational structures, processes, systems, and practices, both formal and informal, to the ability of the firm to continuously replicate the business logic, generating additional growth.

Together the two logics support and reinforce each other such that the cost-effective delivery of the firm's products and services creates a defensible competitive position. Viewed in this way, product and service offerings that are responsive to customer needs, coupled with a comprehensive delivery capability, constitute a platform for growth enabling high levels of organic growth to be realized.

Consider, as an example, the creation of big-box retail stores – a phenomenon of the 1980s that has continued to the present. In Chapter 4, Tom Taylor provides an excellent example of this twin logic with his presentation of growth challenges at The Home Depot. As he describes, the founders, Bernie Marcus and Arthur Blank, developed a remarkable idea for the "do-it-yourself" home improvement market. The idea of a one-stop store was replicable and led to a period of unparalleled growth for The Home Depot, driven primarily by their business logic. However, Taylor indicates that at a certain point, The Home Depot "hit the wall" and growth slowed. After careful analysis, they identified deficiencies in their delivery logic, requiring significant investment in support technologies, distribution capabilities, and procurement to enhance supply chain management. Once the delivery logic was refined and extended, the company regained its earlier growth momentum.

Replicution: a model for organic growth

We refer to this combination of the business logic and the delivery logic directed at executing a strategy of replication as "replication." The term replication emphasizes the duality of the growth strategy – the product and service portfolio must be matched by the execution system. Winter and Szulanski (2001) have titled this the "McDonald's approach," referring to the well-known chain of restaurants familiar to millions across the world that has flourished since Ray Kroc's first design. Winter and Szulanski estimate that over one-third of all retail businesses in the United States are conducted using this strategy.

Replicution begins with the development of a business logic that is carefully honed through trial offerings until the model is close to perfect. Often this original logic takes a great deal of time to be tested and refined before replication can begin. As Winter and Szulanski (2001) point out, this is the time that the replicator firm begins to refine and internalize the business logic at the initial sites and routinizes it in preparation for transferring the logic to successive units. According to Winter and Szulanski (2001: 731): "The transition from the first phase to the second is a critical period in which the task is to create and refine the capabilities that support the more routine replication activities to follow."

The business logic consists of the set of products and services offered by the replicator. Presumably, the linkage between the consumer and the products/services mix is innovative and at least moderately successful in the initial business units offered by the replicator. In several of the cases in this book, the companies have succeeded in transforming their competitive position by bringing a mix of products and services together under one umbrella, providing greater value for the customer. For example, The Home Depot was able to provide the full range of products and services a home-owner would need to complete a home improvement project. Previously a home-owner would have to visit multiple stores to purchase tools and materials, and even contractors to finish a project. The Home Depot provided all of these and with lower prices. Other retail outlets have developed the "big-box" approach including Costco, Sam's Club, and IKEA.

Siemens Medical Solutions offers another example of a business logic that fueled growth. After struggling with poor performance for several years, Siemens concentrated on innovating its product designs and broadening its offerings to include services to support both their equipment in the field and the medical professionals working with that equipment. Information technology was a critical element in their services. The importance of the business logic must be stressed since it is obvious that without a workable business logic, there is nothing to replicate. We hasten to note that the development of a sustainable business logic is quite difficult and that only a small minority of companies that attempt something unique are successful. Undoubtedly, many try this strategy and fail.

Equally important to the success of a replication strategy is the delivery logic. Building on the examples in this book, the major elements of the delivery logic are: enabling technology (often information technology), measurement systems, reward systems, and the training of employees to understand the functioning of both the business and delivery logics. In our view, Winter and Szulanski (2001) do not accord the delivery logic much importance. Of course, they recognize technical subsystems as part of the overall process of replication, but to them, these critical systems are just another routine to be replicated. Based on the findings of this book, we believe that technology and measurement systems in particular stand as equal success factors along with the business logic. In several of the business cases reported in this book, the firms went through a phase of launching the business logic without adequate delivery support, or the delivery support eroded over time. They then found themselves with multiple sites and facilities that were not integrated, with poor execution and deviance from the model that weakened performance. In each case, a crisis or turnaround situation emerged that required the development, refinement, or expansion of the delivery logic that would produce efficiencies and back up the original business logic. This reflects the experience of both The Home Depot and Siemens Medical Solutions.

To us, this is not a process of routinization, but rather a process of innovation and creativity. More thinking and resources may go into the development of this delivery logic than into the original business logic. Consider the example of SYSCO presented by Ed Hess in Chapter 5. Although its growth has been extraordinary, its business logic is rather simple and parallels that of others in the industry – distributing thousands of commodity food products to more than 400,000 customers. However, its delivery logic is clearly its differentiator in the market. As Hess notes, SYSCO's execution appears flawless, indicated by the fact that 99% of deliveries are on time and defect-free. Internal initiatives are designed to make certain that customers receive the products ordered on time and undamaged, that invoices are accurate and timely, and that customer relationships are well managed. SYSCO's business logic, therefore, is enabled by a range of organizational systems and practices that build customer loyalty and facilitate new customer acquisition.

Although not profiled in this book, much has been already written about IKEA (Torekull, 1999), a company that engages in several practices that involve inexpensive delivery of products to customers. For example, all products are made to store in flat boxes. This simplifies shipping, storage in an IKEA store, and packing into customer cars and trucks. Further, IKEA uses a design-to-price approach. They know in advance how the target is priced and innovate to deliver a product at that price. Another example from IKEA is that they market non-IKEA products through the same chain of IKEA stores. The business logic itself may change and evolve because the underlying delivery system offers the capacity to handle other products or services.

At some point, the delivery logic may become a product or service itself and eclipse or extend the original business logic. Consider UPS, described in Chapter 3 by Ed Hess. In order to serve the business and residential delivery markets efficiently, UPS developed, in a decade-long process, an extensive ground and air distribution system that emerged by the 1990s as a global delivery company. Having amassed a distinct set of strategic assets and competencies to serve its customers, UPS then decided to pursue a new growth market providing synchronized commerce services and solutions. This leveraged their expertise in supply chain management and positioned them in an even larger, faster-growing market. This move can be seen as a modification of their business logic that utilizes much of the existing delivery logic.

Building upon the contributions of our colleagues in this book, we have developed an organic growth model, depicted in Figure 14.1. We employ a process perspective here, viewing growth as the result of successful replication. This process begins with the development of the initial business logic and the establishment of an initial set of units, such as stores, facilities, or customer sites. These units are limited in number and likely are located in geographic proximity to the founders and executives of the company. Initially, these are test and trial units. At this stage, the company is determining the mix of goods/services it will offer. After the initial test is completed, the company begins a process of replicating units across multiple geographic settings. Replication itself is problematic and so the company must learn a set of routines on how to replicate (Winter and Szulanski, 2001). This process refines and institutionalizes the approach to replication and sets the stage for further growth. We believe that this phase also may over-emphasize the business logic and under-emphasize the delivery logic. With the right business logic the firm might well replicate quickly, but that growth might outpace the capacity of the delivery vehicle. Ultimately, the firm might "hit a growth wall" when control over the replicated units begins to decline.

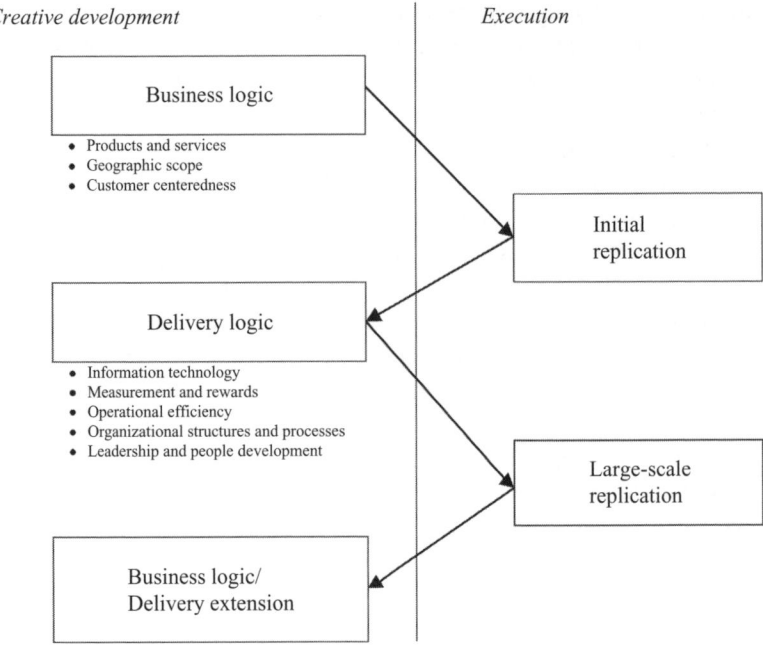

Creative development   *Execution*

Figure 14.1. Towards a model of organic growth.

This requires a second phase of innovation wherein the company develops supporting technologies, measurement and reward systems, and detailed supply agreements with vendors and customers. This second phase is separate and distinct from the business logic that consists solely of developing a unique bundle of products and services. This is not yet full-scale replication, but rather the development of the delivery logic – a robust execution system that needs to be applied in new units and in existing units. As shown in Figure 14.1, this is often accompanied by a major transformation of the organization, as was experienced by Siemens Medical Solutions and by The Home Depot. With both the business and delivery logic in place, large-scale replication can then proceed, generating growth.

As a market saturation point is approached, limiting growth, a company may enter a third phase, in which the company searches for new but related bundles of products and services to serve as the basis for the next round of growth. Consider The Home Depot as an example. The Home Depot's first business logic was evidenced in its well-known home-improvement store. After remarkable success with this concept, The Home Depot refined and extended both its business logic and delivery logic to enter into a similar field. It created Home Expo, a do-it-yourself and contractor-installation store for upscale home improvement. The Home Depot also entered into stores just for contractors, urban stores, and stores for landscaping and gardening. Figure 14.1 points to the possibility that multiple concepts can be leveraged. The business logic can be leveraged by geographic expansion and the delivery logic can be leveraged by expansion into new markets.

Hitting the growth wall

One of the major premises of our conference and this associated book was that many organizations "hit the growth wall" as part of the natural process of growing. This is to say that growth may be significant for a period, and then might be punctuated by a series of events that slow growth, followed by solutions to these events that let the firm grow once again. Many authors suggest that "interruptions to growth" occur when young organizations hit resource constraints. These authors argue that initial success breeds subsequent failure because firms that grow can face shortages of resources at critical points in time. Meyer, Anzani, and Walsh (2005) believe that new and discontinuous technological innovation spurs growth in the initial phases of a new industry. But, technologically driven growth is not enough to sustain the firm. They argue that firms (they use IBM as an example) must go through a renewal phase where they innovate in market segmentation and the development of scalable product platforms that can be shared across segments. Nicholls-Nixon (2005) presents the view that the strains and stresses of fast growth reduce managerial effectiveness in decision-making. Her view is that growth is periodic and strains and stresses need to be overcome before growth can start again.

Figure 14.1 allows us to speculate further on points in the development cycle where a company may hit the growth wall. Following Winter and Szulanski (2001), we believe that replicating the business logic in the first wave of growth is not an easy proposition. The company may begin with one or two units that function well under the entrepreneurs' constant tutelage. When units are extended to other geographic areas, remote from the daily management of experience,

replication may prove difficult. An accepted idea in organization theory is that the transfer of knowledge to a new unit may be difficult
because replicators do not know exactly what aspects of the business
logic are the generators of success and what deviations may be needed
for local tastes. In effect, the business logic is still being investigated and
tested. Growth may be impeded until the replicator has the opportunity
to learn from early replications.

The next possible growth wall occurs when the organization creates
sufficient units to strain the nascent delivery logic. In our understanding
of growth, it is the business logic that first enables growth to occur.
But, ultimately, having a minimum delivery system in place causes a
loss of control in the organization at some later point. Our view of the
delivery logic is that it consists of an advanced platform of information
systems, measurement and reward systems, operational efficiencies,
and carefully selected and developed human assets. Without such an
advanced system in place, the sheer size of the organization, in units,
prevents an understanding of how the system is operating, and whether
firm-wide objectives are being met at the local level. Prior to having the
final delivery logic in place, local management is free to experiment,
but a corporation-wide identity is threatened.

Creating new delivery logic is a form of discontinuous innovation.
It must be experimented with and piloted before being rolled out to
all established units and integrated into the creation of new units. In
a sense, this critical phase is structurally similar to the rolling out of
the business logic. It is a major transformation of the firm. Once established, issues of replication occur again. The new technology platform
must be replicated at the level of established units. As stated above,
replication itself may cause stumbling blocks to occur.

At this point, a growth spurt is likely. The firm now has in place twin
logics. One is concerned with the business itself and the other with how
products and services can be brought to customers. The original mix
will likely be altered incrementally to meet changing needs, but the
essence of the idea behind the business and delivery logics will remain
intact.

Variations on a theme: alternative sequences of development

We have described our growth model, presented in Figure 14.1, in a
linear fashion, suggesting that the development of the business logic

precedes that of the delivery logic, and that subsequent extensions are conducted in a similar way. This approach allows us to explicate each of the two logics in detail as well as to theorize about their interrelationship. Further, it may well describe the growth trajectory of some firms. For example, The Home Depot's growth path largely seems to have mirrored the model as presented. However, in practice, firms may experience different paths through these steps. SYSCO was created in 1969 through the merging of nine separate family-owned companies. At the company's creation, considerable thought and design was directed at both the business and delivery logics, such that the erosion of delivery capability experienced in some firms did not occur at SYSCO. More likely, the business logic and delivery logic were constantly modified and refined in a closely iterative fashion. Its developmental experience suggests that it is quite possible, in fact probably more desirable, to develop the business and delivery logics simultaneously. The developmental path of UPS is similar to that of SYSCO in this regard.

Alternatively, the sequence of business logic to delivery logic to extension of the model to new growth opportunities captures the growth path of some companies. Among the business cases described here, both UPS and The Home Depot concentrated on their core market opportunities until those markets began to approach saturation. Then each identified new, related markets to enter by leveraging and extending their existing logics. However, Siemens Medical Solutions transformed both their business and delivery logics when their performance deteriorated, and used that opportunity to extend their position into new products and services, thereby promoting growth.

Discussion and directions for future research

The role of organizations in the generation of growth continues to be a topic of broad theoretical and practical concern. As most or our contributors have pointed out, growth and innovation are among the essential competitive and organizational challenges facing domestic and international firms today. A major purpose in holding our conference and publishing this edited book was to promote rigorous research to address these growth issues.

Winter and Szulanski (2001) provide us with a rich framework to understand an overall process of growth through replication. We have built upon their ideas by extending their model in such a way that it allows looking at the delivery logic, composed of elements of information technology, the measurement system, and other factors discussed earlier, as an equal partner to the business logic part of the growth equation. We quote from Winter and Szulanski (2001) to highlight the practical and research dimension of understanding replicution:

. . . such a view clouds the strategic subtlety of replication, because replicators create value through activities that fall largely outside its scope. Replicators create value by discovering and refining a business model, by choosing the necessary components to replicate that model in suitable geographical locations, by developing capabilities to routinize knowledge transfer, and by maintaining the model in operation once it has been replicated. The formula or business model, far from being a quantum of information that is revealed in a flash, is typically a complex set of interdependent routines that is discovered, adjusted, and fine-tuned by "doing." Growth by replicating such a "formula" requires the capability to recreate complex, imperfectly understood, and partly tacit productive processes in carefully selected sites, with different human resources every time, facing in many cases resistance from proud, locally autonomous agents. For this reason, replication requires effort, and naturally takes time. Its value is eroded by delay – partly for the simple reason of the time value of money, but also because rivals may seize the best opportunities. Urgency is a hallmark of a replication strategy. However, undertaking rapid large-scale replication of an inadequate business model may backfire and foreclose the opportunity to replicate a suitable one later on. So, the replicator has to decide when to stabilize the business model, abandoning efforts to refine it further, and beginning large-scale replication. When that decision is being made, the value that could be derived by replicating such a business model is speculative and remains so until the model is stabilized and the scope of demand emerges clearly.

Winter and Szulanski's assessment points to the need for more qualitative, case-based fieldwork to address issues of timing, refinement, and technology transfer. The model we have presented should be regarded as just an initial framework with which we can address other issues related to growth. The wide variety of reports from practitioner and academic contributors to this book suggests that the model we have presented is viable, but needs to account for other paths to growth.

There is so little written today about firm growth that any and all models to explain growth would be welcome. We suggest several angles from which academics, working with practitioners, could explore research opportunities. Researchers have published and tested multiple stage-based models of organization growth. The common thread for all of this research is that organizations pass through a series of stages beginning with the initial formation of the organization and ending with decline or stagnation. Each stage is thought to be a unique configuration of organizational attributes suited to the dominant problems the organization faces (Kazanjian, 1988). Every organization passes through these stages; hence they are predictable. Further, transition to the next stage is thought to be preceded by a period of tumultuousness.

While this literature has been regarded as a reasonably good description of growth, it has not addressed other antecedent factors such as the rate of growth the firm is experiencing. We are unaware of any research that examines how fast a firm grows and that tries to understand how growth rates affect management of the enterprise. Valid research questions here might include: At what growth rate do firms experience an over-running of their capabilities? How do firms stretch their human capital and financial capital? When a firm is experiencing extreme munificence, what strategies should it pursue? Should this firm slow down and risk having competitors soak up pent-up demand? Should it engage in alliances or joint ventures?

This book is dedicated to understanding what barriers impede growth, and how firms overcome those barriers. Much of what has been written about growth in the field of economics suggests that growth is self-limiting. Eventually growth is curtailed because the process of learning by doing is based on arguments of diminishing returns. Growth rates are higher earlier in an industry growth cycle because assets invested in growth processes accumulate fast returns from learning. Eventually any given technology is learned to its fullest and growth slows down. For example, markets become saturated, new technologies that underlie products have been fully exploited, and equipment to produce goods has been thoroughly rationalized.

While this dismal description may strike us as mostly true at the level of the industry, at the firm level there are many barriers we need to understand that would allow the individual firm to grow faster. Thus the challenge is not necessarily that growth decreases over time universally, but is the issue of what firms can do to overcome growth barriers faster than their competitors.

References

Anderson, P. & Tushman, M. L. 1990. Technological discontinuities and dominant designs: a cyclical model of technological change. *Administrative Science Quarterly*, 35: 604–633

Chandler, A. D. 1962. *Strategy and Structure*. Cambridge, MA: MIT Press.

Drazin, R., Glynn, M., & Kazanjian, R. K. 2004. Dynamics of structural change. In M. Scott Poole and A. Van de Ven (eds.), *Handbook of Organization Change and Innovation*. Oxford: Oxford University Press.

Eisenhardt, K. M. 1989. Making fast strategic decisions. *Academy of Management Journal*, 32: 543–576.

Hannan, M. T. & Freeman, J. H. 1977. The population ecology of organizations. *American Journal of Sociology*, 82: 929–964.

Kanter, R. M. 1983. *The Change Masters: Innovation for Productivity in the American Corporation*. New York: Simon & Schuster.

Kazanjian, R. K. 1998. Relation of dominant problems to stages of growth in technology based new ventures. *Academy of Management Journal*, 31: 257–279.

Meyer, M. H., Anzani, M., & Walsh, G. 2005. Innovation and enterprise growth. *Research Technology Management*, 4: 34–44.

Nicholls-Nixon, C. L. 2005. Rapid growth and high performance: the entrepreneur's "impossible" dream? *Academy of Management Executive*, 19(1): 77–82.

Penrose, E. 1995. *The Theory of the Growth of the Firm*. Oxford: Oxford University Press.

Prahalad, C. K. and Bettis, R. A. 1986. The dominant logic: a new linkage between diversity and performance. *Strategic Management Journal*, 7: 485–501.

Quinn, J. B. 1992. *The Intelligent Enterprise*. Boston: The Free Press.

Scott, W. R. 1992. *Organizations: Rational, Natural, and Open Systems*, 3rd edn. Englewood Cliffs, NJ: Prentice-Hall.

Stopford, J. M. and Baden-Fuller, C. W. 1994. Creating corporate entrepreneurship. *Strategic Management Journal*, 15: 521–536.

Torekull, B. 1999. *Leading by Design: The IKEA Story*. New York: HarperCollins.

Williamson, O. 1975. *Markets and Hierarchies*. New York: The Free Press.

Winter, S. G. and Szulanski, G. 2001. Replication as strategy. *Organization Science*, 12: 730–743.

Index